Families in America

SOCIOLOGY IN THE 21ST CENTURY

Edited by John Iceland, Pennsylvania State University

This series introduces students to a range of sociological issues of broad interest in the United States today and addresses topics such as race, immigration, gender, the family, education, and social inequality. Each work has a similar structure and approach as follows:

- introduction to the topic's importance in contemporary society
- overview of conceptual issues
- review of empirical research including demographic data
- cross-national comparisons
- discussion of policy debates

These course books highlight findings from current, rigorous research and include personal narratives to illustrate major themes in an accessible manner. The similarity in approach across the series allows instructors to assign them as a featured or supplementary book in various courses.

1. *A Portrait of America: The Demographic Perspective,* by John Iceland
2. *Race and Ethnicity in America,* by John Iceland
3. *Education in America,* by Kimberly A. Goyette
4. *Families in America,* by Susan L. Brown

Families in America

Susan L. Brown

UNIVERSITY OF CALIFORNIA PRESS

University of California Press, one of the most distinguished university presses in the United States, enriches lives around the world by advancing scholarship in the humanities, social sciences, and natural sciences. Its activities are supported by the UC Press Foundation and by philanthropic contributions from individuals and institutions. For more information, visit www.ucpress.edu.

University of California Press
Oakland, California

Library of Congress Cataloging-in-Publication Data

Names: Brown, Susan L., author.
Title: Families in America / Susan L. Brown.
Other titles: Sociology in the 21st century (University of California Press); 4.
Description: Oakland, California : University of California Press, [2017] | Series: Sociology in the 21st century ; 4 | Includes bibliographical references and index.
Identifiers: LCCN 2016057570 (print) | LCCN 2016055431 (ebook) | ISBN 9780520285880 (cloth : alk. paper) | ISBN 9780520285897 (pbk : alk. paper) | ISBN 9780520961241 ()
Subjects: LCSH: Families—United States.
Classification: LCC HQ536 .B774 2017 (ebook) | LCC HQ536 (print) | DDC 306.850973—dc23
LC record available at https://lccn.loc.gov/2016057570

ClassifNumber   PubDate
DeweyNumber'—dc23   CatalogNumber

Manufactured in the United States of America

24   23   22   21   20   19   18   17
10   9   8   7   6   5   4   3   2   1

To my family—Smog (in memoriam),
Sir, Babes, and Ribs

Contents

Illustrations

Acknowledgments

My introduction to the study of family life occurred in 1991 when I enrolled in Steven Nock's sociology of the family course as an undergraduate at the University of Virginia. Even though it was a large lecture class, I felt like Steve was talking directly to me. His lectures were riveting. His guidance led me to pursue graduate study at Penn State in sociology and demography with Alan Booth. Alan was in a class by himself. He offered unparalleled mentoring that I strive to emulate as I train my own students. Both Alan and Steve shaped my career development and I am indebted to them for their support. I hope this book honors the memories of both of them.

I am privileged to have exceptional colleagues and collaborators in the sociology department at Bowling Green State University. In particular, my collaborations with Wendy Manning, I-Fen Lin, Kei Nomaguchi, Gary Lee, Karen Guzzo, and Laura Sanchez have sharpened my thinking about what's happening in today's families, informing both the structure and content of this book. The team that Wendy and I work with as codirectors of the National Center for Family & Marriage Research keeps the national research community updated on the very latest family patterns and trends. I am pleased to include several figures in this book that are from our long-standing series of family profiles. A special thank you to Krista Payne for her assistance with these figures.

When Sociology in the 21st Century series editor John Iceland asked me if I would write a book about families, I immediately said yes because I knew that he was building a collection of works that would likely appeal to a broad audience of readers. I really appreciate the support and feedback that John as well as Naomi Schneider, executive editor at the University of California Press, have given me. Their insights, along with feedback from anonymous reviewers, have greatly improved the book.

Since I began writing this book, my own family life has changed dramatically. My parents moved from the East Coast to Bowling Green, Ohio, to join me and my husband because they both were experiencing significant health crises. It has been deeply rewarding to have my parents nearby and it has brought into stark relief the meaning and importance of families. I am extremely grateful for their love and encouragement over the years. Their support and flexibility allowed me the time to complete this book. I also want to thank my brother for his patience and sense of humor—he manages to make me laugh and groan. Finally, it is difficult to express the innumerable ways in which my husband supports and loves me day in and day out. Let me just say that my mother told anyone who would listen that "Steve is the best son-in-law in the world."

Introduction

Who is in your family? You likely have a ready answer to this basic question. But your answer also is probably unlike that of others. We each have our own unique approach to defining or conceptualizing our family. While our idiosyncratic version helps us to make sense of our own lived experience, we cannot simply extrapolate from that to speak more broadly about the meaning of the family in contemporary society. Families have become more diverse and individualized, which makes generalizations challenging. But the task of achieving an overarching definition of families is also more urgent—deciphering family patterns and trends is essential to understanding what is happening to families. And if we wish to consider how families shape the well-being and future of their members, it is vital that we articulate how family life unfolds across the generations.

Family life is a hotly contested subject that sparks strong views and moral pronouncements. Part of the reason why politicians, pundits, and the public disagree about whether families are declining or thriving these days reflects disparate perspectives on how to conceptualize the family. Some family types are less common today than in the past. The demise of the traditional breadwinner-homemaker family that was emblematic of the 1950s is a prime example. Meanwhile other family configurations are gaining new ground. Perhaps the most striking example is the legalization of same-sex marriage by the U.S. Supreme Court in 2015. What do these changes signal about the state of the family? The answer to this question depends in part on how one thinks about and conceptualizes families.

Regardless, these two examples illustrate that the family is neither uniform nor static. Over time, families have changed profoundly. But family change is not a recent phenomenon. Rather, families have been changing across the centuries. A historical perspective on family life (provided in chapter 1) reveals the pathways and precursors to present-day families. How we think about contemporary family life is embedded in our understanding of families of the past. The structure and functions of families are different nowadays than they were just a half-century ago, but those midcentury families in turn differed from their forebears, too. And it is worth noting that despite considerable change, there are some features of families that endure across time. Whether formed on the basis of an economic alliance, companionship, or love, families offer us close social ties that are reinforced by resource pooling. The family remains the primary agent of socialization for children, providing an environment in which our youngest members of society learn how to interact with others and navigate social relationships. Families are a conduit between the individual and society.

DEFINING FAMILY

To measure family patterns and trends, the Census Bureau relies on a straightforward but arguably narrow definition of family. According to their definition, a family is two or more persons who are related by blood, marriage, or adoption who reside together. A family is distinct from a household, which is the term the Census uses to describe one or more people who share living quarters, whether a house, apartment, or room.[1] In other words, a family is a special case of a household because it stipulates specific types of relationships between household members that are required to constitute a family. Conversely, a household may or may not contain a family. As shown in figure 1, fewer than half of today's households include a married couple, reflecting a significant decline since the

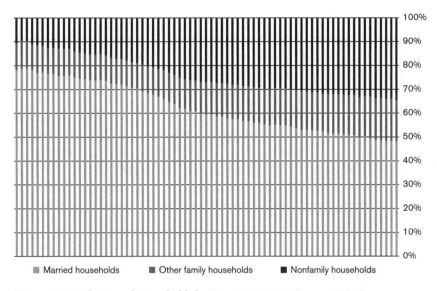

100%
90%
80%
70%
60%
50%
40%
30%
20%
10%
0%

■ Married households   ■ Other family households   ■ Nonfamily households

Figure 1. Distribution of Households by Type, 1947–2015. Source: U.S. Census Bureau, table HH-1, Households by Type: 1940 to Present.

mid-twentieth century when the share was nearly 80 percent. The decline in married households has been offset by growth in both other family and nonfamily households. Other family households include single mothers and their children. Nonfamily households have more than tripled over the past half-century from about 10 percent to more than one-third of all households. They encompass a range of configurations but of particular note is the growing trend of living solo, or the rise of single-person households. Cohabiting couples without resident children are also in the nonfamily-households category and this living arrangement has accelerated in recent decades, too.

The Census Bureau's approach to defining and measuring families probably does not align with how most Americans think about families. Do families have to live together? For ease of measurement, it is understandable why the Census Bureau imposes this constraint in its definition, but family members can span across households. Children who do not live with one of their biological parents nevertheless probably view their non-resident parent as part of their family. Likewise, this approach does not recognize newer family forms, such as cohabitation, that rest on informal ties rather than legal marriage. A sizeable share of cohabiting couples are rearing children together, but from the Census Bureau's perspective these would be single-parent families with children. Prior to the 2015 ruling by the U.S. Supreme Court that legalized marriage for same-sex couples, gay and lesbian couple households would not have counted as families.

Beyond the structural factors and relationship ties, we might also think about the functions or purposes of families as we formulate a working definition. Family members are interdependent and typically share resources. They care for one another, providing social and material support. Families often rear the next generation or are caregivers for the aged.[2] In short, families are integral to individual development, health, and well-being.[3]

How We View Families

As family life has become less uniform, Americans have come to hold diverse views about what constitutes a family. A study by Pew Research Center reveals wide-ranging opinions on recent family change. Nearly one-third of Americans are accepting of today's family patterns. They express no concerns about growth in different-sex or same-sex cohabiting couples rearing children; single mothers rearing children; cohabitation; labor-force participation of mothers of young children; interracial marriage; and childlessness. But an equivalent sized group of Americans rejects these recent family changes, viewing them as detrimental to society. The remainder, about 37 percent, are characterized as skeptical because they are largely accepting but view the growth in single motherhood as problematic.[4]

This range of public opinion about family life is consistent with research conducted by sociologist Brian Powell and his colleagues, who interviewed a sample of American adults to ask them about their views on various living arrangements. As described in their book, *Counted Out: Same-Sex Relations and Americans' Definitions of Family,* the research team presented respondents with numerous living-arrangement configurations to appraise.[5] Is the married couple with biological children a family? For this configuration, consensus was uniform—everyone agreed this group constitutes a family. But this was the only configuration about which respondents completely agreed. A woman (or man) with children was considered a family by nearly all (94 percent) respondents. Likewise, 93 percent viewed a married couple with no children as a family. But other configurations received weaker affirmation. An unmarried man and woman with children were viewed as a family by less than 80 percent. For an unmarried couple without children, the share identifying this configuration as a family was only 31 percent. These patterns illustrate the joint significance of marriage and children. A married, childless couple is viewed as a family whereas a cohabiting couple without children is not perceived to be a family by the majority of Americans. Only when cohabiting couples have children are most adults willing to label them a family. For same-sex couples, the disparity by the presence of children is similar although the absolute levels of support are lower than observed for different-sex cohabiting couples. Only about one-quarter of Americans agreed that two men or two women without children are a family. The inclusion of children doubled support levels to about 55 percent, a notable gain but one that falls short of different-sex unmarried couples with children.[6]

It is possible that levels of support for various configurations are higher today. Powell and his colleagues conducted their study a decade ago. Since then, unmarried cohabitation has continued to rise and same-sex marriage (as well as adoption by same-sex couples) has been a divisive issue in numerous states, culminating in the U.S. Supreme Court ruling that legalized same-sex marriage across the country in 2015. Although the shares of adults who identify cohabiting or same-sex couples (with or without children) as families probably has grown since the study was completed, nonetheless the larger patterns of support likely persist. That is, Americans are expected to be most supportive of married configurations, followed by different-sex cohabiting, and lastly by same-sex cohabiting. Where same-sex married pairings would fit awaits future research.

Why It Matters

It seems that it should be straightforward to identify what constitutes a family. After all, nearly everyone would claim to be part of a family. But our individual experiences are varied and do not lend themselves to abstraction. Certainly it is fair to say that one size does not fit all—there is no singular family type—but how precisely can we distinguish a family? What are the key ingredients that signal that a group constitutes a family? These are challenging questions that reveal the difficulty involved in formulating a definition of the family. "What is a family?" is a deceptively simple question to which there is no one right answer.

Defining the family is not merely an academic exercise. How we as a society conceptualize the family speaks to our morals and values. Which living arrangements do we view as acceptable or desirable? That depends on our definition of the family. A broad definition that encompasses varied configurations signals that we value family diversity. A narrow approach to families, say one that requires marriage, telegraphs a message of conformity and even rigidity because of the narrowness of the criteria for a family. By extension, how we define a family not only testifies which living arrangements are privileged in society but also informs our assessments of the state of families. Are families in decline?[7] The response very much depends on our definition. If we view the family as the traditional breadwinner-homemaker married couple with shared children, then we would conclude the family is in peril. However, if we rely on a more inclusive definition that recognizes variation in family types, we are likely to reach a very different conclusion: families are thriving. The ability of individuals to form families they choose outside of traditional constraints would indicate that family change is beneficial to society.

Apart from moral and evaluative reasons, how we define the family has vital implications for the distribution of economic resources and our legal rights and responsibilities to one another. One of the main reasons why same-sex couples fought for the right to marry was to gain access to the unique benefits that spouses enjoy that are not available to unmarried partners. At the federal level alone, there are more than a thousand unique benefits that accrue to married couples.[8] These range from tax and inheritance laws to access to Social Security and veteran's benefits to family-reunification preferences for immigration. Likewise the disbursement of employee benefits relies on a definition of family. For example, individuals with employer health plans can purchase family coverage which is accompanied by precise definitions of who qualifies as a family member. Another example is the treatment of step-relations by the law. Stepparents typically have no rights to their stepchildren nor are they obligated to care for them unless they have legally adopted the children, underscoring the primacy of biological and adoptive ties from a legal standpoint. In the United States, stepchildren and stepparents are "legal strangers" under the law.[9]

It matters how we count families. Although Americans hold a range of views about the meaning of family, there is a strong consensus among social scientists that families are varied and diverse. We no longer refer to "the family," which implies a singular form. Instead we use the term "families" to convey the plurality of and variation in family life today. Family demographers aim to uncover different types of living arrangements to elucidate patterns and trends in both long-standing and emerging family forms. A cursory review of Census publications reveals how our approach to counting families has evolved over time, shifting from a narrow emphasis on marriage and widowhood to incorporate single-mother families, cohabitation, and most recently same-sex co-residential partnerships. Now that same-sex marriage is legal across the nation, the Census must ensure its measures accommodate this pivotal change in family life. Married couples can be different-sex or same-sex pairings. Our conceptualization of families is not fixed. Instead, social scientists emphasize that families are dynamic and changing. One of the most notable features of modern family life is its uncertainty and instability. These days, children and adults alike more often experience multiple family transitions.[10] A one-time snapshot of families presents a partial view, obscuring movement into and out of various types of families. Family instability is linked to poorer well-being, especially among children.

PLAN FOR THE BOOK

The goal of this book is to provide a dynamic portrait of U.S. family life that emphasizes change and variation to fully capture the diverse experiences that characterize today's families. Our approach is guided by a social demographic perspective that addresses the patterns, timing, and types of union formation and dissolution as well as childbearing. Chapter 1 delves into the historical roots of family life to provide a richer foundation for understanding how the constellation of contemporary families has emerged. It charts the experiences of American families from the seventeenth century to the present, emphasizing how changes in the economy, demography, and women's and men's family and work roles have contributed to dramatic shifts in family life.[11]

The focus of chapter 2 is family formation, which can occur through cohabitation or marriage as well as childbearing. This chapter also addresses alternatives and precursors to union formation, including solo living, intergenerational co-residence among young adults, dating, and living apart together relationships. Increasingly, families are formed outside of marriage through nonmarital childbearing. This chapter concludes with a discussion of fertility trends and explanations for these changing patterns.

Families can be unstable, with many ending through break-up, divorce, or widowhood. Chapter 3 addresses family dissolution and repartnership. It traces the rise of divorce in the United States and explores societal and individual level factors that have contributed to our nation's high divorce rate. It also examines the consequences of divorce for adults and children. Cohabitation dissolution is even more common than divorce and thus the chapter explores separation for different-sex and same-sex couples. Although marital dissolution often occurs through divorce, other marriages end through spousal death. Dissolution is sometimes followed by repartnership, and the chapter concludes with a consideration of remarriage and stepfamilies.

Much of the debate about the state of the American family hinges on the notion that families shape our mental, physical, social, and economic well-being.[12] Families also serve as the core developmental context for children.[13] Chapter 4 addresses the relationship between family patterns and individual health and well-being among adults and children. As family life becomes more complex and unstable, it is important to decipher which features of children's family experiences are instrumental to their healthy development.

Family life unfolds in a specific sociohistorical context marked by public policy initiatives that can help or hurt families. Chapter 5 examines three policy-relevant family issues, including poverty and single motherhood; work-family balance; and family caregiving for the aged. Family policies such as welfare reform and marriage promotion are quintessentially American and represent a unique approach to purportedly supporting disadvantaged members of society. Likewise, the United States is unusual in its (lack of) response to work-family balance issues that affect nearly all families as they attempt to juggle competing demands from employers and family members without a formal, government-mandated safety net to support parents and other caregivers.

The roles of rising socioeconomic inequality and racial-ethnic variation in family patterns and change threads throughout the book. Family patterns tend to vary across racial and ethnic groups and these differences are confounded with socioeconomic status, a factor that is increasingly central to family behaviors. Family experiences are now bifurcated by education, a leading indicator of socioeconomic status.[14] Moreover, the potential benefits (or costs) of various family experiences appear to differ by race-ethnicity.[15] For instance, the health and well-being advantage associated with marriage is larger for whites than blacks. And family policies, particularly welfare reform, have a disproportionate impact on economically marginalized groups and minority populations. The book closes with a chapter about why family change matters and about the prospects for the future of families.

1 Historical and Contemporary Perspectives on Families

During its heyday in the 1950s, the breadwinner-homemaker family with children was described as the singular, preferred family form. Sociologists Talcott Parsons and Robert Bales wrote in 1956 that "it goes without saying that the differentiation of the sex roles within the family constitutes not merely a major axis of its structure, but is deeply involved in both of these two central function-complexes of the family and in their application with each other. Indeed we argue that probably the importance of the family and its functions for society constitutes the primary set of reasons why there is a social as distinguished from purely reproductive, differentiation of sex roles."[1]

Even though this American family "ideal" is not reflective of contemporary families, it remains firmly entrenched in our culture, exemplifying "the good old days": a breadwinning father, a homemaker mother, and their shared children. Typically portrayed in popular culture as white, middle-class, and suburban, we continue to view this family type as the norm and measure other living arrangements against it. In fact, a longer view of the history of families in America reveals that the 1950s, the purported golden age of the family, is actually an aberration. For much of U.S. history, families did not conform to this stereotype.[2]

Yet when cultural critics and policy makers lament the decline of the family, they are referring to the disappearance of the 1950s ideal of the breadwinner-homemaker married couple and their children. This family type is a relic of the past; only about one-fifth of children reside in this "traditional" family form nowadays.[3] In recent decades, the retreat from marriage coupled with the rise in divorce, nonmarital child bearing, and single-mother families have reshaped American families. The ramifications of these changes have generated extensive debate, in both academic circles and the policy arena.[4] Our collective worry about the future of the family and more specifically the consequences of family change for child development not only inform the popular and political discourse but also drive key policy shifts, such as the sweeping changes to the federal welfare system two decades ago (discussed in chapter 5).[5] Indeed, modern-day family and child welfare policy shifts are often proscriptive, designed to encourage a return to what some have characterized as the pillar of society: lifelong marriage. Nevertheless, the prominence of marriage in family life is arguably weaker today than at any point in U.S. history.[6]

These fears about family decline are not new. Concern about family change and marital stability stretches back to Puritan times.[7] Throughout history, family life has shifted in response to broader economic, demographic, and cultural shifts, prompting concerns about the demise of the family. The vulnerabilities of today's families may differ from those of the past, but families have always faced challenges.

This chapter provides an overview of the social history of family life in the United States, tracing the arc of family change from the seventeenth century to the present. Contrary to the persistent notion that there is a "traditional family" and that its structure and function mirrors that which characterized many families of the 1950s, family change has been a constant throughout U.S. history. According to historians Steven Mintz and Susan Kellogg, these changes are largely driven by three factors: the economy, demography, and changing roles of women.[8] The rise of industrialization spurred the shift from a rural, agrarian economy to an urban, cash-based system that fundamentally altered family life by separating work and home.[9] Demographic changes, particularly the drop in childbearing and the aging of the population, also are pivotal. As infant and child mortality improved, the emphasis in families shifted from childbearing to childrearing.[10] Childhood was recognized as a distinctive life stage and women were viewed as uniquely suited to provide the moral training children required.[11] In addition to lower levels of child mortality, rising standards of living for families allowed them to make greater investments in child quality. Another demographic trend with implications for families is the aging of the population. Lengthening life expectancies meant more married couples experienced an empty nest after launching their children into independence and grandparenthood became a meaningful familial role.[12] Finally, women's roles have been transformed over the past few centuries.[13] Women went from being producers alongside their husbands, contributing to the family economy, to housewives and mothers confined to a spiritually elevated, separate sphere with an exclusive focus on home and family. In recent decades, women's attachment to domestic roles has diminished as the rate of employment, especially among married mothers, has grown steadily. As women's roles have changed, our conceptualization of what it means to be a wife and mother has shifted. At the same time, the roles of husband and father have been reconfigured, as men increasingly assume what was once considered women's work: household chores and childrearing.[14]

EARLY AMERICAN FAMILIES

In the seventeenth century, Puritans were settling in New England. The family was the organizing unit of society and individuals were defined by their family or household membership. Families tended to be nuclear in structure, with about two to three children surviving to adulthood, reflecting high infant and child mortality levels because married women typically bore six or more children. Families often included other unrelated individuals such as servants, boarders, or apprentices. The family was governed by a patriarch, the father and husband, who held the legal and social authority to control not just the family land or property but also the family's members, including his wife and children along with unrelated members. During this time period, the family also performed such functions as education and religious training.[15] The household head was required to teach family members to read, and he held prayer and scriptural readings. The family was a producing unit and all family members, including women and children, contributed to the family economy through domestic and agrarian labor. Upon marriage, women were legally subsumed under their husbands according to the law of coverture. They could neither buy nor sell property nor represent themselves in a courtroom. Much like their children, wives were dependents of the patriarch. Young children were viewed as the embodiment of sin who required breaking to ensure their readiness to begin to assume some adult roles at the age of seven. Children of all social classes were fostered out to other families to receive the training and discipline that parents were perceived as incapable of providing.[16]

Patriarchal authority was predicated on the father's control of his property or his craft. Most fathers did not relinquish their land to their sons until they died, which delayed marriage entry among offspring. Marriage was about forging economic alliances, not a love match. But land can only be divided so many times across the generations and still be of sufficient size to support a family. Over time, partible inheritances divided among all sons made agrarian work impracticable for many young men. At the same time, opportunities were emerging in cities because of industrialization. These trends ultimately reduced patriarchal authority, weakening the involvement of parents in the mate-selection process of their offspring. Daughters began to marry out of order and sons were less likely to wait for their inheritance to start their own families.[17]

DEMOCRATIC FAMILIES

As patriarchal authority and wifely obedience waned during the late eighteenth century and into the nineteenth century, the modern democratic family gained prominence among the middle class.[18] Consistent with the Enlightenment period's emphasis on the individual, families during this time period functioned less as a miniature society and more as a retreat from the harsh realities of a capitalist economy. Husbands and wives were companions and friends who were affectionate toward each other. Demarcating the lines between work and family, the roles of husbands and wives became more distinctive. Families were losing their productive roles, as husbands increasingly left the home to earn a wage as breadwinners in factories, mills, and shops. The rise of industrialization led to gender-specific roles. Wives were homemakers and devoted considerable time to rearing children. Childrearing manuals written for mothers framed childhood as a distinctive life stage for growth and development. The birth rate began to decline as children shifted from economic assets engaged in agrarian production to economic liabilities requiring training and education. In 1800, a married woman bore more than seven children, on average. By 1900, the figure was less than four children.[19] In the nineteenth century, women were viewed as morally superior to men and less susceptible to the pressures of the economy, making them uniquely suited to rear children. The cult of true womanhood praised women's key virtues: piety, submissiveness, purity, and domesticity. These shifts contributed to new family tensions, isolating women in the domestic sphere. Wives and children had lost their productive functions and were secluded within the family.[20]

It was during the Victorian era that love became the basis for marriage, particularly among the middle class. Until then, marriage had been about forging ties that maximized wealth and property; it had been an economic arrangement. This economic basis of marriage was now replaced by an emphasis on a love match. Individuals viewed falling in love as a necessary precursor to marriage. This new emphasis on emotions, satisfaction, and fulfillment marked the beginning of the modern approach to matrimony. The stakes were high, and many unmarried women feared a "marriage trauma" if they made a poor match.[21] Widening economic opportunities for women, who attended high school in greater numbers in the nineteenth century and had more access to jobs, enabled many to remain single and avoid marriage altogether. The focus on married love spurred notable changes in family law, such as eased restrictions on divorce, which were followed by an uptick in the divorce rate. The exponential increase in divorce over the course of U.S. history began in the post–Civil War era. Love was a fragile basis for marriage. Historically, children were dependents of their fathers, but the tender-years doctrine meant that children were cared for by their mothers following divorce. And in the mid-nineteenth century, states began passing married women's property acts that allowed married women to control their own earnings and property, another indicator of the diminished influence of patriarchal authority within Victorian marriage.[22]

The rise of companionate marriage and the doctrine of separate spheres in the nineteenth century occurred among middle-class whites.[23] In economically disadvantaged families, wives went to work, often in service to middle-class housewives, and earned paltry wages. Children in working-class families contributed up to half of the family's income.[24] The breadwinner-homemaker family was an ideal that was unattainable for much of society.

For the working class, many of whom were new immigrants, life often meant long hours working in factories. Schooling was a luxury that had to be forgone, particularly for girls, who were sent to work at an early age so that their brothers could remain in school for a few more years. Unlike middle-class families in which wives lost their productive function, wives in working-class families made significant economic contributions, whether by working outside of the home, taking in boarders, performing piece work (so called because they were paid by the unit completed), or doing laundry in the home. Children also contributed to the family economy, delaying their own family formation until they established their own financial security. Many did not marry until their early thirties, and it was common for one daughter to remain unmarried so she could care for her parents during their old age. Kin ties were essential, particularly for immigrant families, who relied heavily on family networks to navigate American life.[25]

Families were also integral to African Americans both during and after slavery. Stable, two-parent families were common, with marriages persisting until spousal death. Legal marriage was not available to slaves, and most slave owners allowed couples to dissolve their unions. But usually it was the owners themselves who separated slave couples. One in six marriages was dissolved through sale. Slave children were even more likely than their parents to be sold away. Parents were constrained in their ability to protect their children from the atrocities of slavery. Around age seven, slave children resided separately from their mothers and began working for their master. Rape and sexual violence against slave women was commonplace, and many owners attempted to encourage childbearing among slaves for their own economic gain.[26]

After the Civil War, African Americans often worked as sharecroppers. Similar to their working-class immigrant counterparts scattered among American cities, many black families had to rely on multiple earners to make ends meet. Despite talk of a family wage to ensure that fathers could support their families, blacks, immigrants, and the working class found the breadwinner-homemaker ideal elusive. Wages peaked early for young men, whose incomes tended to decline as they aged. This meant they were especially vulnerable economically when they had young children (who could not contribute economically to the household) and in their old age.[27]

EARLY TWENTIETH-CENTURY FAMILIES

Industrialization, urbanization, and the transformation of women's roles were in full swing by the onset of the twentieth century, and family life was changing in radical ways. The middle class resided in companionate families that were formed and maintained on the basis of romantic and sexual love between husbands and wives. A majority of middle-class couples used birth control to limit their fertility, indicating both that smaller families were increasingly the norm and that sexual relations for pleasure (as opposed to procreation) were deemed appropriate and even desirable by married couples.[28] Parent-child relations became less formal as children were allowed to be more expressive and autonomous. Children became more focused on their peer groups.[29]

The shift to a market economy solidified the separation between work and family. Urbanization weakened extended family ties as family members migrated to geographic locales with greater employment opportunities. The standard of living began to rise for families during the early twentieth century. New inventions like the automobile provided unprecedented privacy and independence for middle-class young adults, spurring a revolution in morals. Women altered their appearance, adopting a boyish form and bobbing their hair. They relinquished bulky undergarments and wore slimmer clothing that required much less fabric. Premarital sexual activity became more common among women during the early decades of the twentieth century.[30]

The rise in female labor-force participation accelerated during this period, climbing over 150 percent between 1880 and 1920. Women were also pursuing advanced education in greater numbers, and by the early decades of the twentieth century were achieving education levels comparable to men.[31] After decades of struggle through the suffrage movement, women finally won the right to vote when the Nineteenth Amendment to the constitution was ratified in 1920. In short, women's economic and political power were growing, and the widening scope of opportunities available to women chipped away at the traditional, gender-based "separate spheres."

The roles of husbands and wives were recast as couples rejected Victorian-era morality and family ideals that characterized marriage as an institution through which pious, pure women could tame men's animalistic nature. Now, companionate families were predicated on sexual fulfillment. Sexual activity was viewed as integral to marital satisfaction.[32] Nevertheless, the roles and responsibilities of fathers and mothers remained highly gendered. Unlike their predecessors, companionate fathers took a narrow view of their role, defining it in terms of economic provision as the family breadwinner. Whereas fathers in the past were patriarchs who guided the moral and spiritual development of the family, in companionate families these elements were within the purview of mothers, who were wholly responsible for running the household and rearing the children. Fathers, who spent most of their time working, were physically and morally distant from family life during this era.[33]

In the 1920s, sociologists Robert and Helen Lynd first studied the Midwestern town of Muncie, Indiana, and found that nearly all middle-class married couples used some form of birth control, whereas very few in the working class did.[34] Margaret Sanger was leading a nationwide campaign to educate couples about birth control and make it more widely available. Several types of birth control were available, including condoms, douches, suppositories, sponges, and diaphragms. Birth-control proponents trumpeted its benefits for marital happiness, women's autonomy, and infant and child health. But part of the initiative was to encourage greater fertility control for certain groups, namely the economically disadvantaged and immigrants. Abortion was outlawed because the birth rates of middle-class white women were deemed to be too low.[35]

The emphasis of companionate families was on the emotional needs of family members. Married couples expected love and sexual fulfillment from their spouses. By 1920, the divorce rate was fifteen times the rate it was a half-century earlier. Across the nation, 14 percent of marriages ended in divorce. In some urban areas the levels were considerably higher. The judicial system responded by tightening divorce laws, aiming to make it more difficult for couples to end their marriages. But these efforts were essentially futile as the divorce rate continued its ascent.[36]

At the forefront of the Progressive movement, which spanned the late nineteenth and early twentieth centuries, was family life. Experts such as social scientists, educators, physicians, and lawyers believed they could improve family functioning by training Americans how to have a successful marriage, run an efficient household, and raise well-adjusted children. Social problems linked to the modern family were remediable by public health and professional interventions. For example, the growing centrality of sexual fulfillment within marriage combined with concerns about the loosening morals of youth spurred the emergence of sex-education and reproduction courses. Marriage-education courses, counseling, and therapy were designed to enhance marital quality and stability. The principles of scientific motherhood were articulated by medical experts to educate mothers on how to raise their children properly.[37] It was thought that social ills such as juvenile delinquency and poverty were outcomes of poor parenting. In addition to instructing mothers on how to rear their children, domestic scientists heightened the standards of cleanliness which ultimately ratcheted up women's housework. The availability of domestic workers was declining as women gained opportunities in other job sectors. The market economy delivered new appliances such as refrigerators, washing machines, and vacuum cleaners, ostensibly as "labor-saving devices." But women's time spent on housework increased in response to rising expectations for cleanliness.[38] The court system introduced family courts to handle divorce cases in a less adversarial fashion and to ensure that decisions about the custody of children were made in the best interests of the child. Juvenile courts were also established during this era, reflecting the growing recognition that children were developmentally different than adults. New legislation banned child labor and made schooling compulsory. The rapid growth in employment among low-income mothers prompted social reformers to launch day nurseries for children, many of whom were receiving minimal supervision while their mothers were at work.[39]

The beginnings of a modern welfare state first emerged during the early decades of the twentieth century. Several states began providing aid to mothers with dependent children so that the mothers could stay at home and care for their children. These early initiatives primarily served widowed women, not divorced or never-married mothers. Nevertheless, they were the harbingers for the nationwide programs that offered assistance to needy families (discussed in greater detail in chapter 5), which came on the heels of the Great Depression as part of the Social Security Act of 1935.[40]

MIDCENTURY FAMILY LIFE

The Great Depression revealed the limits of the family for ensuring survival during an economic downturn. Even many middle- and working-class families simply could not make ends meet. Economic disadvantage was fairly widespread in the years immediately preceding the Great Depression. The Brookings Institution estimated that about 60 percent of Americans were living at or below subsistence level. What was remarkable about the Great Depression was that it ensnared groups that had been impervious to economic adversity. As factories were shuttered and banks failed, Americans who had been living comfortably were suddenly without a safety net. About 20 percent of banks closed, wiping out individual savings.[41]

Families struggled to maintain their financial footing. According the 1930 Census, about one in three families relied on more than one wage earner, and in one-quarter of families there were at least three earners.[42] Labor-force participation among married women rose in response to losses experienced by their husbands. Economic adversity and male unemployment had repercussions for family functioning by undermining paternal authority. In many families, no members could secure regular work due to a lack of available jobs. Americans were dying from starvation, and malnourishment was common among children. The economic situation was so dire that the family was often unable to shield its members from adversity. Americans needed more than local government and charitable support to survive. The enduring legacy of the Great Depression is a reorientation in thinking about the limits of the family in a time of severe economic crisis. There was a growing recognition that families were suffering in ways that were too substantial to be overcome without federal government intervention.

Indeed, family life was dramatically altered by the Great Depression. Families were dissolving at unprecedented levels. This disruption occurred through desertion, not divorce, which actually declined. People simply left their families and did not come back. Many parents placed their children in orphanages because they could no longer afford to care for them. Families were doubling up to share residences with relatives and pool housing costs. Age at first marriage rose as young adults delayed marriage entry because they were not economically independent. Many married couples who might have divorced under better economic circumstances remained in unhappy, distant marriages. And the birth rate dropped below replacement level for the first time in U.S. history, as couples delayed childbearing because they could not afford it.[43]

The New Deal provided significant relief for many Americans by creating numerous new programs that supported or protected families. For example, the Civilian Conservation Corps provided employment for the young. The Works Progress Administration created jobs for millions of unemployed Americans. State-sponsored family planning programs gained traction, offering contraceptive education to poor and rural mothers who wanted to control their fertility. In 1935, the Social Security Act established many of the social-welfare programs that persist today. Old-age support through the Social Security Administration alleviated poverty among the aged. Aid to Dependent Children (ADC) gave cash benefits to poor, widowed mothers. Disabled and unemployed persons also gained relief.[44]

To be sure, there were criticisms of various features of the New Deal that sound strikingly similar to the opposition expressed today toward government programs. The Social Security Act of 1935 did not address health insurance. The Social Security retirement system was regressive, disadvantaging those on the bottom, and excluded marginalized classes of workers such as those in farm labor. By creating separate programs for the old and the working age, it pitted these two groups against one another. Social Security is not a means-tested benefit, but this is arguably why it is perhaps the most popular. It has been quite successful in reducing poverty among the elderly. Historians Mintz and Kellogg assert that the Great

Depression is noteworthy, not for a particular program or policy, but rather for the way in which it changed our expectations about what a family can do for its members, bringing to the forefront the limitations of the modern family in the face of a crippling economic crisis.[45] Government supports became essential to ensuring the welfare of the nation.

World War II was a tremendous economic engine that substantially reduced poverty. Manufacturing was booming and workers were in high demand as men shipped overseas to fight the war. On the home front, families were moving to urban centers for jobs or to areas with military bases to be closer to relatives in the service. These population shifts contributed to housing shortages that were exacerbated by wartime rationing of materials commonly used in construction. The nation's housing shortage persisted after the war.[46]

The surge in the economy coupled with the urgency of the war resulted in a rapid rise in marriage and childbearing during the early 1940s. The marriage rate shot up as couples rushed to wed before sweethearts were sent overseas. Many young couples were eager to experience marital intimacy before long-term separation because of the war. Still others got married to be eligible to receive Allotment Annies, which were government payments to the spouse and children of servicemen. The growth in the marriage rate coincided with a rising rate of childbearing. Only husbands with a dependent child were eligible to avoid the draft.[47]

Roughly sixteen million men were in the military. The industrial war effort faced a critical shortage of workers. Women did their part in the war effort by laboring in factories performing manufacturing jobs that were traditionally done by men. The influx of women into the labor force was particularly noteworthy because the majority of the new entrants were married women with children.[48] World War II marked the beginning of the long, sustained ascent in married women's employment that unfolded during the twentieth century. Women produced ammunition and built airplanes. The iconic symbol of Rosie the Riveter was created by the federal government to encourage women to join the war effort by working in often strenuous, dirty jobs. Wives of servicemen were especially likely to be working, probably because the Allotment Annies provided by the military were barely adequate to meet basic needs. At the same time, the American housewife was implored to be "a general in her own kitchen," and accommodate wartime rationing that severely limited the availability of various food and household items as well as gas, electricity, and water.[49]

With fathers at war and mothers at work, children were less closely monitored and supervised. Teens were leaving school to go to work.[50] They spent their earnings on entertainment outside of the home. The peer group gained influence as the authority of parents weakened. Public child-care facilities were opened to serve working mothers and their families, but they were underutilized and often poorly run. Mothers were skeptical about institutional care for their children and the costs were prohibitive for many.[51]

Postwar adjustment was challenging for families. Husbands and fathers returning from the war had to reintegrate into civilian life. Wives and children who had forged new family routines during the father's absence had to recalibrate their domestic life when the father returned. After gaining independence through wartime employment, women were often reluctant to give it up. The government told them it was their patriotic duty to relinquish their jobs to the men returning from war, who had to reestablish themselves in the labor market.[52] Many men suffered psychologically and emotionally following the war, which made reintegration into civilian life difficult. These postwar stresses undermined family stability. Many marriages faltered under the strains of postwar adjustment. The divorce rate nearly doubled between 1940 and 1944.[53] Some of the marriages that dissolved were quickie marriages formed right before the war. Others were torn apart by infidelity.

After surviving the Great Depression and World War II, Americans were poised to turn inward toward the family.[54] The family-centered 1950s, marked by early and nearly universal marriage, large family sizes, and low divorce rates, can be viewed as a reaction to the sacrifices and strains so many Americans had struggled with in recent decades. Peacetime and prosperity prevailed and families flocked to the newly built suburbs, isolating themselves from urban employment centers. Historians refer to this era as the golden age of the family, but of course beneath the veneer of the archetypical happy family discontent simmered, particularly over gender roles. The insularity of families in the 1950s ultimately contributed to their unraveling, setting the stage for modern American family life.[55]

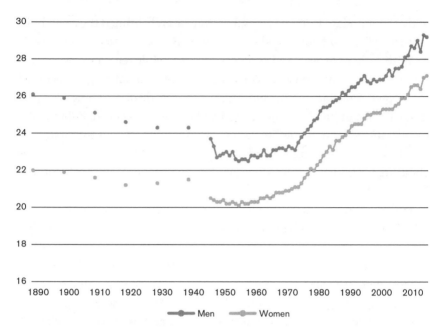

Figure 2. Median Age at First Marriage, 1890–2015.
Source: U.S. Census Bureau, table MS-2, Estimated Median Age at First Marriage: 1890 to Present.

Family patterns of the 1950s are often the benchmark for comparison with today's families. The arbitrariness of this benchmark is magnified when we consider that the marriage, childbearing, and divorce trends of the 1950s were a historical oddity.[56] During this decade, the marriage rate skyrocketed and age at first marriage hit an all-time low of about twenty for women and twenty-two for men. Figure 2 shows the median age at first marriage for women and men from 1890 to 2015. Age at first marriage plummeted during the 1950s and since then it has been steadily rising. Women's fertility rate peaked during the 1950s, as illustrated in figure 3. After more than a century of steady decline that persisted through the Great Depression, the birthrate reversed course and family size expanded, creating the Baby Boom generation (born 1946–64). Families were averaging nearly three children. Almost one in three women experienced a first birth prior to age twenty. The vast majority of these births occurred within marriage. Surprisingly, these early marriages were fairly stable; the

Figure 3. Births per Thousand Women Aged Fifteen to Forty-four, 1940–2013.
Source: Martin et al. 2015, table 1.

divorce rate dropped during the 1950s despite the younger median age at first marriage. Children of the Great Depression were coming of age and eager to start families of their own. The strong economy paved their way to early family formation.[57]

The share of young adults living with their parents declined as they left home to marry and set up independent households. By about age fifty, most parents experienced an empty nest. Meanwhile the proportion of young adults with minor children in their households rose, reflecting the patterns of early marriage and fertility. Married couples typically transitioned to parenthood just a year or two following marriage. Nearly all (90 percent) children lived with both of their parents. Marriages were quite stable during this era. Demographers at the Census Bureau estimated that only about 20 percent of marriages would end through divorce. After divorce, the majority of women and men were predicted to remarry.[58] Marriage was viewed as a key ingredient for individual happiness. Few Americans believed an unmarried individual could be happy.[59]

The resurgence of marriage and childbearing in the 1950s coincided with the growth in the middle class. The robust economy eased the transition from one's family of origin (i.e., the parental home) to establishing a family of procreation (i.e., marriage and children of one's own). Families increasingly had the means to achieve home ownership and low-interest mortgage loans for veterans enabled additional first-time homebuyers. The pervasive housing shortages of the Great Depression and wartime were alleviated by suburban development. Household sizes shrunk as fewer families had to double up. Demand for housing spurred the suburbanization of America, which opened the door to a new way of life that was profoundly child-centered. Families retreated from crowded cities to newly developed suburban areas, enjoying brand new tract housing with green space and populated almost entirely by married couples with young children.[60]

This flight from the urban core isolated families, who relied on automobiles to navigate suburban sprawl. The expanded distance between work and home meant that fathers were spending much of their time either at work or commuting. Rarely at home, fathers were strangers in their own families as mothers ran the household and reared the children. Patriarchal authority was muted. Childrearing experts expressed concern about how this shift in parental roles was altering children's development, particularly for sons. It was feared that by spending so much time with their mothers, sons would become insufficiently masculine.[61]

Women's outsize role in the family did not translate into greater marital power. The companionate family ideal, which trickled down from the upper middle class of the 1920s to the 1950s middle-class suburban family, stipulated that wives and husbands were friends and partners who ideally loved each other, but most wives did not enjoy equality within their marriage.[62] Wives were responsible for the well-being of their husbands and their children. They were to establish and maintain a smoothly functioning domestic realm to soothe their husband and children in the face of the pressures of the outside world. The Cold War era fostered an inward retreat that placed the family at the pinnacle of society.[63] But within many suburban families, women were feeling stymied.

After making significant gains in educational attainment during the earlier part of the century, women traded schooling and economic independence for the security of marriage. Women were expected to derive fulfillment from their roles as wives and mothers.[64] They invested a lot of time in domestic tasks, outpacing previous generations of women, but reaped few rewards for their efforts. Childbearing occurred early and births were closely spaced, freeing married mothers for paid labor. Their options were largely constrained to traditional, part-time positions that might help their families with expenses such as a mortgage or children's college tuition. Women were shut out of various sectors of the labor market that had welcomed them during the war effort. In 1960, about one-third of married women were gainfully employed.[65]

The restlessness felt by many suburban housewives was articulated by Betty Friedan in her 1963 blockbuster book, *The Feminine Mystique*. Friedan wrote about "the problem that has no name," the sense of meaninglessness and loss of identity experienced by middle-class married mothers marooned in their ranch tract homes. The isolation of suburban living, she argued, left women to question their own yearnings without input from others. Discontent was widespread, but women were unaware that others shared their same feelings of frustration. Outwardly, other women appeared content with their family lives, leading women who were questioning their own lives to think there must be something wrong with themselves. Friedan debunked the myth of "the happy housewife heroine" and validated the malaise of suburban women.[66]

Seeds of discontent were already evident by the late 1950s when birth rates peaked and began declining. Age at first marriage also bottomed out and resumed its ascent. By the mid-1960s women were earning roughly 40 percent of all bachelors and masters degrees awarded. And their movement into the labor force accelerated.[67]

Meanwhile, teens and young adults were disrupting the status quo by developing their own subculture that largely was defined in opposition to conventional adulthood. As Baby Boom children came of age, they rejected the conventional pathways favored by their parents.[68] The sedate 1950s gave way to turmoil in the 1960s. Young people called attention to the many forms of oppression facing marginalized groups in society. The women's movement denounced sexism and advocated for equal treatment for women. It questioned the assumption that a woman's place was in the home. For women to achieve equality with men they needed access to the same set of opportunities in the public arena.[69]

The wide availability of the Pill in the 1960s gave women unprecedented control over their fertility, providing them with a nearly foolproof method for avoiding a pregnancy that did not require any involvement from or even the knowledge of their partner. The Pill separated sex and contraception.[70] For married women, this meant they could more realistically achieve their fertility goals, whether they aimed to remain childless, space the births of their children, or avoid future births because they had attained their desired family size. For unmarried women, it changed the calculus guiding relationships by greatly reducing the potential costs of sexual activity. The Pill made the sexual revolution possible, and is viewed as a critical factor in the acceleration of nonmarital sexual activity.[71]

As women sought greater autonomy through the women's rights movement and the sexual revolution, they achieved viable alternatives to the traditional, gendered life pathway of marriage and childbearing. The recognition that they could forgo marriage, pursue a career, or combine work and family fundamentally altered women's life trajectories. Beginning in the 1960s, women gained unprecedented freedom to chart their own lives. An unplanned pregnancy could derail a woman's future plans by disrupting her schooling or employment. According to Kristin Luker, "once [women] had choices about life roles, they came to feel that they had a right to use abortion in order to control their own lives."[72] Thus, access to legal abortion became a central cause of the women's movement. The guiding slogan was "the personal is the political," underscoring the role of women's rights in the abortion debate. In 1973, the U.S. Supreme Court ruled in *Roe v. Wade* that a woman's right to privacy under the Fourteenth Amendment included the choice to have an abortion. Since then, women's access to abortion has steadily eroded as abortion opponents have worked at the state level to limit the availability of abortion services. In 2011, the abortion rate was at its lowest level since 1973.[73]

CONTEMPORARY FAMILIES: DIVERSITY AND CHANGE

The family changes that began emerging in the 1960s and 1970s were harbingers of today's contemporary families. Subsequent chapters in this book detail the trends in U.S. families so for now the goal is to briefly sketch these recent family changes and then contextualize them by examining the sociopolitical discourse on families, namely the enduring culture wars waged in recent decades about whether the family is in decline. The chapter concludes with a discussion of the second demographic transition theory, which informs our understanding of how these historical changes unfolded and their ramifications for family life in the coming years.

The retreat from marriage has marked the past half-century as the marriage rate in the United States descended in rapid free fall beginning around 1970. This coincided with a rise in the median age at first marriage. Scholars debated whether marriage delayed would translate into marriage forgone. In other words, if an individual did not enter into marriage as a young adult, did the likelihood of marriage essentially become infinitesimal? In 1986, *Newsweek* published a cover story with a headline that a forty-year-old, college-educated, white single woman's chance of getting married was smaller than her chance of being killed by a terrorist. This unleashed a firestorm reaction. The calculations that supported such a dramatic analogy turned out to be erroneous.[74] But the damage was done. Although the term *spinster* was not invoked, the effect was the same and the message was clear: if a woman had not married by a certain age, she was relegated to a life of singlehood.

Since the 1960s, young men and women have had alternatives to marriage besides singlehood. The share of adults "shacking up" or living together unmarried was modest around 1970, but grew exponentially in the coming decades such that premarital cohabitation is now normative.[75] Rapid growth in cohabitation was thought to contribute to the delay in marriage entry as couples lived together to test-drive their relationship for marriage. Couples pointed to the ability to gauge their compatibility for marriage as the primary reason for cohabitation.[76]

They had good reason to be skittish about marriage and fearful of divorce. By the early 1980s, the divorce rate reached an all-time high and roughly one in two marriages was ending in divorce.[77] Divorce was viewed by some as emblematic of the breakdown of the family. But for others, divorce signaled liberation and freedom from the patriarchal institution of marriage. Much of the debate centered on the changing roles of women. As they achieved higher levels of education and became more attached to the labor force, women's bargaining position in marriage shifted. They could demand greater equality and had the resources to call it quits if the marriage was untenable.

Economists such as Gary Becker argued that the rise in married women's labor-force participation was destabilizing marriage.[78] Wives were no longer economically dependent on their husbands. With their own incomes, they could support themselves outside of marriage. Marriage was less compulsory. Unlike spouses in traditional marriages in which husbands exchanged their breadwinning for housewifery and childrearing by wives, now spouses were less interdependent. Becker and others insisted that specialization was key to marital stability because it was not only efficient but also encouraged (inter)dependence. According to the independence hypothesis, the growth in women's employment was undermining marriage as an institution by weakening the ties that encouraged couples to stay married. These arguments gained traction as the growth in married women's employment mirrored the rise in divorce during the 1970s and early 1980s.

Other scholars, including sociologist Valerie Oppenheimer, maintained that wives' employment was a rational response to a labor market that was increasingly precarious, especially for men. During the 1970s, men's wages stagnated. Inflation was high. Families kept pace with rising costs by having a second earner: the wife. According to Oppenheimer, the vagaries of the economy necessitated two earners for many families to achieve even a modest standard of living. Moreover, staying in the labor force offered wives a hedge against divorce. If the odds were roughly as likely that a marriage would succeed as it would fail, then dropping out of the labor force to run a household and raise children was a risky proposition for women. A husband's breadwinning enhanced his own human capital and was portable to another marriage. In contrast, a wife's homemaking skills did not pay comparable dividends and children were a liability in the remarriage market for women.[79]

The divorce revolution resulted in the growth of single-mother families. By 1983, about 20 percent of children resided with single mothers and this was the second most common living arrangement for children after the two-biological-married-parent family.[80] Of course, the rise in single-mother families was not solely due to high levels of divorce but also to growth in unwed childbearing. The share of births to unmarried women rose from only 5 percent in 1960 to nearly 20 percent in 1980.[81] Single-mother families and their children suffered extremely high poverty and this disadvantage persists today. About one-half of children living with single mothers are poor.[82] The shaky economic situation of single-mother families was compounded by other factors, such as lack of involvement on the part of many fathers, whether in terms of child-support payments or visitation. These largely absent and uninvolved fathers were labeled "deadbeat dads." Mothers often carried a heavy burden as solo parents, raising concerns about how children fared in single-mother families. Numerous studies documented small but consistent deficits for children living outside of two-biological-married-parent families and this adversity had enduring effects through adulthood.[83]

Single motherhood and "deadbeat dads" were at the heart of the political debate over the decline of the American family. A leading critic of the state of contemporary family life, David Popenoe lamented the marginalization of the family, which he maintained was losing functions and authority.[84] Over time, families had relinquished the traditional functions of religion, education, and work to specialized institutions. These losses, however, according to Popenoe, were not as alarming as the diminished role of the family in childrearing and the provision of emotional support and affection. The downfall of the nuclear family, "the last vestige of the traditional family unit," according to Popenoe, could be catastrophic.[85] Essentially, families were disappearing. They were smaller in size, much less stable, and therefore endured for shorter periods of time. Individuals seemed reluctant to make the investments required to ensure family success and stability, instead preferring to invest in themselves. These changes were to the detriment of children, in particular, who increasingly had only one parent to raise and love them, and the dire ramifications of this "'end-of-the-line' family decline" could persist for generations to come.[86] In other words, Popenoe viewed single motherhood as the centerpiece of family decline. Conceding that adults could successfully live outside of traditional families, he asserted that children simply could not. They needed to be raised in a nuclear family to ensure they developed into successful adults.

This dire portrait of the American family was rejected by many social scientists. Sociologist Judith Stacey offered a trenchant critique of Popenoe's assessment of the state of the family, arguing that his premise rested on a faulty definition that reified the traditional breadwinner-homemaker couple and their children. Stacey rejected this prescriptive, narrow view of the family and advocated for conceptualizing the family more ephemerally as "an ideological, symbolic construct" rooted in history and politics.[87] As noted in the introduction, how the family is defined shapes our assessments of which family configurations are socially valued (and which are not). The definition also informs our evaluation of the family—is it in decline? Stacey and others did not share Popenoe's worries about the demise of the nuclear family.[88] Instead, they denounced the fundamental basis of the traditional family: gender inequality. Marital instability was a signal that the nuclear family was out of step with egalitarianism. Women were not just demanding equality in the workplace but also on the home front. They were less willing to be subordinate to their husbands and had the resources and power to avoid it if they chose. Divorce provided women a way to escape a hostile marriage. Egalitarian marriages may be difficult to form and sustain. Regardless, public policy could do more to minimize the disadvantage associated with divorce and single motherhood, Stacey maintained, by providing social and economic supports for all families, including mothers and their children.[89]

These culture wars of the 1980s and 1990s were not merely academic debates. As described in detail in chapter 5, concerns about rising levels of nonmarital childbearing and single motherhood shaped sweeping welfare-reform legislation that was signed into law by President Bill Clinton in 1996. The reform was multifaceted, but undergirding the legislation was the broad goal of promoting the formation and maintenance of stable, two-parent married families.

TWO AMERICAS: SOCIAL CLASS AND CONTEMPORARY FAMILY LIFE

As the culture wars rage on, we have seen the emergence of what could be described as "two Americas," in which family life is increasingly bifurcated

by social class. At one end of the spectrum, family life follows the traditional script: marriage rates are high and divorce and nonmarital childbearing are low. This pattern characterizes those with a high level of education, defined as a college degree or more. Those with less education
typically experience a different set of family patterns. For this group, marriage is much less common. A sizeable share of children are born to
unmarried parents and reared by single mothers whose economic situation is insecure. Many of these single mothers have children with more
than one man.

These "diverging destinies," as sociologist Sara McLanahan has labeled
the widening gap between advantaged and disadvantaged families, have
long-term implications for children.[90] Children in financially secure married-couple families enjoy unprecedented levels of parental involvement,
particularly from fathers. In contrast, children in disadvantaged families
often reside with a single mother and receive little financial support from
or social interaction with their father. According to McLanahan, "The people with more education tend to have stable family structures with committed, involved fathers. The people with less education are more likely to
have complex, unstable situations involving men who come and go."[91]

This bifurcation of family life is a key factor in rising economic inequality. As marriage is increasingly confined to the privileged classes, some
estimates indicate that this shift could account for upward of 40 percent
of the rise in inequality. Nonmarital childbearing has accelerated most
rapidly among white women with lower levels of education. The racial gap
in the share of children born outside of marriage has decreased in recent
decades. Unwed childbearing trends are converging, particularly for
Hispanic and white women with lower levels of education. Although the
shares among black women are higher across the education spectrum, the
racial gap is closing.[92]

Nowadays, the educational divide is driving family patterns. In the late
1960s, nearly all (95 percent) children in the upper and middle third of
the income distribution lived in two-parent married families. Even 77 percent of the bottom third was in this family form. Today, 88 percent of children in the top third are living in married-parent families, but the levels
in the middle and bottom thirds have dropped precipitously, falling to 71
percent for the middle and 41 percent for the bottom third. In short, the

middle now more closely resembles the bottom, according to Bruce Western, evidence of the growing gap between the privileged and the disadvantaged.[93]

FAMILY CHANGE DURING THE SECOND DEMOGRAPHIC TRANSITION

Contemporary family patterns, such as high levels of cohabitation, a rising age at marriage, widespread divorce, and subreplacement fertility rates, are collectively characterized as emblematic of the second demographic transition (SDT).[94] Marriage is no longer universal. Individuals can pursue partnerships outside of marriage through cohabitation or living apart together (LAT) relationships, or remain single. Marriages are also less stable these days, with nearly one-half ending through divorce. And fewer divorced people eventually remarry, although increasingly they postmaritally cohabit. Childbearing is no longer confined to marriage. Over 40 percent of U.S. births are nonmarital and more than half of these births occur within cohabitation. Having children is optional. Childlessness is commonplace today and among those who have children family sizes are smaller. The early-1960s marked the end of the Baby Boom and ushered in a downward trajectory in fertility. Now, many developed countries are experiencing subreplacement fertility rates. Immigration is not sufficient to offset population loss due to declining fertility. Indeed, below replacement fertility coupled with lengthening life expectancies translate into population aging.[95]

The SDT is not only affecting the United States, but also has swept across western and eastern Europe and now is entering Asia and South America. Cultural changes have been pivotal in the SDT. Secularization and weakening social cohesion have opened alternative life-course pathways. Individuals now have the opportunity to make choices about their family lives, or to avoid family altogether. They are no longer obligated to follow a singular path, constrained by tradition. Now, autonomy reigns supreme and women and men alike are free to pursue their own individual desires. A rising standard of living, greater gender equality, and the sexual revolution along with waning influence by major social institutions (e.g., religion) have spurred the SDT.[96]

CONCLUSION

Throughout U.S. history, marriage has been the basis for organizing families. Initially marriage was an economic alliance between families. By the mid-nineteenth century it began to shift toward companionship and over time the emphasis on a love match took precedence over other factors, including economic ones. Marriage was the setting for childbearing, and children were integral to family life. In recent decades, marriage has become individualized, a union in which couples define their own roles and seek self-fulfillment.[97] Childbearing is disconnected from marriage. Instead, couples increasingly have children in cohabiting unions or choose to remain childless. It is remarkable how much marriage has receded from the center of family life. As discussed in next chapter, several living arrangement options are available in lieu of marriage, which is increasingly out of reach for many, even though most continue to profess a desire to marry. These changes are redefining family formation, altering long-standing patterns and trends.

2 Pathways to Family Formation

Historically, the path to family formation was relatively straightforward, if only because few socially accepted alternatives existed. A marker of adulthood, marriage was nearly universal through the 1960s. Many Americans viewed single men and women with derision and pity, affirming the popular belief that these individuals were mentally ill because they were not married. A 1957 survey revealed that 80 percent of adults viewed those who preferred singlehood to marriage as "'sick,' 'neurotic,' or 'immoral.'"[1] Living outside the boundaries of marriage, then, was not only unusual but also cause for concern.

The family landscape has shifted dramatically in recent decades. Nowadays, slightly less than half (48 percent) of all households are headed by a married couple. By comparison, roughly two-thirds of households were headed by a married couple in the 1970s.[2] Americans are spending less time than ever before in history in the married state. They wait longer to enter marriage, are less likely to stay married, and increasingly do not remarry following a divorce.[3] For a growing share of Americans, marriage is no longer the defining feature of family life.

Instead, we form families outside of marriage. Couples live together unmarried in cohabiting unions. Some of these couples eventually tie the knot, but more often they split up.[4] Childbearing is no longer confined to marriage. Two out of every five children is born to an unmarried mother.[5] In the past, unplanned pregnancies prompted "shotgun marriages," hastily formed to legitimate the birth. These days, couples often respond to a pregnancy by forming a cohabiting union, a middle ground that allows couples to live together without committing to the formal legal ties necessitated by marriage.[6] In short, family formation today reflects families we choose. The traditional tendency toward conformity through marriage has given way to less conventional pathways. Family living arrangements nowadays are diverse and fluid, often held together by informal ties and spanning across households. New family living arrangements are always cropping up. An example featured in the *New York Times* is divorced couples living on different floors of the same brownstone for the sake of their children. One mother stated, "The benefits are that we do not need to pick up or drop off the girls, they just use the stairs from one apartment to the other." Her former husband summed it up succinctly: "We're still a family."[7]

This chapter traces the varied arcs of family formation. It charts the rise of singlehood and solo living, along with changes in the mate-selection process, from courtship to dating to the varied strategies guiding today's couples to the altar—or allowing them to avoid marriage altogether. More couples these days are choosing to remain unmarried. Cohabitation is now a normative feature of the family life course, although its meaning and purpose continues to evolve. The emergence of long-term, committed non-co-residential unions, termed living apart together (LAT) relationships, are yet another indicator of the declining centrality of marriage and the growing emphasis on individualized, pure relationships that preserve partners' autonomy and flexibility. Indeed, individuals often are not in any kind of partnership—married or unmarried—and instead are going solo, living alone.

SINGLEHOOD, DATING, AND LIVING APART TOGETHER

Solo Living

Living alone is a luxury that a growing share of Americans can afford. It reflects our cultural emphasis on privacy and autonomy and the rising economic fortunes of a select group of Americans who are able to purchase this form of privacy. Until recently, single living was extremely rare. In 1850, about 2 percent of all households contained just one person. A century later, fewer than one in ten households held a sole occupant. But in 2010, the share was a whopping 27 percent. More than one in four households in the United States today is a one-person household.[8]

Solo living is attractive to a broad range of Americans but tends to be concentrated among younger and older adults.[9] Young adults who can afford to live independently prefer to do so rather than co-reside with parents or roommates. Likewise, older single adults, most of whom are widowed women, prefer to live independently rather than with an adult child. Widows who are the most financially secure are the most likely to live by themselves.[10] Economist Kathleen McGarry told a *New York Times* reporter that "when [older adults] have more income and they have a choice of how to live, they choose to live alone. They buy their independence."[11]

The going-solo trend not only reflects the rising economic fortunes of Americans, particularly among the aged, but also key shifts in the cultural meanings of family. In particular, the growth in singlehood is consonant with the declining centrality of marriage in modern society and the increased emphasis on individualism. Family ties are less compulsory and more flexible today than in the past.[12] Individuals with the economic resources to live alone may be less compelled to marry because they do not need to rely on a spouse for financial support. Indeed, solo living is especially common among the never-married, a group that appears to be growing.

The percentage of American adults who are never-married has followed a U-shaped trajectory during the past century. After a sustained decline in the share of persons ages 35 and older who were never married began in 1920, the trend reversed course and steadily rose beginning in 1980. As of 2010, 14 percent of men and over 10 percent of women ages thirty-five and older had never been married. By comparison, the historic low point occurred in 1980, when only about 6 percent of men and women aged thirty-five and older were never married.[13] Essentially, we can view this as an indicator of growth in nonmarriage. Few people marry for the first time after age thirty-five. Some experts anticipate that upward of one in four Millennials will never marry. This estimate represents a significant retreat from marriage relative to the patterns observed for older generations. Over 90 percent of Baby Boomers, for example, have married at least once.[14]

The reasons never-married adults provide for why they are not currently married vary by age. In a 2014 study, the primary reason reported by young adults aged eighteen to twenty-four was that they were not yet ready to settle down or were too young for marriage (33 percent). For never-married adults aged thirty-five and over, the main reason was that they hadn't found what they were looking for (41 percent). Only 11 percent reported a reluctance to settle down. Financial preparedness is also a factor and plays the largest role for individuals aged twenty-five to thirty-four.[15]

This retreat from marriage is much more pronounced among blacks than whites. In 2010, about 25 percent of black men and women aged thirty-five and older were never married versus about 12 percent of white men and slightly more than 6 percent of white women. The race gap in 1980 was quite small by comparison with never-marrieds aged thirty-five and older accounting for 10 percent of black men, about 8 percent of black women, and roughly 5 percent of white men and women.[16] The widening racial gap in the never-married status is not entirely understood, but is at least partially due to racial differentials in the availability of marriageable men. According to the Pew Research Center, blacks and Hispanics are more likely than whites to view having a steady job as a "very important" characteristic in choosing a spouse. In 2014, roughly three-quarters of blacks and Hispanics versus just 59 percent of whites wanted to marry someone with a steady job. Yet, not only do blacks face a less generous sex ratio (the number of men per hundred women) than whites, Hispanics, or Asians, the ratio is even more lopsided when restricted to employed men. For never-married individuals aged twenty-five to thirty-four, there were just 51 employed black men per 100 employed black women in 2012. By comparison, the ratio stood at 102 for whites, 107 for Hispanics, and 100 for Asians.[17] Thus, for blacks in particular, there is what William Julius Wilson termed a shortage of marriageable men.[18] This presumes most never-married individuals would like to get married, but it appears that this desire is waning somewhat. In 2014, only 53 percent of never-marrieds expressed a desire to marry versus 61 percent in 2010.[19]

There are viable alternatives to marriage these days. Indeed, not all never-marrieds are living alone—many are cohabiting. About 14 percent of never-marrieds in 2014 were living with an opposite-sex partner compared with 7 percent in 1995.[20] Still others may live with family members, primarily parents. Multigenerational living soared during the Great Recession and continues to remain popular, especially among young adults.

Boomerang Young Adults

The rise in solo living has occurred at the same time as the increase in young adults returning to the parental nest. Multigenerational living is now more common among young adults than among the oldest Americans.[21] Although some young adults are able to go it alone and support themselves, others do not have the resources to live independently. Economic duress often propels them back to the parental home.

Since the 1960s there has been a modest increase in the share of young adults who reside with their parents, as shown in figure 4. In 2010, 51 percent of men and 47 percent of women ages eighteen to twenty-four lived in their parent's household. Among those ages twenty-five to thirty-four, the shares were 19 percent among men and 15 percent among women. Most young adults living in the parental home are single. Married young adults are less than half as likely as unmarried ones to live at home. Still, there has been a notable uptick in co-residence with parents among married young adults. Whereas only about 5 percent of marrieds ages eighteen to twenty-four resided in the parental home in 1980, in 2010 about 20 percent of married men and women ages eighteen to twenty-four lived in their parent's household. By comparison, the figure for singles was roughly 50 percent in 2010 versus about 55 percent in 1980.

Adult children who live with their parents are slightly more likely to be enrolled in school than those who live independently, but the difference is modest. The earnings gap is more substantial, with the median earnings of young adults who live independently about two and a half times higher than for adult children living with their parents. Not surprisingly, those in the parental home are less likely to be employed full-time than those not co-residing.[22] In short, young adults who co-reside with their parents presumably rely more heavily on their parents for economic support.

The economic situation of young adults has become more tenuous since the Great Recession, which took place from December 2007 to June

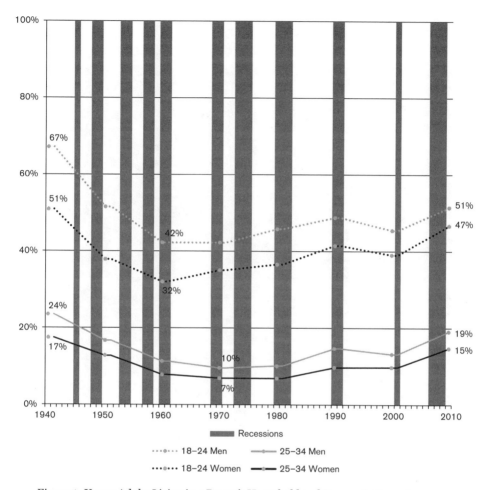

Figure 4. Young Adults Living in a Parent's Household and Economic Recession Years by Sex and Age, 1940–2010. Source: Payne 2012, figure 1.

2009. Regardless of whether they lived in the parental home, young adults typically experienced a tremendous decrease in their earnings. As depicted in figure 5, for those ages eighteen to twenty-four, median earnings dropped by 28 percent (from more than eleven thousand dollars to eight thousand dollars) between 2006 and 2011. Young adults ages twenty-five to thirty-four experienced a 10 percent decline in median earnings, which fell from roughly thirty-one thousand dollars to twenty-eight thousand

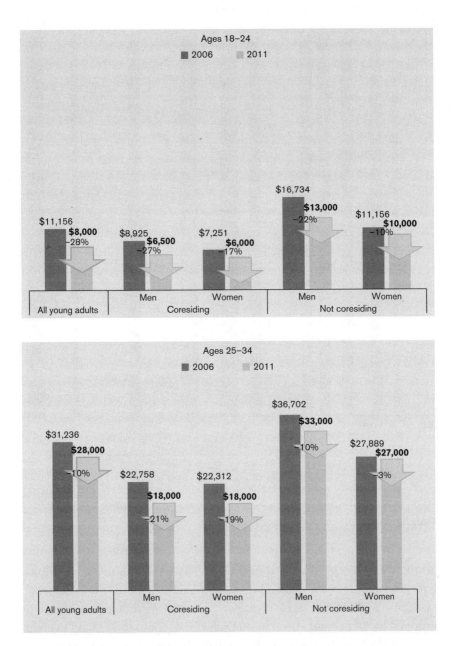

Figure 5a–b. Unemployment Rate of Young Adults Pre- and Post-recession by Co-residence and Sex. Source: Payne and Copp 2013, figure 2.

dollars. Declines were steeper among those living with parents, suggesting that the economic well-being of these young adults is especially precarious. Parents may be helping to fill the void by providing additional economic resources beyond a place to live.

Many of the adult children living with their parents are boomerang kids who left home to attend college, for instance, but returned after graduating. Even college-educated young adults have been finding the path to independence shaky as they struggle to pay down large student-loan debt and gain meaningful, well-paid employment that takes advantage of their degree and skills.

A photo-essay feature in the *New York Times Magazine* in 2014 revealed some of the challenges confronting today's college graduates.[23] Sarah, a recent college graduate with a degree in biology and fifty thousand dollars in student-loan debt noted that while she loved her parents, "it's just hard trying to transition into adulthood while still living with them. As a 24-year-old, I often feel like I'm being treated as a 10-year-old. When their kids are living in their house, that's what they're used to. It gets difficult sometimes with each of us understanding what that means and how to act while trying to still hold the roles." Young adults and their parents are navigating uncharted terrain, attempting to negotiate appropriate behavior and expectations for quasi-independent children who are adults living under their parents' roof.

The financial burdens young adults carry today can impede their transition to adulthood, including marriage. A twenty-seven-year-old named Annie who had seventy-five thousand dollars of student-loan debt said, "Two years ago, I was dating this guy long distance from Wisconsin, and he told me that he would never marry me because of my debt. I was just dumbfounded and taken aback." A twenty-two-year-old man with a bachelor's in economics lamented, "It's just like I'm stuck. I have a girlfriend, but she's living at home, too, because she's almost in the same boat as I am. She is actually rolling in debt right now." Others pointed to the difficulties that living at home presented for dating. Gabriel, a twenty-two-year-old with more than a hundred thousand dollars in student-loan debt said "I date, but it doesn't really ever last long. . . . It's kind of weird, because I don't even want to bring girls over to my house with my mom, so like that kinds of prevents it. . . . Most times I end up just hanging out with my two guy friends."[24]

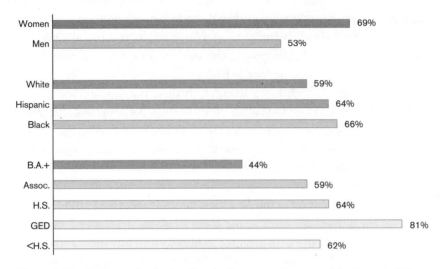

Figure 6. Family Formation by Age Twenty-five across Demographic Characteristics. Source: Payne 2011, figure 1.

Although it is now more common, living at home as a young adult remains undesirable for most individuals. A key indicator of a successful launch from childhood to adulthood is living independently without parental support. Traditionally, this would have meant forming one's own family through marriage, but marriage is no longer a prerequisite for adulthood. By age twenty-five most (61 percent) young adults have formed a family through either cohabitation, marriage, or parenthood, as shown in figure 6. But marriage is the least common pathway. Just 27 percent of adults have married by age twenty-five whereas nearly half (47 percent) have cohabited and one-third have had a child. Family formation by age twenty-five is somewhat more prevalent among Hispanics (64 percent) and blacks (66 percent) than whites (59 percent). Moreover, education is inversely associated with family formation, meaning that the college-educated are least likely to have formed a family, at 44 percent. In contrast, nearly two-thirds of those with a high school degree or less have either cohabited, married, or had a child by age 25.

These patterns not only illuminate the diverse pathways to family formation but also reveal the social-class gradient in family life. Young adults investing more time and energy in their education tend to delay family formation until later ages. With the median age at first marriage at a record high of late twenties for men and women alike, young people are spending years single (or perhaps cohabiting) before eventually entering into marriage.[25] Increasingly, it seems that much of this time is spent, not searching for a potential spouse, but rather "playing the field" and enjoying oneself. Most college students, for instance, insist that they are not looking for a marital partner; nor do they anticipate getting married soon after college. Instead, they are concentrating on their career advancement, and marriage will come later if at all. Marriage is secondary to establishing oneself in a career, according to today's college students.

This approach is not unreasonable, considering the tight job market young adults face. Unlike their parents, today's twenty-somethings are not expected to experience upward mobility. In fact, economists predict that young adults will lose economic ground, achieving less than what their parents did.[26] Their devotion to cementing their career is well placed to ensure their own economic stability as they age. In a 2015 study, roughly 70 percent of young adults in their twenties reported that they had not progressed as far as they would have liked in their careers, and close to 80 percent felt they didn't earn enough money. Not surprisingly then, nearly one-half of young adults receive financial support from their parents.[27]

Dating

Online dating is a burgeoning industry that caters to nearly every demographic imaginable. There are dating websites for Christians, Jews, and Muslims. Some sites serve seniors, other are designed for the divorced. There is even a website for married individuals looking for an extramarital affair. Young adults form liaisons through apps such as Tinder, Tumblr, and Snapchat. The ever-widening range of specialty dating websites coupled with the continued growth in membership in omnibus sites, such as OKCupid, Match.com, and eHarmony, attest to the popularity of searching online for dating partners. It is the go-to source for many, particularly those who are in specialized markets, such as those searching for a same-sex partner or who are in middle adulthood. Online sites provide a deeper pool of available mates than can be identified through more traditional social intermediaries such as family, work, religion, and school. They are changing the way individuals initiate partnerships, especially when they face what have been termed "thin markets."[28]

Now commonplace, online dating has shed much of its stigma. These days only a minority of internet users view online dating as an act of desperation. Rather, most agree that this is a viable approach for meeting people and that online dating actually can help to identify a higher-quality match for an individual. This favorable view toward online dating may reflect the fact that regardless of whether they have experienced it themselves, more Americans now know someone who has had success with online dating. In 2013, nearly 30 percent of Americans reported knowing a person who had formed either a long-term relationship or marriage as a result of online dating, which was twice the level reported in 2005.[29]

A 2013 study by Pew Research found that one in ten Americans has used an online dating site. Among adults who are currently single and searching for a partner, nearly 40 percent have tried online dating. Young people are more likely to use online dating websites than older people. And, online daters tend to be concentrated in metropolitan areas. The college-educated are about twice as likely as those with less education to engage in online dating.[30] The gender imbalance in the use of online dating sites is negligible, although at least one pundit worries that the ready supply of potential dates may serve as a deterrent to forming serious relationships for men.[31] Why settle for one when there is an endless supply of fish in the sea of online dating?

Online daters are not necessarily looking for a spouse. Rather, a majority report using either an online or mobile dating website to meet people with whom they have common interests, hobbies, beliefs, and values. About half (46 percent) are using dating websites to find "someone for a long-term relationship or marriage," while another quarter seek "fun without being in a serious relationship." The share of partnerships that began online remains modest, with estimates ranging from 11 percent to 18 percent among those who formed a relationship in the past decade.[32] Most couples who meet online do not go on to marry. Of course, this trend is not unique to the online dating world but instead is characteristic of the decoupling of dating from the mate selection process. Today's daters are not necessarily in the market for a spouse.

Indeed, the way in which we select our marital partners has changed considerably over time. Prior to 1900, courtship occurred under the watchful eyes of the young woman's parents, who played a prominent role in the selection of a spouse, particularly in the middle and upper classes. Young women and men could socialize casually at a large public gathering, such as a dance or festival. But courting took place at the woman's home in the presence of her parents. In this sense, courting was a more visible, public process in which women and their parents had substantial control. Successful courtships culminated in marriage, which was nearly universal during the eighteenth and nineteenth centuries in the United States.[33]

Courtship was transformed by broader economic and cultural shifts that unfolded at the turn of the twentieth century. In a rapidly urbanizing society in which people migrated from sparsely populated rural areas to more densely habited cities, the potential for meeting partners widened and the ability of parents to orchestrate their children's mate selection dwindled. Young adults enjoyed more autonomy as they earned cash wages in the industrial economy. Dating, which shifted the balance of power to men who were in charge of organizing and sponsoring an activity outside of the home, emerged as the dominant approach for finding a spouse. Parents were marginalized as the couple developed their relationship both in public venues such as the movie theater or restaurant and in personal spaces, particularly the automobile, which provided young couples with unprecedented privacy.[34]

Still, dating and courtship shared the same ultimate goal: marriage. These relationships either progressed to marriage or ended. During the post–World War II era, dating reached its zenith, with young couples meeting in their teens, going steady, and then tying the knot soon thereafter. Age at first marriage was at an all-time low during the 1950s, when half of all young men and women had married before age twenty.[35] One educational film produced in 1950 by the National Council on Family Relations, the professional organization of family scholars, recommended group dating to find a steady partner, providing specific suggestions for group date activities, such as decorating for a school social event and hosting a weenie roast. The next step would be going steady, meaning the couple was in an exclusive relationship that may eventuate in engagement and, of course, the crowning achievement would be marriage.[36]

Beginning in the 1960s, the linkage between dating and marriage began to disintegrate. Age at first marriage ticked up. This decade was marked by tremendous cultural upheaval with the emergence of the civil rights and women's movements as well as the Vietnam War. The Baby Boom generation came of age during the 1960s, urging their peers not to trust anyone over the age of thirty. The Boomers rewrote the script for young adulthood, jettisoning traditional, gendered approaches to mate selection and family formation in favor of "free love." Women's rights groups critiqued marriage as a patriarchal institution designed to keep women subordinate to men. Gloria Steinem famously rejected the traditional role of wife, popularizing the feminist slogan that "a woman needs a man like a fish needs a bicycle." In other words, women can manage without a man. Women enjoyed unprecedented freedom as educational and employment opportunities became more widely available, allowing them to support themselves economically instead of relying on a husband.[37]

The sexual revolution led young people to reject long-standing norms that largely forbade premarital sexual activity. The availability of the Pill for contraceptive use in 1960 gave women (and their male sexual partners) a reliable, discreet method to control their fertility. For the first time in history, sex was separated from the control of reproduction. Premarital sexual activity shot up and, at the same time, the age at first marriage began its ascent. Sex was no longer confined to marriage; couples could enjoy sex outside of marriage with relatively few strings attached.[38]

Nowadays, young couples engage in sex without any relationship expectations at all. "Hooking up" describes a sexual encounter that occurs between two people who are not in a romantic relationship. Although it is akin to a one-night stand, it may or may not include sexual intercourse. The term is purposively vague and can describe a range of sexual activities. Hooking up can be a one-time event that happens at a party or other social event since hook-ups often involve alcohol. Or, it could be a friends with benefits arrangement, which describes sexual activity between two people who label themselves as "just friends" and not in a romantic relationship. These forms of sex outside of any relationship seem to have supplanted dating relationships from a half-century ago, at least among college students. Half of all college students report having engaged in at least five hook-ups compared with just three dates.[39] But mounting evidence suggests that hooking up may serve as a pathway to more traditional, dating-type relationships among young adults.[40] The historical pattern of relationship progression that involved meeting someone, forming a relationship, and then engaging in sexual activity has reversed course. College students often initiate sexual activity with someone they do not know very well through a hook-up. Or, the relationship is strictly friends with benefits and does not involve any type of commitment. Euphemisms such as "Netflix and chill" gloss over the true purpose of the hook-up: a sexual encounter. Increasingly, sex precedes the formation of a romantic relationship.

Some experts express concern about how this reversal may impact young adults' ability to form and maintain long-term, committed relationships. How will young adults learn to cooperate, negotiate, and support one another if they do not form close, personal relationships? This concern partially stems from the debate over whether the hook-up culture is bad for women, an issue that has generated considerable controversy. Women experience less sexual pleasure in hook-ups than in relationships, in part because they feel less comfortable asserting themselves in sexual encounters.[41] At the same time, hook-ups relieve both women and men from the obligations of relationships. Many prefer hook-ups because relationships require a lot of time, a precious commodity for college students feeling pressure to succeed academically and achieve broader career goals.

The emergence of the hook-up culture is further evidence that young adults are in no hurry to find a spouse. Sex is not only decoupled from marriage but is now available outside of relationships altogether. Many young adults are not interested in a serious, committed relationship because it is too time-consuming and would compete with other activities. Those who are interested tend to approach relationships tentatively. Undergraduates engage in "talking," which often occurs through texting and some face-to-face interaction, to assess whether they want to form a relationship. Marriage is typically not an expected outcome.

The evolution of mate selection, from courtship to dating to hooking up and other forms of relationships available today, illustrates the rise of what Giddens termed "the pure relationship."[42] This is a relationship formed and sustained solely to satisfy the self, not to placate others. Relationships are optional these days and pursued not because of social expectations or pressure from family and friends but from one's own desire. Relationships persist only so long as they are mutually satisfying. It is a postmodern era of intimate relationships.

Living Apart Together (LAT) Relationships

The flexibility of intimate partnerships is exemplified by living apart together (LAT) relationships, an emerging partnership type that does not involve co-residence. Although some scholars have defined LAT relationships so loosely that they are indistinguishable from dating, others have conceptualized the LAT relationship as a committed, long-term union that is unlikely to eventuate in either cohabitation or marriage.[43] LAT partners maintain separate domiciles, not because they are necessarily less committed to their relationships than couples who co-reside, but rather to preserve their autonomy. LAT partners value the freedom to be independent and do their own thing. Cohabitation and marriage are viewed are less desirable by LATs because these unions are predicated on dependence and obligation. A LAT relationship enables partners to privilege their individual needs and desires. Spending time apart helps LATs to avoid tension and appreciate the time they do share together. An older woman in a LAT relationship described it this way: "I want to do things together with him, and I'm thinking that would be nice to be in a place where we're together all the time that's not just a trip or a weekend or something. . . . But then I think of the times when we are together, and like I said, I need to be apart."[44]

LAT relationships appear to be gaining momentum among middle-aged and older couples for whom marriage and even cohabitation may hold comparatively few benefits. A combination of companionship and independence is attractive to many who have experienced breakups through separation or divorce. For women in particular, avoiding co-residence helps to ensure that the relationship does not settle into a pattern of traditional, gendered division of labor in which women are responsible for domestic tasks and care work.[45] Middle-aged and older adults are more likely to have the resources to afford to maintain separate residences. A sixty-four-year-old woman in a LAT relationship articulated her unwillingness to marry: "Marriage is a problem when you're older because, okay, if Eli and I got married now, what happens if he goes into a nursing home and if suddenly my assets are his assets because we're married and it sucks it all away, and the money that I intended for my nursing home is now gone? Or if I managed to have assets still intact at the time of my death, it would go to my son. What if I'm married? No, then it goes to the partner. You know, there are complications there and, and legal, and financial entanglements that for me, I just feel like unless the guy's really wealthy, marriage is just not an option, especially if you are looking toward taking care of yourself in your old age and/or leaving something to your children."[46]

Do LAT relationships represent a new family form? Scholars have drawn varied conclusions about the meaning of LAT relationships, with some arguing that LATs signal a disruption in conventional notions of the family. Even LATs themselves vary in their willingness to embrace their relationship type. Some older LATs are ambivalent about their partnerships or actually would prefer to be married or at least living with their LAT partner.[47] But LAT relationships are a telling example of how far we have moved from the narrow confines of marriage as the exclusive path to family living. A few decades ago, couples who lived together unmarried were considered unconventional, but, as described in the next section, cohabitation is commonplace these days and a majority of marriages are preceded by cohabitation, not dating. LAT relationships offer an alternative to both cohabitation and marriage, removing the obligation of co-residence and allowing the couple to stake out the level of commitment and obligation they have to each other. This is the new frontier in individualized relationships in which norms and expectations for partnerships are negotiated by the couple, not imposed by society. LAT relationships offer an unprecedented level of flexibility and autonomy, pillars of modern relationships.

COHABITATION

Cohabitation, which describes couples living together outside of marriage, is "the new normal," according to NBC News. A young woman interviewed for the segment said of her decision to live with her boyfriend: "It was definitely a no-brainer for me. It was always something I planned to do."[48] Living together unmarried has moved from the margins to the mainstream with nearly 70 percent of women ages nineteen to forty-four having experienced cohabitation. A quarter-century ago, just 30 to 40 percent had ever cohabited.[49] Once described using pejorative terms such as "living in sin" or "shacking up," cohabitation is not only accepted by a majority of Americans but actually viewed as a desirable living arrangement. Nearly two-thirds of Generation Xers (born 1965–80) and Millennials (born 1981–2000) believe that living together before marriage is a good idea because it could help to prevent divorce.[50]

The growth in cohabitation has accelerated over time. Figure 7 illustrates the rise in opposite-sex cohabiting couple households (same-sex cohabitation is described later in this chapter). In 1970, there were roughly half a million cohabiting couples. In 2015, there were more than 8.3 million cohabiting couples in the United States, representing a sixteen-fold increase over four decades. The skyrocketing number of cohabiting households is underscored by the corresponding increase in the percentage of single people who are cohabiting. From 2000 to 2015, the share of unmarried adults living in a cohabiting relationship rose from under 8 percent to 13 percent.[51] This pattern is evident regardless of age, although cohabitation is most common among younger singles.

Cohabitation challenges the traditional notion that family ties are established through marriage. Living together provides couples with many of the benefits of marriage, including co-residence with an intimate partner, the opportunity to pool resources, and the chance to bear and rear children together. Cohabitation is often a testing ground for marriage, a dress rehearsal of sorts for couples to assess the relationship's viability for marriage.[52]

Although cohabitors forgo the formal legal advantages that accrue with marriage, at the same time they avoid having to obtain a divorce in the event that the relationship dissolves. Ending a cohabiting union is a private affair that typically occurs outside the confines of the law. In fact, many people are so afraid of divorce that they choose to cohabit precisely because then they do not have to worry about the possibility of divorce.

Now that cohabitation is commonplace, family demographers have widened the lens that was narrowly focused on marriage to encompass cohabitation, using the umbrella term "unions" to describe cohabiting and marital relationships. Over one-quarter of women of childbearing age are

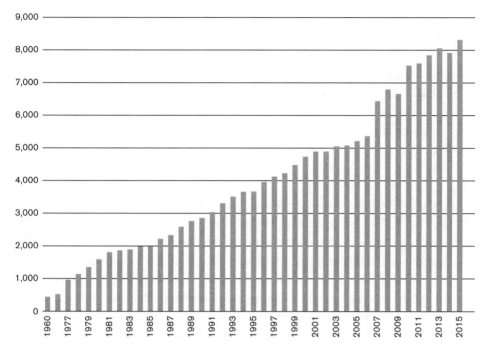

Figure 7. Number of Different-sex Cohabiting Couples Households by Year (in Thousands). Source: U.S. Census Bureau, table UC-1, Unmarried Couples of the Opposite Sex, by Presence of Children: 1960 to Present.

in a cohabiting union—more than twice the level documented twenty years ago.[53] Of all couple households in the United States, 13 percent are cohabiting and 87 percent are married households.[54]

Americans are waiting longer to marry, but the median age at first cohabitation has remained steady over the past three decades at about twenty-two years old for women and nearly twenty-four years old for men. Increasingly, the unions that young adults form are cohabiting relationships rather than marriages. Roughly three-quarters of first unions are cohabitations, not marriages. These patterns hold across racial and ethnic groups, but there is some variation by education. The college-educated are distinctive, with later ages at first cohabitation (twenty-four to twenty-five years old), reflecting their delayed union formation in favor of investment in education.[55]

Cohabiting unions tend to be rather short-lived, lasting just one or two years, on average, before ending either through separation or marriage.[56] The short duration of most cohabiting unions aligns with the primary reason couples say they are cohabiting: to test whether the relationship is viable for marriage. If it is, the couple transitions to marriage. Otherwise, the couple often breaks up rather than continue to cohabit. Over time, the share of cohabiting unions that are formalized through marriage has declined. In the 1980s, about 60 percent of cohabitations "ended" through marriage. Today, just 40 percent of cohabiting couples get married. A majority break up.[57]

One of the key reasons why fewer cohabitations eventuate in marriage is that the bar for marriage entry has risen. Couples have high expectations for what constitutes a marriage-worthy relationship. Specifically, they are desirous of stability and security. Relationships plagued by disagreement, distrust, and violence are unlikely to become marriages. Couples want to feel established financially, meaning they have completed their schooling, obtained jobs, and saved enough money not only to pay bills on time but also to have a big wedding and purchase a home. Ultimately, everything must be in place prior to marriage as a hedge against divorce. As one young mother said, "I am only doing it once! I'm only getting married once."[58] The presence of children is not a deterrent to marriage. Actually cohabiting couples with children are more likely to marry than their childless counterparts. Still, low-income cohabiting parents identified the same prerequisites for marriage; financial resources were paramount. Marriage is a marker of achievement, a signal to others that the couple has "'arrived' in a financial sense," according to one study.[59]

Qualitative research poignantly illustrates the hurdles facing many cohabiting couples, particularly those who are poor or working class. In interviews with cohabitors in an Ohio city, the salience of money was a recurrent theme. One cohabitor lamented, "The love is there, uh . . . trust is there. Everything's there except money." A young cohabiting woman explained: "Um, we have certain things that we want to do before we get married. We both want very good jobs, and we both want a house, we both want reliable transportation. . . . We're trying. We just want to have—we gotta have everything we need before we say 'let's get married.'"[60] Financial security is a key requirement for marriage. Moreover, economic stability paves the way to marriage by helping to ease relationship tensions. Stress and conflict about meeting financial obligations often dominate the relationships of those lacking adequate resources.

Given the high bar for marriage these days, perhaps it is not surprising that most cohabiting couples never make it down the aisle. Instead, they break up. The instability of cohabitation has resulted in the emergence of a relatively new phenomenon, serial cohabitation, which describes individuals who cohabit with one partner, break up, form a new union with a new partner, and so forth. Just as many who divorce subsequently remarry, the decoupling of cohabitation and marriage, as evidenced by the shrinking share of cohabiting unions that are formalized through marriage, has coincided with a rise in cohabitors who repartner.[61]

Serial cohabitation grew almost 40 percent between the late 1990s and early 2000s. During this same time period, the increase in cohabitation was comparatively modest at 26 percent. Nonetheless, most women have not experienced serial cohabitation. It is somewhat more common among never-married versus ever married women, at 30 percent versus 22 percent, respectively, which aligns with the expectation that serial cohabitation might operate as an alternative to marriage. Among married women, three-quarters of those who premaritally cohabited only lived with their spouses.[62] Even though the increase in serial cohabitation has been dramatic, nonetheless most women only cohabit once, typically with the man whom they will eventually marry.

By 2002, cohabitation with multiple partners was especially likely among the women who were least likely to marry, that is, those who ended their first cohabitation by splitting up. Indeed, serial cohabitation was concentrated among disadvantaged segments of the population. Early sexual debut and nonmarital childbearing were linked to serial cohabitation.[63] Serial cohabitors were unlikely to plan to marry their partners and in the event that they did get married, their risk of divorce was high.[64] As fewer cohabiting unions are formalized through marriage, we can expect serial cohabitation to continue its ascent.

The diffusion of cohabitation across the population has firmly cemented this union type in the family life course. Cohabitation is a family form that in many regards operates similarly to marriage and often serves as a setting for childbearing and childrearing. But cohabitors are not a monolithic group and the meaning of cohabitation is variable. Cohabitation serves different purposes for different groups. Researchers have identified several typologies of cohabiting unions.[65] Perhaps the most common one is that cohabitation serves as a prelude to marriage. A majority of cohabitors report plans to marry their partner and these plans are especially likely to be realized when the male partner expresses marital intentions.[66] Yet cohabiting unions less often culminate in marriage than they did decades ago, suggesting that cohabitation as a stepping stone to marriage may be losing ground.

Some researchers have maintained that cohabitation is best conceptualized as an alternative to singlehood.[67] Cohabitors share many of the same sociodemographic characteristics as singles do and their unions are typically short-lived. From this vantage point, cohabitation is akin to intensive dating. These couples do not have plans to marry and often are in relationships of poorer quality than their counterparts in cohabiting unions that serve as a precursor to marriage. Some fraction of these cohabitors have formed their union in response to a pregnancy—this occurrence has been described as "shotgun cohabitation."[68] Couples who are not ready for marriage take a more tentative step toward commitment by cohabiting rather than getting married. Eventual marriage is not a primary concern; rearing their shared child is. Childbearing in cohabiting unions is actually associated with reduced odds of marriage, probably because at the pivotal moment—pregnancy—couples hesitated, so to speak, about making an ostensibly permanent commitment through marriage.[69] After the birth of the child, the magic moment has passed and the difficulties of rearing a young child set in.

For a small group, cohabitation operates as a substitute for marriage, providing a long-term alternative to tying the knot. Less than one in ten cohabiting unions persists for at least five years.[70] Couples in this type of cohabiting union are typically divorced and older. Many are disillusioned by the institution of marriage but want to be in a co-residential intimate partnership. In a 2012 study, this scenario was most common among cohabiting couples over age fifty, who were unlikely to either wed or break up. A union transition for these cohabitors was most likely to result from one of the partners dying.[71] Older cohabitors have less incentive to marry than younger cohabitors. Young cohabitors usually have few assets and build their nest egg together as a couple. For older couples, asset accumulation is largely complete and a primary goal is to pass along an inheritance to the next generation. In fact, adult children often discourage a parent from marrying later in life to avoid the economic and legal obligations marriage entails. Cohabitation is a way for older couples to enjoy many of the benefits of marriage without ceding their economic autonomy and possibly losing Social Security or pension benefits from a former spouse.[72] Since 2000, the number of adults ages fifty and older who are cohabiting has more than tripled, and researchers anticipate this upward trend will persist as Baby Boomers, the first to cohabit in large numbers as young adults (and many of whom have experienced divorce during middle adulthood), move into old age.[73]

Cohabitation is reshaping family life, providing couples with alternatives to both singlehood and marriage. The preeminence of marriage is dimming as couples increasingly pursue cohabitation and less often marry. Family sociologist Steven Nock borrowed Andrew Cherlin's term *incomplete institution* to describe cohabitation because it lacks the shared norms and expectations governing marriage.[74] Cherlin had applied this concept to stepfamilies, positing that as they became more common, they would also become more institutionalized. Nock extended this logic to cohabiting relationships, and drew on this concept to explain why cohabitors often report poorer relationship quality than marrieds. Cohabitors have to actively construct and negotiate the parameters of their relationships such as the division of labor and decision-making power. Despite common knowledge of the traditional, gendered approach to marriage, this is of course no longer the default option. Married couples too have to establish their own set of rules for their relationship; one size no longer fits all. Indeed, Cherlin concludes that marriage is now deinstitutionalized.[75] In this sense, cohabitation and marriage have become more similar. They are both individualized relationships that are built on a precarious foundation of personal fulfillment.

Even though cohabitation less often culminates in marriage, the most common path of entry into marriage is through cohabitation. Two-thirds of married women of childbearing age cohabited with their spouse before marriage.[76] During most of the twentieth century, couples dated prior to marriage. Although premarital sexual activity among engaged couples was the norm, co-residence was not in the cards. Setting up house and sharing a bed occurred after the wedding bells rang. Nowadays, marriage presumably offers few surprises because couples have already been living together. The relationship quality of married couples who cohabited premaritally appears to be comparable to that of cohabiting couples intending to marry. The two groups report similar levels of happiness in their relationships. And, both report comparable levels of disillusionment with their relationships. Couples who marry directly without any premarital cohabitation are uncommon. They tend to report somewhat higher-quality marriages than married couples who did initially cohabit. At the other end of the spectrum, cohabitors who do not plan to marry suffer from the poorest relationship quality and are quite likely to break up.[77] Few cohabitors without marriage plans go on to marry.[78] This constellation of findings illustrates the blurred boundaries between some types of cohabitation and marriage. Most couples who marry cohabit first, and most cohabitors report marital intentions. These two groups constitute the majority of unions and are largely indistinguishable in terms of relationship quality. These blurred boundaries are further evidence of the deinstitutionalization of cohabitation and marriage alike.

According to diffusion theory, as cohabitation becomes more prevalent in the population it is necessarily less selective.[79] That is, the characteristics of the individuals who cohabit are not especially distinctive from those who do not cohabit. This theory has been applied to the linkage between cohabitation and marital dissolution. In the 1980s and 1990s, when cohabitation was less common, numerous studies documented an increased risk of divorce for those who cohabited prior to marriage.[80] Whether this linkage reflected a causal effect of premarital cohabitation, meaning that something about the experience of cohabitation per se heightened the odds of divorce, or whether the greater risk was merely due to selection of certain kinds of people into cohabitation was unclear, as the former is nearly impossible to test empirically.

From the diffusion perspective, the likelihood of dissolution should form a U-shaped curve, with cohabitors most likely to face higher odds of dissolution when cohabitation is either very rare or nearly universal in the population. The lowest point should be when about half of the population cohabits. Support for the diffusion perspective has been found in European and U.S. contexts.[81] In the United States, the association between premarital cohabitation and the risk of divorce has been negligible for couples who married after 1998, a stark contrast from the patterns documented just a couple of decades ago when premarital cohabitors faced higher odds of divorce.[82] How cohabitation is tied to other family behaviors, such as divorce, depends in part on how prevalent it is in the population. Its growing popularity has diminished the role of selection to such an extent that some scholars have argued that we should be examining who chooses not to cohabit, since they are the unusual ones.[83] This shift represents a dramatic change in family life in just a few short decades, fundamentally altering the family landscape.

MARRIAGE

The marriage rate in America has sunk to an all-time low. The National Center for Family & Marriage Research pieced together how the marriage rate (per 1,000 unmarried women) has changed over more than a century, as shown in figure 8. Between 1890 and 1970, the pattern was characterized by undulating fluctuations but was pretty stable on the whole. Beginning in 1970, there has been a precipitous, steady drop-off, with the marriage rate plummeting by roughly 60 percent.

This downward trend in marriage may come as a surprise to the wedding industry, which has successfully stoked demand for ever more elaborate—and expensive—weddings. A ceremony followed by a cake and punch reception in a church basement is a relic of the past. Nowadays, there are destination weddings held at lavish resorts, and wedding events that span entire weekends. The typical wedding rang up at a whopping $31,213 in 2014, according to TheKnot.com. Wedding costs have risen although the number of guests at a wedding has shrunk to 136 from 149 in 2009.[84]

Of course, a couple does not need to have a fancy wedding to get married. They can simply go to the courthouse and pay a nominal fee for a marriage license. But social scientists find that most couples are not interested in a mere "downtown marriage." One young, working-class cohabitor dismissed a courthouse marriage, declaring it "the poor people

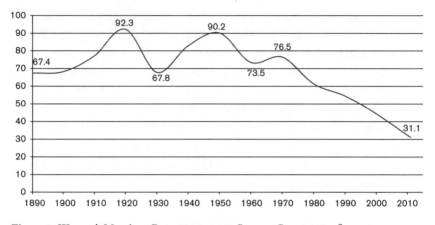

Figure 8. Women's Marriage Rate, 1890–2011. Source: Cruz 2013a, figure 1.

way."[85] Instead, couples want a wedding celebration that is commensurate with the milestone achievement that marriage signifies in modern society. Dream weddings are symptomatic of the meaning of modern marriage. Marriage is a public statement: we've arrived, and we're living the dream.

Today's brides and grooms can afford to celebrate. Once nearly universal, marriage is now the province of the elite. A majority (60 percent) of college-educated women are currently married compared with less than half of those with a high school degree or some postsecondary schooling. Fewer than three in ten women who did not finish high school are married. A half-century ago, educational variation in marriage was modest and college-educated women were the least likely to be married. Since 1990, women with college degrees have had the highest marriage rate.[86]

Similarly, marriage patterns have been diverging by race-ethnicity since the 1950s, with especially precipitous declines for blacks. The share of black women who were married fell from more than 60 percent in 1950 to just 26 percent in 2011. The declines in the percentage married for Asians, whites, and Hispanics have been relatively modest. In 2010, slightly more than 40 percent of Hispanic women, 50 percent of white women, and more than 55 percent of Asian women were married.[87] These racial-ethnic and education patterns provide clear evidence of the socioeconomic divide that is emblematic of contemporary marriage.

Couples used to marry young and build their lives together. In the 1950s, the median age at first marriage was in the early twenties. As of 2015, age at first marriage was at an all-time high for women and men at twenty-seven and twenty-nine, respectively.[88] There is no educational variation in the median age at first marriage; less-educated women are just as likely to delay marriage entry as their college-educated peers.[89] Only thirty years ago, in the late 1980s, women with less than a high school degree married six years younger, on average. The marriage ages of less-educated women have converged with college-educated women. However, the education gap in the proportion of women ages thirty-five to forty-four who have ever married widened between 1988 and 2006-10, indicating that marriage delayed by less-educated women may ultimately translate into marriage forgone. College-educated women moved from the least likely ever to have married, at 89 percent in 1988, to the most likely, at 89 percent in 2006–10. In contrast, among women who did not finish high school, about 90 percent had ever married in 1988 versus less than 80 percent in 2006–10. The difference in the proportions of women ever married by education grew from a trivial difference of a couple of percentage points in the late 1980s to 10 percent by 2006-10. Racial and ethnic variation in the proportion of women ever married also rose during this time period. In 1988 the share of women ages thirty-five to forty-four who had ever married was only about 10 percent higher for whites and Hispanics than blacks. Now, the gap has more than doubled, with 85–90 percent of Hispanic and white women, respectively, ever having married by ages thirty-five to forty-four versus 66 percent of black women.[90]

The declining marriage rate and rising age at first marriage largely reflect the pivotal role that financial security plays in couples' assessments of their readiness for marriage. Men and women alike want to marry someone who is a good economic provider. In most marriages, both husbands and wives are working outside the home. In fact, in nearly one-third of married couples, the wife out-earns the husband.[91] For many couples, wives' economic contributions to the marriage are essential to achieve a middle-class lifestyle, particularly as men's earning power has diminished in recent years. Marriage remains out of reach for most couples without stable employment. It is a capstone event that occurs only after everything else in life has fallen into place—an advanced education, a job, no debt, and maybe even home ownership.[92] This is why marriage patterns today mirror the growing socioeconomic divide.

Rising economic inequality has contributed to the marriage free fall. Although couples usually want to get married, many feel they cannot afford to. Cohabitation offers several of the benefits of marriage while couples strive to achieve a financial footing. For those with lower levels of education working low-wage jobs, financial security may remain elusive, meaning that marriage ultimately is not feasible.

But even the most advantaged segments of society in the United States find the path to marriage perilous. Young adults are spending more time in school, pursuing a college (and often graduate) degree that traditionally has been a ticket to the middle class. They are racking up record levels of debt as the cost of college has skyrocketed, only to graduate to a job market in which unpaid internships are increasingly the norm.[93] Economists have warned that the Great Recession will have enduring effects on the lifetime earnings of today's young adults. Millennials are returning to the parental nest and delaying first-home purchases. The sluggish economy is also likely to impede their trip to the altar. A recent survey shows 15 percent of young adults have postponed getting married because of student-loan debt.[94]

This bleak portrait of marriage in America belies the optimism most of us express about marriage. A majority of young Americans report a desire to marry even as fewer actually do tie the knot. The Monitoring the Future study has interviewed high school seniors annually since the mid-1970s. Researchers at the National Center for Family & Marriage Research tracked marriage attitudes from 1976 to 2008.[95] In response to how important it is to have "a good marriage and family," the trend is stable with over 70 percent of high school seniors agreeing it is extremely important. Another item taps the viability of marriage by asking seniors to agree or disagree that "one sees so few good or happy marriages that one questions it as a way of life." Only a minority of seniors agree, although there has been a modest uptick in the late 2000s when the proportion rose from 30 percent to 35 percent.[96]

Among unmarried adults, a majority (61 percent) reports wanting to marry. Another 27 percent are unsure. Only 12 percent do not wish to marry, according to a 2013 study by Pew Research. The most cited reason for marrying is love, which 84 percent of singles deem a very important reason for marrying. Making a lifelong commitment and having companionship come in second and third place, respectively. Having children and achieving financial stability are less often cited as very important reasons for marriage.[97]

Our cultural emphasis on marriage is pervasive. Not only do most Americans privilege marriage in their personal lives, but so too does our social policy. Over the past two decades, the federal government has spent more than $600 million on healthy-marriage promotion and fatherhood activities. Healthy-marriage programs are designed to provide relationship-skills training to low-income couples to help enhance their relationship quality and stability in the hopes that some couples will view themselves as ready for marriage. These large intervention programs appear to have had few lasting effects.[98]

Moreover, marriage is unlikely to be a panacea for poor women with children. Poor mothers who get and stay married fare better than their single counterparts, but mothers who marry and later divorce are worse off than if they had never married.[99] Given the high rates of divorce for low-income couples, marriage among poor mothers is a risky proposition that is not likely to pay off in terms of economic stability. These patterns are consistent with poor women's fear of divorce, a recurring theme in low-income and poor women's narratives about marriage. For instance, a young single mother whose child's father was not able to find a job remarked, "My whole idea about it is, if we get married, we going to have [to] be serious about it, 'cause I don't believe in divorce. And I can't get divorced."[100]

Despite substantial federal and state investment in marriage promotion, the retreat from marriage continues. Social scientists have posited numerous explanations for the decline in marriage. One of the earliest arguments was developed by William Julius Wilson, who pointed to the shortage of marriageable men, particularly for black women, to explain why marriage has fallen precipitously for blacks. High rates of mortality and incarceration for young black men coupled with their relatively poor economic prospects account for some, but not all, of the racial gap in marriage.[101]

Other scholars have focused on changing roles for women and men. As was described in chapter 1, the economist Gary Becker maintained that marriage is most likely when spouses are interdependent, exchanging financial provision for homemaking and childrearing.[102] This traditional, gendered marriage bargain is less common today, as wives are more often in the paid labor force and husbands are involved fathers. Women who were economically independent would have less of a reason to get married; their gains from marriage would diminish because they could achieve for themselves what husbands traditionally provided: financial security.

Although this argument, termed the women's independence hypothesis, is intuitively appealing, it is not supported by empirical evidence. Since the 1980s, the women who are most likely to get and stay married are those with the highest levels of education and the most economic resources.[103] Indeed, as spouses have rejected the traditional marriage bargain in favor of individualized marriage, men and women alike are searching for the same characteristics in a potential spouse.[104] Economic provision is no longer the sole purview of men. Nowadays, men want to marry women who will be economic contributors to the marriage. Financial security increasingly requires two incomes. Women's economic independence affords women the opportunity to wait longer for a desirable spouse, contributing to the rise in age at first marriage that has occurred in recent decades.[105] Both women and men delay marriage as they secure their own financial footing and search for a spouse whose economic resources mirror theirs.

Marriage is now a capstone event, a status marker that signals to others that one has achieved sufficient economic security and stability to enter into marriage. It is increasingly the purview of a select group of Americans who can afford to get and stay married. Once universal, contemporary marriage is a luxury item attainable only by those with the most economic resources. The shift in who marries and who does not, which we might describe as marriage inequality, mirrors the rise in income inequality in the United States.[106] The widening gap between the rich and the poor is exemplified in the growing gulf between the married and the unmarried. Economic advantage translates into a greater likelihood of getting and staying married. Conversely, economic marginalization is compounded by low levels of marriage. Although marriage is universally held in high esteem in the United States, it is a status that is increasingly difficult to achieve for those with fewer resources.

The prevalence of marriage has certainly declined, yet its symbolic significance has remained high. In fact, the symbolic value of marriage played an integral role in the struggle over same-sex marriage. Supporters argued that marriage is a fundamental human right that should not depend on the gender of one's spouse. Opponents maintained that allowing same-sex couples to marry was at odds with "natural law," which stipulates marriage is a union between one man and one woman, formed largely for the purposes of procreation. The extension of marriage to same-sex couples would undermine the value of traditional marriage, according to opponents. These clashing viewpoints reveal how the symbolic meaning of marriage informed both sides of the issue. Supporters and detractors alike pointed to marriage as a key social institution and status marker to buttress their arguments for or against the legalization of same-sex marriage.[107]

The landmark decision by the U.S. Supreme Court in the *Obergefell v. Hodges* case in June 2015 legalized same-sex marriage across the nation, erasing the patchwork of laws that had existed across states since the mid-1990s. Justice Anthony Kennedy wrote the majority decision, in which he pointed to the symbolic value of marriage in affirming that the Constitution grants same-sex couples "equal dignity in the eyes of the law": "no union is more profound than marriage, for it embodies the highest ideals of love, fidelity, devotion, sacrifice, and family."[108]

Prior to the Supreme Court ruling, thirty-six states and the District of Columbia allowed same-sex marriage. The first state to legalize same-sex marriage was Massachusetts, in 2003. In that same year, most other states had gay-marriage bans. By 2009, same-sex marriage was legal in just five states (Massachusetts, Connecticut, Iowa, New Hampshire, and Vermont) and the District of Columbia.[109] In short, access to same-sex marriage spread rapidly across states from this time to the Supreme Court decision.

The widespread adoption of same-sex marriage by most states and the ultimate decision by the Supreme Court to allow same-sex marriage across the entire country aligns with the tremendous shifts in public opinion on this topic. In 2009, most Americans opposed same-sex marriage. Only 37 percent expressed support, according to a survey by Pew Research Center. The level of support varied across generations, with younger adults more likely to support same-sex marriage than older generations. By 2015, a slight majority (57 percent) of Americans were supportive but generational differences persisted. Whereas nearly three-quarters of Millennials and 59 percent of Generation Xers supported same-sex marriage just 45 percent of Baby Boomers and 39 percent of the Silent Generation expressed support. However, about a month before the Supreme Court ruling, there was broad consensus that same-sex marriage was "inevitable," with about three-quarters of Americans expressing this sentiment, regardless of political affiliation.[110]

Now that same-sex marriage is legal, should we expect an increase in the marriage rate? There might be a modest uptick in marriage in response to the Supreme Court decision, reflecting pent-up demand for marriage among same-sex couples. Roughly one-half of lesbian, gay, bisexual, and transgender (LGBT) adults report that they would like to marry. Similar to the general population, the vast majority of LGBT adults view love and companionship as core reasons for getting married. But LGBT adults are about twice as likely as the general public to point to legal rights and benefits as a reason for getting married. Relative to the general public, LGBT adults place less emphasis on having children or having one's union recognized in a religious ceremony as reasons for getting married.[111]

Family scholars who study marriage will need to adjust their lens to include same-sex married couples. Right now, social scientists lack even a basic understanding about marriage formation and stability among same-sex couples. Which same-sex couples will decide to tie the knot? Will same-sex marriage patterns mirror those of different-sex marriages, with couples who wed being highly educated and economically secure? How stable are same-sex marriages? Although same-sex marriage has been legal in some states for several years, few studies have addressed these questions. Moreover, patterns may differ somewhat across states depending on when same-sex marriage first became available.

The struggle over same-sex marriage underscores the significance of marriage in the United States. Paradoxically, the privileged status associated with marriage has emerged as a shrinking share of adults are married. Many pundits worry that this decline will persist, ultimately leading to the demise of marriage and, by extension, the family. But marriage is unlikely to fade away even though it is much less widespread than it was just fifty years ago. Instead, Cherlin sagely concluded that marriage is deinstitutionalized.[112] It is more flexible and individualized; spouses are no longer expected to conform to rigid gender roles. Marriage may be desirable, but it is not socially obligatory. Rather, it is one in an array of options.

CHILDBEARING

Much like marriage, childbearing is now less obligatory. Fewer women are having children and those who do more often have them outside of marriage in cohabiting unions. Similar to the delay in marriage entry, women are waiting longer to have a child, too. The free fall in the marriage rate is mirrored in the birth rate, which is now at a record low. Childbearing was at a high point in 1960, the height of the Baby Boom, when the fertility rate was 118.0 per 1,000 women. The typical American woman bore three children during this time period. Over the next twenty years, it plummeted to about 65 per 1,000, fluctuating modestly.[113] After rising slightly prior to the Great Recession of 2007–9, the number of births per 1,000 women of childbearing age (fifteen to forty-four) sunk to a new low of 62.5 births per 1,000 women in 2013 and rose ever so slightly to 62.9 in 2014.[114] A state-level analysis reveals that those hit hardest by the recession also experienced the biggest drops in birth rates, illustrating the role of economic distress on childbearing patterns.[115] This decline in birth rates followed economic slumps in the 1970s and 1990s, too.

For the first time in U.S. history, childbearing levels are below replacement. Demographers define replacement fertility as 2.1 children per woman. Essentially, two children are needed to replace the mother and the father. The extra 0.1 offsets losses due to infant and child mortality. In 2013, there were just 1.86 children born per woman.[116] Assuming the death rate and net migration rate remain constant, the U.S. population would be expected to decline in size in the coming years because there are not enough children being born to offset other population flows. Fertility has been below replacement level in the United States since 2007. Of particular concern is the drop in childbearing among the Millennials during the Great Recession. Between 2007 and 2012 the birth rates of women in their twenties fell by 15 percent. This decline occurred across all racial-ethnic groups.[117]

In contrast, childbearing has continued to rise among older women, even during the Great Recession. The birth rates for women ages thirty to forty-four are now at record high levels. In other words, women who give birth tend to be older these days than they were a decade or two ago. In 2014, the birth rate was highest for women ages twenty-five to twenty-nine (105.5 per 1,000), closely followed by women thirty to thirty-four years old (98.0 per 1,000). Until the early 2000s, women ages thirty-five to thirty-nine had a lower fertility rate than teenage women ages fifteen to nineteen. Since then, the differential has reversed and the gap is growing as the birth rate for women ages thirty-five to thirty-nine continues its ascent and the rate for teens remains in freefall. In fact, the only group of women with a lower birth rate than teen women is women ages forty to forty-four. And, this gap has shrunk considerably since 1990, when the birth rate for teens was more than ten times that of women forty to forty-four versus just 2.5 times higher today. Women ages thirty-five and older are more likely to give birth than are teen women.[118]

The precipitous decline in teen childbearing is one of the most notable shifts in childbearing patterns in recent decades. The teen birth rate dropped by half after 1990 and this tremendous decline was evident among all racial and ethnic groups. In 2013, there were just over 273,000 babies born to mothers ages fifteen to nineteen. The decline in the teen birth rate came on the heels of a sustained effort to reduce childbearing among adolescents. Bearing a child as a teenager cuts the likelihood of graduating from high school nearly in half. And children born to teen mothers are at greater risk for adverse outcomes during childhood. The decline in the teen birth rate over the quarter-century from 1990 to 2016 reflected a couple of factors. First, fewer teens were engaging in sexual intercourse and thus the risk of a pregnancy and birth had shrunk. Second, teens who were having sex were more likely to be using contraception.[119]

Apart from the sharp decline in teen childbearing, the age distribution of fertility among women in their twenties, thirties, and forties flattened as the first births were delayed to later ages. Childbearing trends also converged by race-ethnicity with birth rates varying modestly from 59 per 1,000 women among whites to 65 per 1,000 for blacks and 73 per 1,000 for Hispanics.[120] The decline in fertility was especially swift among Hispanics, who exhibited birth rates roughly 40 percent higher than whites in 1990.

At the same time that the overall fertility rate declined, the share of childless women rose. From the mid-1970s to 2010, the proportion of women ages forty to forty-four who were childless had doubled to nearly 20 percent. After 1995, childlessness rose among all racial and ethnic groups and increased among women of all educational levels except for those with a college degree. Among college graduates, 27 percent of women ages forty to forty-four were childless in 1995 versus 22 percent in 2010. Thus, highly-educated women were less likely to be childless than they had been a generation earlier. Although childlessness ticked up modestly among currently and formerly married women during this time period, it dropped considerably among never-married women, falling from 66 percent to 51 percent.[121]

These fertility patterns are another manifestation of the delayed timing of family behaviors. Just as couples have postponed marriage, so too are women waiting longer to have children. But the fertility delay has been outstripped by the delay in marriage entry. The median age at first birth rose from 22.6 in 1980 to 25.3 in 2010. The age at first marriage rose even faster during this time period, climbing from 22.0 to 26.6 between 1980 and 2010. Thus, there was a crossover in the age at first birth and age at first marriage. Historically, women tended to marry first and then have children, meaning that women were younger at first marriage than first birth. Prior to 1991 the age at first marriage was younger than the age at first birth. Since then, the pattern has reversed. The age at marriage is now increasingly older than the age at first birth. This reversal, shown in figure 9 and termed "the great crossover" by the National Center for Family & Marriage Research, illustrates the dramatic shift in the timing and sequencing of family events.[122] The old adage about love, marriage, and a baby carriage has been turned upside-down. These days, women are often younger when they have a child than when they get married, reflecting the reordering of key family life events. Childbearing often precedes marriage.

By 2005-9 , well over half of first married women with no more than a high school diploma had a premarital birth and about one-third of first married women with some college had a child before marriage. In contrast, only 5 percent of first married women with a college degree had a premarital birth. This is a growing trend among less-educated women, but for those with a college degree the share with a premarital birth has not changed much in recent decades. For both white and black women, the share of married women with a premarital birth has climbed steadily since the 1960s.

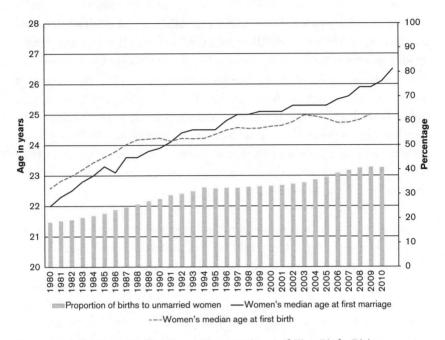

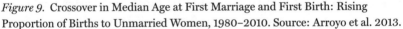

Figure 9. Crossover in Median Age at First Marriage and First Birth: Rising Proportion of Births to Unmarried Women, 1980–2010. Source: Arroyo et al. 2013.

About 20 percent of white women and more than one-half of black women in first marriages experienced a premarital birth. Overall, nearly three in ten first married women have given birth before marriage.[123]

Indeed, perhaps the most profound change in childbearing patterns in recent decades is the shift in the relationship context of births, which occur less often in marriage and more often outside of marriage. Childbearing and marriage have been decoupled. In 1960, just 5 percent of all births were to unmarried women. In 1980, the share was roughly 21 percent. By 2013, more than 40 percent of births were to women who were not married.[124]

This growth has occurred for all women, regardless of race or ethnicity. Keep in mind that marriage has declined for all racial-ethnic groups, particularly blacks. This retreat from marriage has implications for the relationship context in which births occur. Consistent with their lower levels of marriage, black women are most likely to have births outside of marriage.

Yet the rise over time in nonmarital births has been steepest among white women. The share of births that were to unmarried white women increased from 12 percent to 29 percent between 1980 and 2013. For black women, the increase was comparatively modest but the levels were already relative high. From 1980 to 2013, the share of unmarried births rose from 62 percent to 75 percent for black women. Hispanic women were in the middle with 21 percent of births to unmarried women in 1980 versus 60 percent in 2013.[125] Here again, there is evidence of convergence by race and ethnicity. The racial-ethnic differentials in nonmarital fertility are less pronounced today than they were three or four decades ago.

More striking differences emerge when we consider variation by maternal education. The share of births that are to unmarried women have risen regardless of education level, but the education differentials are more bifurcated than linear, reflecting the diverging-destinies concept described in chapter 1. In 1980, there was a clear education gradient, with the share of unmarried births steadily declining as women's education level rose. Now, the distinction is simply college-educated women versus all others. This bifurcation emerged because the growth in unmarried births has been greatest among women with either a high school degree or some college, and these women now appear more similar to women without a high school diploma. Among those who did not finish high school, nearly two-thirds of births are to unmarried women. For those with a high school diploma, over half of births occur outside of marriage. And among women with some college, more than two out of five births are unmarried. In contrast, just 11 percent of all births to college graduates are outside of marriage. For the most-educated women, childbearing continues to be closely tied to marriage.[126] Nearly all births to college-educated women occur within married unions. The distribution of unmarried childbearing, much like marriage, has diverged by education with college-educated women exhibiting high levels of "traditional" family behaviors: they are most likely to marry and least likely to have a child outside of marriage.

The rapid acceleration in unmarried childbearing is largely driven by corresponding increases in cohabitation. Unmarried births can occur to either single, unpartnered mothers or to cohabiting women who co-reside with the father of the child. Cohabitation is a family context and roughly half of all cohabiting unions include shared biological children. The birth

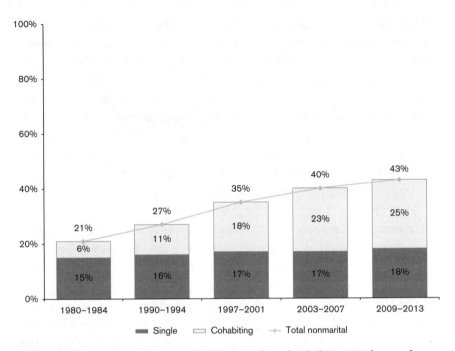

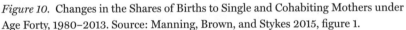

Figure 10. Changes in the Shares of Births to Single and Cohabiting Mothers under Age Forty, 1980–2013. Source: Manning, Brown, and Stykes 2015, figure 1.

rate among cohabiting women is nearly as high as that for married women of childbearing age.

Until the mid-1990s, most unmarried births were to single rather than cohabiting mothers. From the late 1990s to the early 2010s, births to cohabiting mothers outpaced those to single mothers, as illustrated in figure 10. The overall trend in the share of births to single mothers was marked by a slow increase, rising from 15 percent of all births in the early 1980s to 18 percent of births in the early 2010s. Meanwhile, the share of births to cohabiting mothers quadrupled over this time period, from 6 percent to 25 percent. In short, nearly all of the recent increase in unmarried births has been due to the rise in cohabiting births, not births to single women. Most births still occur to women in intimate unions, but these unions are more often cohabiting relationships, not marriages.

In 2009-13, there was notable racial and ethnic variation in cohabiting births. For black women, most unmarried births were to single, unpartnered mothers whereas for Hispanic and white women a majority of unmarried births were to cohabiting mothers. Among black women, 46 percent of births were to single mothers whereas just 29 percent were to cohabiting mothers. Among Hispanic women, only 20 percent of births were to single mothers and 40 percent were to cohabiting mothers. The pattern was similar among white women with 11 percent of births to single mothers and 29 percent to cohabiting mothers.[127]

Unmarried births occur disproportionately to cohabiting rather than single mothers, regardless of education level. At all education levels, more than one-half of the unmarried births in 2009-13 were to cohabiting women. In fact, roughly a third of all births to mothers with a high school diploma or less occurred within cohabitation. Among women with some college, one in four births was to a cohabiting mother. Cohabiting births remained quite rare among college-educated mothers, accounting for a mere 8 percent of all births. Of course, births to single, unpartnered women with a college degree were even more unusual, comprising just 3 percent of all births to these women in 2009-13.[128]

The demographic composition of women differs by birth context. Women who have an unmarried birth tend to be more disadvantaged, on average, than those who experience a marital birth. According to a study by Cruz, women who gave birth outside of marriage tended to be younger, with one-half under age twenty-five. In contrast, a majority (57 percent) of women who had a married birth were aged thirty or older. Among women who gave birth in 2011, just 7 percent of those with an unmarried birth had a college degree compared with 43 percent among those who had a married birth. One-half of women who had an unmarried birth were living in poverty versus just 14 percent of women who had a married birth.[129]

Several factors account for the dramatic growth in unmarried child-bearing. As outlined in the 1995 Report to Congress on Out-of-Wedlock Childbearing, there are five key reasons why nonmarital fertility is on the rise. One factor is delayed marriage. Although the age at marriage has risen, young adults tend not to wait until marriage to engage in sexual intercourse. Most young adults initiate sexual relationships beginning in their late teen years, which exposes them to the risk of a nonmarital birth. The longer young adults wait to marry, the greater the exposure to the risk of a birth outside of marriage. High rates of divorce have also contributed to the rising nonmarital birth rate. Following divorce, women are likely to have sexual partners, particularly in cohabiting unions. About one-third of nonmarital births are actually postmarital, occurring among previously married women. A third factor is nonmarriage. Some women never marry at all, meaning they spend their entire reproductive years single and eligible to have a birth outside of marriage. A fourth factor is cohabitation. Nearly all of the increase in nonmarital childbearing has occurred within cohabiting unions. Cohabitation offers access to a regular sexual partner, increasing the chances of a birth. Finally, shifts in pregnancy resolution are linked to the rise in nonmarital childbearing.[130] Adoption and abortion are less common today than a few decades ago, largely reflecting the decreased stigma surrounding unwed pregnancy and childbearing. Also, abortion access is more restricted in many states and there are fewer providers, which makes it difficult for women, particularly those with fewer economic resources, to obtain an abortion.[131] Increasingly then, women carry their pregnancies to term and rear their children.[132]

The decoupling of marriage and childbearing has contributed to the emergence of multiple partner fertility (MPF), a term that describes having children by more than one partner. In the past, this phenomenon might have occurred within the context of remarriage, but these days it takes place outside of marriage, too. Many mothers and fathers who experience multiple partner fertility have never been married. Parents who have two or more children are eligible to have MPF. About one-quarter of men and women in their forties who have at least two children have MPF. MPF is especially common among those who had an early first birth as well as those whose births were unintended. The prevalence of MPF is greater among younger cohorts, signaling a rise in family complexity.[133] Much like the upward trends in serial cohabitation and partnering, MPF is akin to serial fertility.

Parenthood is achieved through varied contexts, including singlehood, cohabitation, and marriage. Regardless of the context in which it occurs, having a child is a marker of adult status. Part of the reason why the birth rate is somewhat low is because our culture emphasizes child quality and expects parents to make considerable investments of money and time in the upbringing of their children. In fact, large family sizes among the wealthy seem to be on the upswing. Writing in the *Boston Globe*, Kara

Baskin used the term "posh procreation" to describe what some believe is a new trend: "having multiple children is a status symbol." One woman she interviewed remarked "If you're wealthy enough, four is the new three, and three is the new two."[134] These large families signal that parents have the resources to support several children at a very high standard of living.

At the other end of the economic spectrum, parenthood is a defining identity for disadvantaged women and men. The pathway to family formation for many low-income individuals is through childbearing rather than cohabitation or marriage. According to Kathryn Edin and Maria Kefalas, whose in-depth study of motherhood among poor women is the subject of their book *Promises I Can Keep: Why Poor Women Put Motherhood before Marriage*, mothers

> credit their children for virtually all that they see as positive in their lives. Even those who say they might have achieved more if they hadn't become parents when and how they did almost always believe the benefits of children far exceed the costs. . . . Motherhood still offers a powerful source of meaning for American women. This is particularly true for low-income women . . . who have little access to the academic degrees, high status marriages and rewarding professions that provide many middle- and upper-class women with gratifying social identities. . . . The absolute centrality of children in the lives of low-income mothers is the reason that so many poor women place motherhood before marriage, even in the face of harsh economic and personal circumstances. . . . Marriage is a longed-for luxury; children are a necessity.[135]

For low-income men, impending fatherhood is a stage of relationship progression. As couples become more serious, they often use birth control sporadically or not at all. Pregnancy and childbirth help to cement the couple's relationship, at least in the short term. But the stressors and strains that accompany the transition to parenthood, combined with the weak relationship commitment for many of these couples, ultimately destabilizes these partnerships. The couple relationship often fizzles and the ties between fathers and their children are tenuous. Nonetheless, fatherhood is integral to low-income men's identity. In their book *Doing the Best I Can: Fatherhood in the Inner City* Edin and Timothy Nelson find that "fatherhood is not merely a desired status but an eagerly embraced role."[136] These fathers want to marry a soul mate, but do not tend to view the mothers of their children as potential spouses. Edin and Nelson conclude that it is fatherhood, not the couple relationship, which is of primary importance to low-income men. Whereas fatherhood and marriage (or a partnership) are part of a package deal for middle-class men, there is no such package for low-income men. Fatherhood assumes center stage and the relationship with the mother of the child is secondary.

CONCLUSION

The conventional path to family formation is now the road less taken. Fewer adults follow the once-standard script of dating, marriage, and childbearing. Nowadays, many young people are not looking for a spouse but instead are bolstering their career prospects by staying in school longer. Increasingly, young adults are living with their parents as they struggle to gain a foothold in the economy and shoulder the burden of educational debt. Those who can afford to often go it alone, preferring to maintain their independence. The growth in solo living has been phenomenal and signals the viability of opting out of family living. Hooking up offers intimacy without expectations. LAT relationships are another example of how individuals are striking a new balance between autonomy and close relationships. Long-term committed unions do not always eventuate in cohabitation or marriage.

Fewer than half of U.S. adults are married, telling evidence that marriage is far from the universal experience it was just a few generations ago. The rapid acceleration in cohabitation has contributed to the delay in marriage entry and offers a viable alternative to marriage, particularly among older adults for whom marriage holds fewer benefits and often entails significant economic costs. Cohabitation is now the most common pathway to marriage but fewer cohabiting couples are marrying these days. Even though most Americans want to get married, fewer do. The high bar for marriage is shutting out all but the most advantaged. The meaning of marriage has morphed, elevating its symbolic significance. Marriage is an achievement that signals economic success and stability. As such, it is a distant, elusive goal for more Americans.

It is striking how much family patterns are diverging by social class. The growing economic divide is reshaping family life, particularly for those who do not have a college degree. The moderately educated (high school degree or some postsecondary schooling) now appear similar to the least educated in terms of their family formation behaviors. Marriage has plummeted among these groups while cohabitation and nonmarital childbearing have skyrocketed. The college-educated are now distinctive for their "traditional" family patterns of relatively high marriage rates and nearly all births within marriage.

The family landscape is diverse, reflecting varied pathways to partnership and parenthood. Of course, neither union formation nor childbearing are compulsory. The retreat from marriage and rise in childlessness has been pronounced in recent decades. Our culture is more accepting of families formed outside of marriage. At the same time, marriage has become more inclusive and flexible. Same-sex couples can marry and enjoy the benefits previously available only to different-sex couples. Married couples are free to construct individualized marriages with roles and expectations that suit their own purposes. The flexibility characterizing contemporary family formation may help to solidify family ties. Alternatively, it may be indicative of our reluctance to "go all in" and fully commit to our partners. The next chapter considers the trends in and consequences of union dissolution, including divorce, the dissolution of cohabiting unions, and widowhood, and how these experiences set the stage for subsequent repartnership.

3 Union Dissolution and Repartnering

The family-formation patterns described in chapter 2 are inextricably tied to trends in union dissolution and repartnership that are the subject of this chapter. For example, the rise in premarital cohabitation in recent decades was partially spurred by young adults' fears of divorce.[1] Having come of age during the divorce revolution in the 1970s and early 1980s, many young people had experienced parental divorce and were anxious to avoid their own divorces. Cohabitation was viewed as a way to test drive a relationship and appraise its fitness for marriage. It also served as a stop-gap to marriage. As one cohabitor put it, "Marriage is a big step. . . . But if you get married, I don't want to be one of those couples that gets married and three years later gets a divorce."[2] Couples who cohabit actually face very high levels of instability and a shrinking share ultimately marry their partner. Instead, they experience cohabitation dissolution.[3]

In some ways, family formation and dissolution are two sides of the same coin. That is, marriage and divorce trends are interwoven. Individuals are marrying at later ages, which helps to reduce their risk of divorce.[4] The shifting composition of who gets married shapes marital stability. Because marriage is now largely the province of the most advantaged in society, marital stability has increased. Divorce is no longer rising and actually has declined for younger adults, reflecting the advantaged profile of today's married couples.[5] Following divorce, individuals may remarry, form a cohabiting union, or remain unpartnered. Part of the reason the overall marriage rate has shrunk is because previously married individuals are less likely to tie the knot again.[6] Remarriage is declining, particularly among younger people.[7] Still, remarriage remains associated with a higher risk of divorce than first marriage for myriad reasons described later in this chapter.[8] And it is a leading factor in the recent "gray-divorce" phenomenon, divorces that occur among individuals aged fifty and older. The gray-divorce rate has doubled since 1990.[9]

This chapter addresses union dissolution and repartnership. Union dissolution occurs through either divorce or spousal death among those who are married. And for those in cohabiting unions, dissolution results from separation. The next section traces the historical arc of divorce, which accelerated until the 1980s and has essentially plateaued since then.[10] Why do marriages end through divorce? Both macro-, societal-level factors and individual risk factors for divorce are considered. What are the consequences of divorce? Divorce can be an extremely stressful, disruptive experience with wide-ranging implications for the well-being of adults and their children in both the immediate aftermath of divorce and over the long haul.[11] Similarly, marital disruption through widowhood negatively affects the surviving spouse and actually increases his or her risk of death.[12] The implications of cohabitation dissolution are less well understood but are examined here, too. Union dissolution may be followed by repartnership, whether through remarriage or postmarital cohabitation. The chapter closes with a section on remarriage trends and an explication of the significant challenges surrounding remarriage and stepfamily living that ultimately destabilize many of these repartnerships.[13]

DIVORCE

When Americans take their marriage vows, they promise to stay together "until death do us part." But nearly half of all marriages in the United States end through divorce.[14] Divorce is so widespread that many young couples delay or even forgo marriage altogether simply to avoid the possibility of having to experience it.[15] The fear of divorce appears to have contributed to several notable changes in contemporary family life: the growth in cohabitation, the rise in age at first marriage, and the small but growing trend of nonmarriage. Although Americans are quite accepting of divorce—and many experience divorce themselves—nonetheless they appraise it as a tremendously stressful life event, ranking below only spousal death.[16]

Divorce is not a recent phenomenon. It has a long history in the United States that can be traced back more than 150 years. The trend in the proportion of marriages that end through divorce is one of exponential increase. From the 1860s to the 1980s, the divorce rate accelerated, picking up speed in the post–World War II era. Estimates indicate that roughly 5 percent of marriages in 1860s ended through divorce. By 1900, the share had more than doubled to 12 percent. Another doubling occurred over the next forty years, with 25 percent of marriages having ended in divorce in 1940.[17] By 1960, nearly 40 percent of married couples divorced and by 1980, the widely cited 50 percent level was reached.[18] Roughly one in two marriages were ending through divorce by the early 1980s. Marriages were as likely to fail as they were to succeed.

Most people believe that divorce is continuing to climb. It has become more difficult to assess recent divorce trends because the United States stopped collecting state-level divorce statistics in the mid-1990s, citing prohibitive costs associated with gathering the appropriate data from states. Scholars suggested that the divorce rate was stable or possibly even declining slightly.[19] Most estimates pegged the risk of divorce as somewhere around 40 to 45 percent, with younger people in first marriages least likely to get divorced. In fact, researchers maintained that young, highly educated married couples were at lower risk of divorce than their counterparts were a generation ago.[20]

A new study by demographer Sheela Kennedy and historian Steven Ruggles has called into question the broadly accepted notion that the divorce rate was stable over the past few decades. Using age-adjusted divorce rates, they concluded that divorce is still rising. The patterns of divorce differed across age groups with those under forty less likely to divorce today than a generation ago whereas those over forty were increasingly likely to experience divorce.[21] This trend in part reflects the growing selectivity of marriage. Only the most stable and secure young adults are choosing to tie the knot and they now enjoy higher marital stability than did their parents.

In contrast, the rate of divorce among married persons ages fifty and older has doubled over the past two decades. This trend, termed the gray-divorce revolution, is redefining who gets divorced. In 1990, less than 10 percent of people who got divorced were age fifty or older. Today, one in four people getting divorced are in this age group.[22] Of course, the U.S. population is older today than it was twenty years ago, but much of the shift in the age distribution of those getting divorced reflects the doubled gray-divorce rate. The causes and consequences of the gray-divorce revolution are not well understood, but researchers are beginning to investigate how divorce in later life may be linked to health and well-being.[23] Later-life divorce coincides with other life transitions such as launching children from the parental nest, retirement, and deterioration of physical and cognitive health.[24] Whether gray divorce diminishes the capacity of individuals to adapt to these life transitions is a key question that researchers need to address to ensure the well-being of what could be an increasingly vulnerable, socially isolated older population.

In addition to age variation in the divorce rate, divorce patterns differ by race-ethnicity and education. The divorce plateau that emerged around 1980 was driven by falling divorce among well-educated whites. For blacks and those with lower levels of education, the divorce rate continued its ascent.[25] Although the chances of divorce have declined for women with at least a college degree, the risks have climbed for women with less education, signaling a bifurcation in divorce. The education gradient in divorce has magnified over time.[26] Likewise, the risk of divorce for blacks is persistently higher than that of either whites or Hispanics.[27] The explanation for this racial differential is not entirely clear. Part of the gap is explained by racial variation in age at marriage, education, and premarital childbearing, but these compositional factors alone do not fully account for the differential.[28]

Explaining the Rise in Divorce

The historical rise in divorce has coincided with broad, societal level changes.[29] Shifting views of marriage and divorce are two primary reasons why divorce accelerated over much of the twentieth century. Rising labor-force participation among women also has been linked to the divorce revolution, largely because economic independence provides wives with the financial means to leave unsatisfying marriages. Moreover, the growth in paid employment among women has redefined the roles of women and men in marriage. Nowadays, the roles of wives and husbands are more variable and less prescriptive than in the past.[30] Gender boundaries are blurred in many contemporary marriages, with wives engaged in bread-winning and husbands actively rearing children.[31]

ATTITUDES TOWARD MARRIAGE

One reason why divorce has increased is the change in what constitutes a successful marriage.[32] More than a century ago, marriage was institutional, an economic alliance forged between two families. The basis of marriage was not romance and love. Instead, couples were bound together through economic dependence, duty, and obligation. Patriarchy governed marriage, anointing the husband as the head of the family. Wives were legally subsumed under their husbands and in the eyes of the law were dependents akin to minor children. Indeed, divorce was available to men, but not to women, reflecting the prevailing view that wives were an economic asset of their husbands. The grounds for divorce were narrow: desertion, adultery, and cruelty.[33]

Beginning in the twentieth century, the meaning of marriage increasingly centered on companionship and romantic love as the foundation for matrimony. Marriages became more fragile as couples emphasized love matches.[34] Love and companionship moved from the margins to the center and became the defining feature of a good marriage. A loveless marriage may be endured, but it was not desirable. This rise of companionate marriage in the twentieth century corresponded with a sustained increase in divorce as couples more often called it quits when they fell out of love.[35]

In recent decades, the bar for marriage has only continued to rise, as companionate marriage has been replaced by individualized marriage, which stresses the centrality of personal fulfillment through marriage. Americans have very high expectations for their unions, as described in chapter 2. It is no longer enough to effectively perform one's role as a wife or husband. The marriage itself must provide individual satisfaction and a sense of self-fulfillment, ultimately enhancing personal well-being. Marriage does not rest on roles or obligations but instead is individualized, constructed according to the inclinations of the couple. A good marriage offers love and happiness. When marriage fails to meet one's emotional needs, then divorce is a viable solution.[36]

The prerequisites for marriage are difficult to meet for many Americans, let alone sustain over several decades. Some might deem these expectations too high and ultimately unrealistic. Family scholar Norval Glenn described this as the marriage paradox.[37] Our fear of divorce leads us to hold back in our marriages, to not fully invest ourselves in the union. This reluctance to "go all in" has the unanticipated consequence of actually destabilizing the union. Without having fully given ourselves over to marriage, we have our defenses up, rendering the foundation of the union more fragile, and ultimately facilitating its eventual demise. From Glenn's perspective, our fear of divorce is essentially a self-fulfilling prophecy, undermining marital stability.

ATTITUDES TOWARD DIVORCE

As our expectations for marriage have changed and evolved over time, so too have our views of divorce. Historically, divorce was rare and stigmatized. Few Americans looked favorably on divorce, especially for married parents. Divorce represented a personal or moral failing that reflected poorly on the couple.[38] Of course, nowadays divorce retains no real stigma in the United States. The vast majority of Americans believe divorce is an acceptable resolution to an unhappy marriage, even when children are involved.[39]

Why have Americans become so accepting of divorce? Many point to the emergence of no-fault divorce laws. The grounds for divorce expanded greatly over the course of the past century, culminating in the passage of the first no-fault divorce law, in the state of California in 1969.[40] This landmark legislation enabled couples to divorce without having to stipulate that one spouse was at fault, or had committed one of the few acts that were required to be granted a divorce by the state. Now, couples did not have to prove that one spouse had wronged the other. Instead, they could simply point to "irreconcilable differences," a term that essentially means the couple does not get along and cannot resolve their grievances. They are no longer happy with each other or their marriage and are ready to call it quits.

Many worried that no-fault divorce would open the floodgates, causing a huge spike in divorce. As other states followed California's lead, no-fault divorce became more widely available. New York was the last state to enact no-fault divorce, but it did not do so until 2010. Scholars have struggled to establish the order of events. Was the run-up in divorce during the 1960s and 1970s a result of new no-fault divorce laws? Or, did the new legislation simply reflect the contemporary mindset of Americans, which held that divorce was a decision to be made by the couple, without the state's interference? Prior to the passage of no-fault divorce laws, many couples engaged in sham divorce proceedings, pretending one spouse was adulterous, for instance, to obtain a divorce.[41] Many legal experts maintain that the emergence of no-fault divorce was in direct response to the increasing number of divorce cases in which neither spouse had actually committed a violation that was grounds for divorce. From this standpoint, no-fault divorce was a response to broader social change that was already underway. Rather than subject couples to a drawn out, expensive, and ultimately deceitful divorce process, by enacting no-fault divorce laws, the divorce process was simplified and became less onerous for couples.[42]

WOMEN'S LABOR-FORCE PARTICIPATION

One of the most profound social changes to occur during the twentieth century was the rise in female labor-force participation. As noted in chapter 1, during the early decades of the twentieth century women often worked until they married. Upon marriage, most women eschewed their role as workers in favor of their new roles as wife, homemaker, and eventually mother. The middle-class ideal at that time was for wives to devote their efforts to the home and family rather than earning a paycheck. But by the mid-twentieth century women were returning to work en masse. America was engaged in World War II and working-age men were overseas fighting, which left huge vacancies in the workplaces on the home front, including the factories that produced goods essential to the war effort. The federal government called on all women, even married women with children, to do their patriotic duty and go out to work. Women got a taste for independence and their own paycheck, and many were reluctant to retreat to homemaking once the war was over and men returned to reclaim their jobs.[43]

Historical employment data show that one in eight wives was in the labor force in 1940. By 1950, the share had climbed to one in five. About 30 percent of nonwhite married women were in the labor force in 1950. Married women with a young child under age six were about half as likely to be in the labor force, regardless of race.[44] The surge in married women's labor-force participation during World War II did not diminish in the coming decades. In fact, young women increasingly remained in the labor force following marriage and even the birth of a child. By 1975, about 47 percent of mothers with minor children were working. This fraction grew to about 70 percent in the mid-1990s and has remained pretty steady over the past few decades.[45] For mothers of children under age six, about 60 percent are working nowadays. This proportion holds for married and single mothers alike.[46] In short, most mothers today are working in paid employment.

This dramatic shift in women's roles has implications for divorce. Wives are increasingly economically independent, providing them with the financial means to escape a bad marriage.[47] By achieving financial autonomy, wives are no longer dependent on their husbands for support. Their financial independence affords them a pathway out of marriage. Recall from chapter 1 that some scholars pointed to a wife's employment as destabilizing to marriage.

But we should be cautious about concluding that wives' employment is a trigger for divorce. Dual-earner married couples enjoy higher household incomes than do single-earner couples. And, financial security is integral to marital stability. Couples with inadequate or unstable financial resources are at high risk for divorce. As men's incomes have eroded in recent decades, families have compensated by sending wives to work. Wives' employment is strategic, providing a hedge in case the husband loses his job or becomes too ill to work. Dual-earner marriages are arguably advantageous in an economic environment in which workers are expendable and have less job security than previous generations enjoyed.[48] For these reasons, we might expect wives' employment to be linked to a reduced chance of divorce.

In fact, wives' employment does not lead to divorce. The linkage only emerges among unhappily married couples.[49] For those women who are dissatisfied in their marriage, being employed is tied to an increased chance the couple will divorce. But for happily married wives, their employment status is immaterial. Their risk of divorce is the same regardless of whether they are workers or homemakers. Moreover, wives' absolute and relative income is positively associated with marital happiness and overall well-being.[50] Thus, employment simply allows women to call it quits when they are involved in a miserable marriage.

CHANGES IN WOMEN'S AND MEN'S ROLES

Although the rise in women's labor-force participation has not led to the "breakdown" of the American family, public perception ties women's liberation to divorce.[51] The sexual revolution of the 1960s and 1970s decoupled sex and marriage. Men and women could experience sexual intimacy outside the confines of marriage, reducing the rewards of getting and staying married. The fact that couples could share a bed or live together without tying the knot reinforced the concept of individualized marriage. An individualized marriage is worth maintaining only so long as it enhances one's happiness and satisfaction.

The gender revolution not only shook things up in the bedroom but also transformed the roles of husbands and wives. Through the first half of the twentieth century, most wives were homemakers and husbands typically were breadwinners. This scenario left wives economically dependent on their husbands. Many housewives felt stifled and adrift, suffering from "the problem with no name," as Friedan termed the isolation many wives experienced from an exclusive focus on housework and intensive childrearing.[52]

Despite the simmering tension and discontent that often lurked beneath the veneer of happy families during the golden era of the 1950s, divorce remained relatively uncommon and stigmatized. From an economic standpoint, housewives were invested in relationship-specific capital, namely rearing their children, caring for their husband, and managing the household. In contrast, husbands specialized in market work and served as a primary breadwinner. In the event of a divorce, husbands could easily transfer their market skills to a new marriage. But housewives did not enjoy this possibility of readily transferring their capital to another marriage. On the contrary, children from a prior marriage are a barrier to remarriage for women.[53] New household economics proponent Gary Becker thus concluded that specialization among husbands and wives was the ideal because it maximized marital stability.[54] Stated differently, the economic dependence of wives on their husbands discouraged women from seeking a divorce.

But the dramatic growth in women's labor-force participation during the 1960s and 1970s paved the way for women and, to a lesser extent, men, to begin to reshape the gender dynamics of marriage. Some couples still favor a traditional path, with the wife specializing in homemaking and the husband serving as the sole breadwinner. However, most couples nowadays rely on dual earning. The division of household labor ranges widely among couples. In short, traditional, gender-based marital roles are largely relics of the past. Contemporary married couples must negotiate their own set of expectations, navigating a balance of paid and unpaid labor, an approach that aligns with individualized marriage. This deinstitutionalization of marriage has contributed to the fragility of marriage. The foundation of individualized marriage is precarious because it depends on the continued agreement of the couples about their roles and obligations to one another.[55]

INDIVIDUAL-LEVEL RISK FACTORS

Not all marriages are equally likely to end through divorce. A host of individual risk factors are linked to divorce and thus some couples are more likely to divorce than others. There are demographic, economic, and interpersonal factors that are associated with heightened (or reduced) odds of divorce.[56]

Demographic factors. The age at which one married is linked to one's chance of divorce. In particular, marrying young places couples at greater risk.[57] It is well established that teenage marriages are especially likely to end in divorce.[58] Teens are still maturing and developing. With time, they often grow in different directions. Teens also usually have few financial resources, which places an economic strain on the marriage. Some research shows that marrying at a relatively old age for the first time also may be associated with a higher risk of divorce.[59] These individuals have lived outside of marriage for so long that they have become set in their ways and are less flexible and willing to compromise with their new spouse. Another factor linked to divorce is marriage order, which indicates whether the marriage is a first or higher order marriage, meaning a remarriage.[60] First marriages are more often successful than are remarriages. Remarriages are less stable in part because they are composed of individuals with divorce experience. Having successfully weathered a previous divorce, these individuals know that if the marriage does not work out, getting a divorce is not the end of the world. In contrast, some fraction of those in first marriages are in empty-shell marriages—unhappy unions that will never dissolve because the individuals do not believe in divorce.[61] Another reason why remarriages are more likely to end in divorce is because they often involve the formation of a stepfamily, which is usually beset with relationship challenges. Navigating the complex relationship dynamics stepfamilies entail is often so difficult that the couple calls it quits.

Several other demographic factors are tied to divorce. Marital homogamy, which refers to spousal matching on key characteristics such as age, education, race ethnicity, and religion, appears to encourage marital stability. Dissimilarity between husbands and wives on these indicators is associated with an increased risk of divorce.[62] Children of divorce are more likely to experience divorce themselves. This intergenerational transmission of divorce appears to reflect both social learning and perhaps intergenerational transmission.[63] The birth of a first child exerts a braking effect on divorce.[64] But children born prior to marriage are related to a higher risk of divorce, perhaps because they were not a product of the current marriage. Notably, studies have demonstrated that couples are more likely to divorce when they do not have a son; couples with only daughters are a greater risk of divorce.[65] This surprising finding appears to reflect fathers' greater closeness to and involvement with sons than daughters. In turn, father involvement is associated with better marital quality for mothers.[66] Until recently, premarital cohabitation was linked to an increased risk of divorce. But for marriages formed since 1998, there appears to be no effect of premarital cohabitation, reflecting its broader diffusion across the population.[67]

Economic factors. Financial security is critical to marital stability. With income inequality at its highest level in nearly a century, it is no surprise that the risk of divorce is diverging by education level. Among the college-educated, divorce has declined tremendously in recent decades. By comparison, the chances of divorce for less-advantaged couples with lower levels of education has risen since the 1970s.[68] Similarly, married couples' income and wealth help to buffer life strains and are negatively associated with the risk of divorce.

Interpersonal factors. Couple relationship dynamics, including marital quality, are linked to divorce.[69] Marital conflict and the frequency of marital disagreements are predictors of divorce. All couples experience at least occasional disagreements, but couples differ in their ability to effectively manage relationship conflict. Spouses who criticize, are defensive about their own behavior, or withdraw emotionally from the relationship are especially likely to get divorced. And those who speak contemptuously to their spouse, for example by name calling, are the most likely to see their marriages end through divorce.[70] In addition to marital conflict, infidelity or drug or alcohol abuse can destabilize marriages. Trust and commitment are key ingredients for a long-lasting marriage. One study showed that not all couples who divorce were unhappily married, but they did have other risk factors for divorce such as having experienced the breakup of their parents' marriage and being in a remarriage.[71]

Marital quality tends to decline shortly after marriage, continuing its slow, steady descent until couples experience an empty nest, at which time many enjoy a slight upward reversal in marital quality. Marital duration exerts an independent effect on the risk of divorce, with divorce most likely to occur during the first few years following marriage. It does not take couples long to realize they made a mistake by getting married, and many cut their losses quickly and seek a divorce. Couples who survive the first few years of marriage can look forward to a sustained decline in their risk of divorce over time; the longer a marriage remains intact the less likely it is to end through divorce.[72]

Consequences of Divorce

In her extensive treatise on the family that appeared in *The Atlantic* in 1993, Barbara Dafoe Whitehead articulated how family change, and in particular divorce and unwed childbearing, was to the detriment of society. Lamenting that "it is nearly impossible to discuss changes in family

structure without provoking angry protest," Whitehead proceeded to enu-
merate the ways in which "family disruption . . . threatens a child's well-
being and even survival." She noted that

> children in single-parent families are six times as likely to be poor. . . .
> [They] are two to three times as likely as children in two-parent families to
> have emotional and behavioral problems. They are also more likely to drop
> out of high school, to get pregnant as teenagers, to abuse drugs, and to be in
> trouble with the law. Compared with children in intact families, children
> from disrupted families are at a much higher risk for physical or sexual
> abuse. Contrary to popular belief, many children do not "bounce back" after
> divorce or remarriage. Difficulties that are associated with family breakup
> often persist into adulthood. Children who grow up in single-parent or step-
> parent families are less successful as adults, particularly in the two domains
> of life—love and work—that are most essential to happiness. . . . Given its
> dramatic impact on children's lives, one might reasonably expect that this
> historic level of family disruption would be viewed with alarm, even
> regarded as a national crisis. Yet this has not been the case. . . . If we fail to
> come to terms with the relationship between family structure and declining
> child well-being, then it will be increasingly difficult to improve children's
> life prospects, no matter how many new programs the federal government
> funds. Nor will we be able to make progress in bettering school performance
> or reducing crime or improving the quality of the nation's future work
> force—all domestic problems closely connected to family breakup.[73]

Such alarming predictions about the dire consequences of divorce are
largely overstated. Although it is true that divorce is often associated with
poorer outcomes for both adults and children, this is only part of the story.
The gap in well-being is typically quite modest. The vast majority of children and adults who experience divorce turn out just fine.[74] In fact,
divorce is not always detrimental to individual well-being. Sometimes,
divorce is the best possible outcome in a worst case scenario. For example,
children exposed to high-conflict marriages tend to fare better in the long
haul if their parents split up rather than remaining married. Removing
children from a volatile, hostile environment can be beneficial.[75]

Moreover, it is important to consider how children are faring prior to
parental divorce. Oftentimes, the family environment disintegrates along
with the marriage. Children whose parents divorce exhibit poorer outcomes in the years leading up to the dissolution.[76] These predivorce

differentials in well-being arguably stem from the family distress, but also may reflect other unmeasured factors linked to both poor child outcomes and parental divorce (i.e., a selection effect). Divorce is best construed as a process that unfolds over a period of time. To be sure, couples can point to a specific date on which their divorce became final, but that is often less meaningful than the preceding months or even years during which the marriage unraveled.

THE CRISIS PERIOD

The divorce process is a stressful period for the entire family, straining adults and children alike. For adults, this holds regardless of which spouse initiated the divorce. Psychologist Weiss characterized the emotional experience of divorce as "separation distress," which is evidenced by feelings of depression, anxiety, and ambivalence, punctuated by occasional bursts of euphoria during the year or two following divorce. He likened the marital bond to the parent-child bond, to underscore the severity of the emotional consequences of marital disruption.[77]

During this crisis period, which typically lasts for one or two years following divorce, effectiveness of parenting often declines. Single parents, typically mothers, face three key stressors in their everyday lives. First, they encounter responsibility overload because they must now make decisions on their own. There is no spouse to confer with; single parents are the sole adult in charge. Second, single parents experience task overload, meaning they must perform household tasks alone. There is no second adult to assist with chores. Single mothers may need to rely more heavily on children to assist with household tasks. Third, single parents grapple with emotional overload, the psychological isolation most experience. The day-to-day social and emotional support once provided by a spouse is no longer available. There is no shoulder to cry on, no one with whom to commiserate about the challenges of parenting and life in general.[78]

As single mothers struggle with these forms of overload, their ability to engage in consistent parenting that provides children with high levels of support and moderate levels of control can be compromised. They tend to spend less time with their children and exercise weaker control over them than do mothers in two parent families.[79] The routines that once governed family life are often cast aside as single mothers take on new demands such as more hours in the paid labor force. Children tend to fare best when parents establish an orderly and consistent routine. It often takes a year or two for families to achieve a new equilibrium.[80]

STANDARD OF LIVING

Divorce is costly for families. The economies of scale that couples enjoy during marriage disappear with divorce. Each spouse must live independently and absorb the costs of running a household. This means that spouses often experience a decline in their standard of living following divorce, and this is especially true for women, who typically earn less than men and have been less attached to the labor force in recent years, further diminishing their earnings potential. Several studies have attempted to estimate the changes in standard of living experienced by men and women following divorce. For men, the shift has been quite modest and on balance represents no more than a 10 percent increase in their standard of living. Following divorce, men are no longer supporting their exwives and are only responsible for partially supporting their children. In contrast, women tend to experience a drop in their standard of living after divorce that is on the order of 30 percent.[81] Part of this decline reflects their lower earning power. Another portion stems from the fact that women are usually the resident parent and absorb much of the costs of childrearing. Most fathers are court-ordered to pay child support, but many fathers do not pay support consistently or at all, leaving mothers on the hook to bear the costs of rearing children.[82]

As women's labor-force participation has become normative, the legal system is less likely to offer divorcing women alimony. Instead, women are expected to support themselves even when they have been out of the labor force for years. Not only does this create economic distress in the short term, it also has long-term consequences. The financial toll of divorce persists across the life course, with many divorced women confronting retirement with inadequate nest eggs. Older divorced women are especially likely to experience economic disadvantage in later life.[83]

CONSEQUENCES FOR CHILDREN

Parental divorce is associated with poorer outcomes for children. This linkage is well established and persists across multiple domains of child well-being. Children whose parents divorce tend to fare worse in terms of educational, emotional, behavioral, social, and health outcomes relative to children raised by married parents. Moreover, the negative outcomes associated with parental divorce often have enduring consequences for well-being into young adulthood. Children of divorced parents tend to achieve less schooling, have weaker ties to their parents, and are more likely to experience divorce themselves. The magnitude of these differences, however, is consistently modest. The well-being gap for children whose parents divorce versus children who grow up with married parents is small. Nonetheless, most children of divorce are well adjusted and grow into successful adults, reflecting the resiliency with which children typically respond to parental divorce.[84]

From a divorce-stress-adjustment perspective, the short-term stresses and longer-term strains of the divorce process unfold over a period of time.[85] Their potential ramifications for children vary, depending on how swiftly children adjust to the parental breakup. Consistent with this perspective, children whose parents eventually divorce actually exhibit lower levels of well-being prior to divorce. The predivorce family environment can be negative and stressful for children, contributing to increased depression and anxiety and worsening their performance in school. A 2002 study of adolescents showed that three years prior to parental divorce, teens performed worse on standardized tests than their counterparts whose parents did not eventually divorce.[86] This predivorce differential largely accounted for the well-being gap that was observed postdivorce. In other words, much of the negative child outcomes that are attributed to divorce actually preceded the divorce itself. Similarly, children's psychological outcomes were relatively poor leading up to parental divorce but recovered following the divorce.[87] However, other work suggests that children's depression and anxiety levels remain high after divorce.[88] The pace at which children rebound from parental divorce is unclear and likely varies across children.

A key determinant of how children adjust to parental divorce appears to be the quality of the predivorce family environment. According to a study from 1991, children who were aware of the strains in their parents' marriage because they were exposed to parental conflict fared better in young adulthood if their parents got divorced than if they remained married.[89] Prolonged exposure to a stressful environment is damaging to children over the long term. In contrast, in the same study, children who were oblivious to their parents' impending divorce because the outward appearance of the parental marriage was harmonious and conflict-free, often did not fare well when their parents got divorced. These surprise divorces are devastating for children because they call into question the child's understanding of the family's reality—the child viewed the family as happy and cohesive. This type of parental divorce has enduring negative consequences for children, who exhibit much lower levels of well-being as young adults than do their counterparts whose parents were not in outwardly conflictual marriages and remained married.[90]

UNION DISSOLUTION AMONG COHABITORS

Increasingly, unions are formed outside of marriage through cohabitation. Cohabiting unions tend to be highly unstable. This instability may in part reflect the purpose of many cohabiting relationships: to test whether the relationship is viable for marriage. But as cohabitation has grown in popularity, the share of cohabiting unions that culminate in marriage has declined. In the 1980s, roughly 60 percent of cohabiting relationships resulted in marriage. Nowadays, the share is about 40 percent. Thus, a majority of cohabiting unions end through separation.[91]

Cohabitors' union outcomes differ by race. Black cohabitors are less likely to marry but more likely to remain cohabiting than their white counterparts. The two groups do not differ in their risks of separation—black and white cohabitors are similarly likely to split up.[92] These patterns align with racial variation in the purposes cohabitation serves. Cohabitation is less often a prelude to marriage for blacks compared with whites, for instance. For Hispanics, cohabitation often operates as an alternative to marriage but they are no more likely to marry than whites. And their risk of separation is comparable to that of whites and blacks.[93]

Cohabiting relationships typically do not last long, averaging just a year or two in duration. The risk factors for dissolution among cohabitors are similar to those documented for marrieds. For example, couples with fewer economic resources and, more specifically, male partners who are economically disadvantaged, are at greater risk of separation.[94] And, similar to the situation in marriage, the presence of children is positively associated with relationship stability in cohabitation.[95] Cohabitors' marital intentions are linked to their likelihood of breakup, with couples lacking plans to marry the most likely to separate.[96]

The consequences of cohabitation dissolution are manifold, with outcomes comparable in some ways to divorce. For instance, the economic consequences of cohabitation dissolution are negative for both men and women, who typically experience reductions in their economic standing after the breakup.[97] Cohabitation dissolution is associated with declines in physical and mental health, mirroring the outcomes for marrieds who divorce.[98] The breakup of a union is a stressful life event that can take a toll on one's health.

Union Dissolution and Divorce among Same-Sex Couples

Same-sex marriage is now legal in all U.S. states, which should make divorce among same-sex couples a relatively seamless process. Before the U.S. Supreme Court issued its ruling legalizing same-sex marriage in 2015, it was not entirely clear how married same-sex couples could get divorced if they resided in a state that did not recognize same-sex marriage. Many of these couples had no legal recourse to obtain a divorce. Instead, they had to file for divorce in a state that recognized same-sex marriage, which sometimes required fulfilling residency requirements.[99] Most states did not address complex issues related to divorce such as child custody, creating insurmountable barriers to divorce. These obstacles should now be alleviated given that same-sex marriage is legal around the nation.

Of course, most same-sex couples are not married. Nearly 80 percent of same-sex co-resident couples are cohabiting.[100] Many of these cohabiting couples might transition to marriage now that it is legal. For this reason, it is possible that same-sex cohabiting unions might be more stable, on average, than different-sex cohabiting unions. Same-sex couples also enjoy relatively high education and income levels which may contribute to relationship stability. However, same-sex couples have fewer barriers to break up in that they are less likely to have resident children and tend to be more heterogamous, meaning they are less closely matched on key demographic characteristics (e.g., age and race-ethnicity) that are linked to relationship stability. Moreover, same-sex cohabiting unions are arguably less institutionalized than different-sex cohabiting unions, and the former face greater stigma. These factors might also undermine relationship stability.[101]

The stability of same-sex unions has been studied in the European context, but is only beginning to receive attention in the United States. It appears that the stability of same-sex cohabiting unions is largely comparable to that of different-sex cohabiting unions, according to studies published in 2014 and 2016.[102] Particularly during the first few years of the cohabiting union, same-sex and different-sex unions are similarly stable. Not surprisingly, both union types were less stable than different-sex marriages. Going forward, research on union dissolution and divorce will need to encompass same-sex relationships, too.

WIDOWHOOD

Marriages that do not end through divorce ultimately dissolve when one of the spouses dies. Unlike divorce, which remains high and is accelerating among older adults, widowhood is waning. Over the past half-century, the share of adults aged sixty-five and older who are widowed has steadily declined, according to the U.S. Census. This pattern is evident for women and men alike, although the levels differ considerably by gender, as depicted in figure 11.[103] Women are more often widowed than men largely because women typically marry men older than themselves and women live longer, on average, than men. Additionally, widowed women are much less likely to remarry than their widower counterparts. In 1960, about 53 percent of older women were widowed versus just 40 percent in 2010, representing a 20 percent decrease. For men, the proportion widowed fell by about one-third, from roughly 19 percent to less than 13 percent over this time span. Even today, older women are three times as likely as older men to be currently widowed.

The drop in widowhood for women and men reflects a confluence of factors. First, many marriages end through divorce before either spouse dies. Roughly 45 percent of marriages are dissolved by divorce, meaning

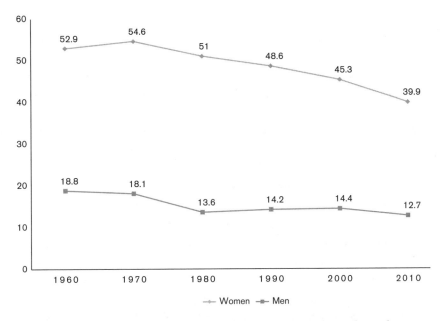

Figure 11. Percentage Widowed among Population Aged Sixty-five and Over by Gender, 1960–2010. Source: U.S. Census Bureau 2014, figure 5-1.

that only slightly more than one-half end through widowhood. Second, fewer people are exposed to the risk of widowhood because of the decline in marriage. Specifically, the drop in remarriage following divorce means that a shrinking share of adults is currently married and at risk of widowhood. In fact, the percentage of older adults who are divorced grew from less than 2 percent to roughly 10 percent between 1960 and 2010.[104] Finally, longevity increasing has forestalled widowhood. As individuals continue to live longer, fewer in a given year experience marital disruption by spousal death. All of these factors have contributed to a dramatic decline in widowhood in recent decades.

This is good news because widowhood has been considered the most stressful life event that adults can experience.[105] Spousal loss, whether anticipated or unexpected, has significant ramifications for the well-being of the surviving spouse. The separation distress that is characteristic of divorce also occurs following widowhood, which is associated with steep declines in psychological well-being. Involuntary separation through spousal death often leads to depression and loneliness. In fact, widowhood is preceded by elevated levels of depressive symptoms. Longitudinal studies following married people over time show that those who eventually become widowed are already more depressed, on average, than their counterparts whose spouses do not pass away, perhaps reflecting the long path to death that is increasingly the norm, now that more people die of chronic rather than acute diseases. Husbands and wives experience similar trajectories of depressive symptoms both pre- and post-widowhood.[106]

Importantly, most widowed persons recover psychologically. Their levels of depressive symptoms return to their pre-widowhood baseline levels within about two years. Even when confronted with such a devastating experience as widowhood, people are nevertheless resilient. Social support from friends and family helps widowed persons to recover, largely by assuaging feelings of loneliness.[107] Immediately following spousal death social support is high as friends and family try to fill the gap left by the deceased spouse. Loneliness tends to decline over time, particularly when widowed persons receive social support from friends. Unlike family ties, which are typically defined on the basis of blood and marriage, friendships are formed and maintained voluntarily according to shared interests and other commonalities, and thus offer a unique form of social support for widowed persons.

The psychological distress of widowhood often spills over into the realm of physical health. Spousal loss is tied to poorer health outcomes relative to being continuously married.[108] Moreover, widowhood is a huge risk factor for mortality. There are three explanations for this linkage.[109] First, the association between widowhood and mortality may be an artifact of selection. Shared household characteristics, such as economic disadvantage, may contribute to both spousal loss and one's own death. Selection also operates in terms of who remains widowed versus who exits widowhood through remarriage. Those who remarry are likely to be more advantaged and in better health than the individuals who stay single. Second, there could be a direct causal effect of widowhood on mortality. When individuals are consumed by the stresses and strains of widowhood, they are unlikely to take good care of themselves and may engage in risky health behaviors such as drinking or not taking medications as prescribed. Many widowed persons are exhausted from extensive caregiving prior to a spouse's death, and this raises their own risk of illness. Third, widowhood requires adjustments in daily living. The surviving spouse has lost the deceased spouse's social, material, and task support. Basically, widowed persons must reconfigure their routines to compensate for the loss of their spouse, which can worsen physical and mental health, raising the risk of mortality. The risk of mortality is highest immediately following widowhood, and the risk dissipates over time. The elevated risk is partially a function of selection with about one-third of the mortality differential between widowed and married persons accounted for by economic differences between the two groups. This means most of the risk is due to the stress of widowhood and the life changes it necessitates.

Socioeconomic status is a protective factor for widowed persons, and some researchers have likened it to a form of social support.[110] One of the most significant consequences of widowhood is the loss of economic resources, especially among women. Although the labor-force participation of wives has increased over time, nonetheless husbands are still the primary earners in most marriages and this is especially true for older generations. Most previously married women receive Social Security through spousal or widow benefits rather than their own contributions.[111] The Social Security benefits accruing to widowed men exceed those to widowed women, reflecting men's higher earnings and greater attachment to the labor force over the life course. Minority widowed women are particularly economically disadvantaged, in part because they had fewer resources pre-widowhood compared with whites.[112]

The economic circumstances of widowed persons often improve with remarriage, but most do not repartner. Estimates indicate that only about one-third of widowed persons form a new marriage or cohabiting union in the United States. The levels are similar in Canada.[113] Widowed women are much less likely than men to repartner, largely because of the gender asymmetry in available partners. Women tend to partner with older men, meaning that as women age, their pool of eligibles shrinks. In contrast, men partner with younger women, and thus men enjoy a widening pool of mates as they age. Beyond demographics though, women are less enthusiastic about repartnering than men. Many express reluctance about remarriage, citing their unwillingness to provide care to a new partner. Women have a "been there, done that" attitude.[114] They were the primary caregiver for their first husband and do not wish to experience the ordeal again. Indeed, for wives, the old adage "a woman's work is never done" remains salient across the life course, and arguably intensifies with age. For men, their traditional responsibility—economic provision—ends upon retirement. Their working days are behind them and they subsist on savings, investments, a pension, and Social Security benefits. For wives, caregiving responsibilities increase with age. These distinctive gender dynamics account for much of the gendered patterns of later-life repartnership.

REMARRIAGE

As of 2012, nearly one in three marriages was a remarriage for at least one spouse.[115] Despite the high level of divorce, many Americans remain enthusiastic about marriage. A majority of people who get divorced eventually remarry, with men more likely to remarry than women (78 percent versus 69 percent).[116] These figures may overestimate remarriage though because they are based on data that are from the 1990s, when the remarriage rate was much higher. Unfortunately, newer estimates are not available.[117]

We do know that since 1990, the remarriage rate has plummeted by 40 percent.[118] This downward trend is most pronounced among younger adults and attenuates with age. For those over age fifty-five, there has been little change in remarriage rates in the past two decades. Women's rate of remarriage continues to lag behind men's, and this pattern holds regardless of education status or race-ethnicity. Remarriage rates are higher among those with more education. The rate is a bit lower for blacks than for other racial and ethnic groups.[119]

The education composition of those remarrying differs from those entering first marriages, as shown in figure 12. Relative to those getting married for the first time, individuals who are forming a higher-order marriage are less educated. Only one-quarter of those remarrying had a college degree in 2010, versus more than one-third among those forming a first marriage. Those entering a first marriage are more racially and ethnically diverse, as illustrated in figure 13, with less than two-thirds identifying as white in 2010. By comparison, nearly three-quarters of those forming a remarriage in 2010 were white. Nearly all first marriages in

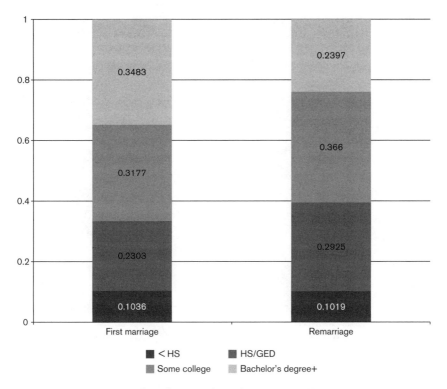

Figure 12. Marriage Type by Educational Attainment, 2010. Source: Cruz 2012a, figure 1.

2010 were to individuals aged forty-five and younger. In contrast, 40 percent of those remarrying were older than forty-five.[120]

Repartnering

Although the remarriage rate has declined, repartnering remains popular. Increasingly, couples choose to cohabit rather than form a remarriage. Many couples opt for cohabitation to avoid the possibility of divorcing again. Still others form cohabiting unions after divorce because they are disenchanted with marriage as an institution. Regardless, the sustained decline in remarriage in recent decades is more than offset by a corresponding increase in postmarital cohabitation. Cohabitors are nearly as

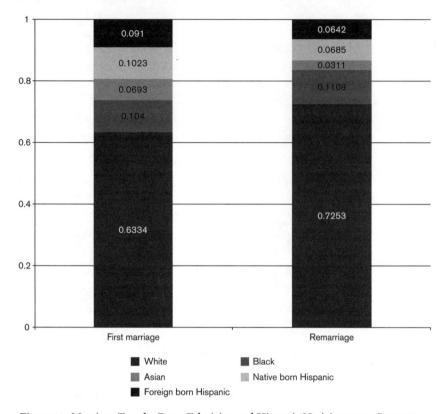

Figure 13. Marriage Type by Race, Ethnicity, and Hispanic Nativity, 2010. Source: Cruz 2012a, figure 2.

likely to be formerly married as never married.[121] Given the instability of cohabiting unions, couples who select cohabitation over remarriage do not insulate themselves from a breakup.

Family demographer Andrew Cherlin characterized the American propensity to form multiple partnerships over the adult life course as "the marriage-go-round," which is also the title of his 2009 book on the state of contemporary marriage.[122] Compared with our European counterparts, Americans are more likely to form and dissolve unions. About half of children whose parents dissolved their cohabiting or marital union formed a new partnership within three years. In Europe, repartnership so soon after a dissolution was much less common, ranging from a high of one-third in Sweden to a low of 8 percent in Italy.[123] Stated differently, U.S. children are nearly twice as likely as children in Europe and Canada to experience two or more parental partnerships. Multiple partnerships are particularly worrisome for children, because the negative effects of family transitions on child well-being accumulate (see chapter 4 for more detail). For this reason, Cherlin urges us to: *"slow down.* Don't rush into having children with a boyfriend/girlfriend or a partner you've recently started living with. If you are already single and raising children, choose your next live-in partner or spouse carefully. Introduce your partner gradually to your kids, and don't try to make him an instant parent."[124]

Stepfamily Living

From a child's perspective, parental remarriage results in the formation of a stepfamily, in which the child resides with a biological parent (typically the mother) and a stepparent (usually a stepfather).[125] Stepfamilies face numerous relationship challenges, which is one of the central reasons why remarriages are more likely to end through divorce than are first marriages. The relationship hurdles are so formidable that many stepfamilies are never able to surmount them and instead are ultimately undone by them.

The relationship challenges confronting stepfamilies center on the various ties between family members for which clear norms and expectations are lacking.[126] In a nuclear family, there is a shared understanding about how the mother, father, and children are to act toward one another. For example, there is no question about whether a biological parent can discipline her or his child. But is a stepparent allowed to punish a child for misbehaving? It depends. In stepfamilies, the norms are less clear and usually must be negotiated, opening the door to disagreement and conflict. The newly remarried couple must navigate unfamiliar terrain in both their own relationship—after all, now they are married and have to decipher what it means to be husband and wife to one another—and their relationships to their own and each other's children. For example, a mother might have focused her attention exclusively on her children while she was single but now that she is remarried her relationship to her own biological children may change as she devotes time to cementing her spousal relationship. And she may need to help smooth the way for her children to establish a relationship with their stepfather. The stepfather's rights and obligations to his stepchildren (i.e., the mother's children) need to be agreed upon by the couple and be accepted by the stepchildren. Returning to our earlier example, is the stepfather allowed to discipline his stepchildren, or does that task fall exclusively to the children's mother? Once the couple has decided on their approach, they have to convey it convincingly to the children to ensure that the children understand and accept the mother's and stepfather's authority. Finally, children have to adjust to having new stepsiblings, particularly if they are co-resident. There may be competition for parental attention and conflict over the distribution of resources. Stepfamilies are precarious largely because family members have to build and sustain their relationships to one another. This process is stressful and can undermine family cohesion and stability.

Stepfamily boundaries span across households. The formation of a stepfamily has ramifications for the coparenting relationship between the two biological parents. Whether it is the resident mother who forms a stepfamily, or the nonresident father who repartners, the two parents must renegotiate their roles and determine the level of involvement the new stepparent will have in parenting their children. In general, mothers view stepfathers (i.e., their own partners) or stepmothers (i.e., the new partners of the biological father of their children) as "junior partners or secondary figures in the coparental support network."[127] Nonresident stepparents play a greater role in childrearing when they reside near the children. Additionally, adolescent children are often quite vocal about which parents they want to spend time with, and this can shape the level of stepparent involvement.

The myriad relationship challenges inherent in stepfamily living reflect the incomplete institutionalization of remarriage.[128] The norms we have that guide nuclear-family life are not readily translated to remarriage. In stepfamilies, members are left to piece together their own relationship ties, but constructing them is exceedingly difficult, and many families ultimately do not succeed. This is one reason why, despite having more financial resources than single-parent families, children do not seem to fare any better in remarried stepfamilies. The economic benefits of having two parents are offset by the poorer relationship dynamics characterizing most stepfamilies.[129]

The incomplete-institutionalization-of-remarriage argument applies to cohabiting stepfamilies, too. In fact, cohabiting stepfamilies are characterized by even more uncertainty about family members' roles, expectations, and obligations to one another precisely because these families are formed outside the boundaries of marriage.[130] The cohabiting relationship may have less legitimacy in the eyes of children, potentially undermining the relationships between children and their parents. Some children appear to be reluctant to acknowledge the presence of a cohabiting stepparent. Among teens whose mothers reported their family type as cohabiting stepfamily, only one-third agreed with their mothers' reports. Most often, these teens reported living in a single-mother family, effectively discounting the presence of a cohabiting parent. This boundary ambiguity about who is in versus who is out of the family is consequential. It tends to be associated with worse family functioning.[131]

Maternal repartnering through cohabitation is linked to declines in mother-child closeness. But the bond between mother and child does not diminish following remarriage, suggesting that the path to repartnering is important for children.[132] Children in cohabiting stepfamilies tend to fare worse than their counterparts in married stepfamilies.[133] This differential partially reflects the economic disadvantage characterizing cohabiting versus married stepfamilies. Children in cohabiting stepfamilies are much more likely to be poor and to experience material hardship than children in married stepfamilies.[134] The relationship dynamics of cohabiting stepfamilies are also particularly strained, as children are more reluctant to accept a cohabiting than a married stepparent.[135]

The pathways to stepfamily living are diverse. Stepfamilies can be formed through either marriage or cohabitation. In 2013, 5 percent of children resided in married stepfamilies and 4 percent lived in cohabiting stepfamilies. There is little racial and ethnic variation in the shares of children living in married or cohabiting stepfamilies. Asian children are about half as likely as white, black, and Hispanic children to reside in a stepfamily.[136]

Nearly all of the research on stepfamilies focuses on families with minor children, but stepfamily formation also can involve adult children who become a member of a stepfamily when their aging parent forms a new partnership.[137] An emerging literature indicates that stepfamilies formed in later life are marked by unique strains. For example, adult children may be less willing to provide support and care for aging parents and stepparents because of weakened intergenerational bonds.[138] When stepfamilies are formed in later life, adult children typically will have never co-resided with the stepparent, contributing to weaker norms of filial expectations. Increasingly, older adults have complicated relationship histories that include divorce and repartnering.[139] Although there are no current national estimates of later-life stepfamilies, we can expect their prevalence to rise in the coming years given the recent growth in gray divorce and cohabitation among older adults.

CONCLUSION

Recent decades have witnessed a rise in union instability. Divorce rates peaked in the 1970s. Although the rate seemingly stabilized beginning in the 1980s, adjusting for the aging of the population reveals that divorce continues to climb.[140] Perhaps what is most intriguing about recent shifts in divorce patterns is the countervailing trends observed for young versus middle-aged and older adults. The former are now less likely to divorce than their predecessors from earlier generations, whereas the latter are experiencing their own divorce revolution. The retreat from marriage among young adults reverberates in their divorce trends; marriage is now selective of the most financially secure individuals, which helps to minimize divorce for this age group. Similarly, the Baby Boom's marriage patterns over the life course have enduring consequences. Following the divorce revolution of the 1970s, many remarried, a factor integral to the emergence of the gray-divorce phenomenon.[141]

These disparate age-related trends in divorce may reshape how we think about the consequences of divorce. Existing research on divorce outcomes focuses almost entirely on minor children and their parents, ignoring the experiences of older adults who call it quits. Yet, the ramifications of later-life divorce are arguably significant because traditionally older adults have relied on spouses as caregivers. Gray divorce is likely to jeopardize the health and well-being of older adults. And it will mean children or society at large will need to fill the care gap, straining intergenerational relationships and adding to the costs of an aging population.

In addition to thinking in new ways about divorce patterns, it is clear that our focus must widen to accommodate the dissolution of unmarried unions. Cohabiting relationships are highly unstable, leading to serial cohabitation for many adults as they form and dissolve multiple unions. Cohabitation tends to end through separation rather than marriage. Even less is known about the dissolution of same-sex partnerships. Emerging evidence indicates that the stability of different-sex and same-sex cohabiting unions are largely comparable. Now that same-sex couples are able to marry, it essential that researchers address both the antecedents and consequences of divorce for this group.

Although divorce is a stressful life event, most who experience it do go on to remarry eventually, or at least they did a couple of decades ago. We lack good data on today's patterns of remarriage. Remarriage is an opportunity to start afresh, but many couples, especially those in stepfamilies with children from prior relationships, eventually dissolve their unions.

Widespread divorce and remarriage mean that the marital biographies of today's adults are more varied and complex than in the past. Marriages less often end by spousal death these days. Children, too, experience family instability as their parents form and dissolve new relationships. The next chapter addresses how these family patterns are linked to the health and well-being of adults and children.

4 Adult and Child Well-being in Families

Despite the complex patterns characterizing contemporary family living arrangements, presumably they all share an important commonality: families ideally provide shelter from the harsh realities of modern society, operating as a buffer between the individual and the larger community. Christopher Lasch famously described the family as "a haven in a heartless world." He explained this analogy in the opening sentences of his 1977 book:

> As business, politics, and diplomacy grow more savage and warlike, men seek a haven in private life, in personal relations, above all in the family—the last refuge of love and decency. Domestic life, however, seems increasingly incapable of providing these comforts. Hence the undercurrent of anxiety that runs through the vast and growing body of commentary on the state of the family. Much of that commentary attempts to show that although the family is changing its form and structure, it serves important needs and therefore has a long life ahead of it. Yet the divorce rate continues to climb, generational conflict intensifies, and enlightened opinion condemns the family as a repressive anachronism. Do these developments signify merely the "strain" of the family's "adaptation" to changing social conditions, or do they portend a weakening of the social fabric, a drastic disorganization of all our institutions? Does the family still provide a haven in a heartless world?

Or do the very storms out of which the need for such a haven arises threaten to engulf the family as well?[1]

Lasch questions the implications of family change for individual well-being. Are families able to meet the needs of their members? From his standpoint and that of many other conservative commentators, family change signals family decline. But regardless of their structure, families are designed to serve as a primary source of social and economic support and to facilitate cooperation in raising the next generation. They provide members with love and companionship, persevering through good times and bad. When couples take their marriage vows, they pledge to stay together for better, for worse, for richer, for poorer, in sickness and in health, underscoring the long-term commitment inherent in marriage. Certainly not all families achieve this ideal. Some families are dysfunctional, marred by conflict and even violence. Families can be burdensome and stifling. Nowadays, fewer adults are even residing with family members; there has been record growth in solo living.[2]

The dramatic structural changes in family life have spurred considerable attention to how marital status is related to adult well-being.[3] Do the married fare better, on average, than the unmarried? If so, what factors account for this marriage advantage? These questions may seem straightforward but the answers, which are detailed in the next section of this chapter, are actually rather complex. Some groups appear to benefit from marriage more than others do. Moreover, marital status is embedded within an individual's marital biography, capturing prior union formation and dissolution experiences that often have long-term influences on health and well-being.[4] Union disruption in particular has enduring negative consequences that are not offset by repartnership.

Parental union formation and dissolution patterns shape children's family environment and are critical to children's development and well-being.[5] Children reside in an array of living arrangements and increasingly experience family transitions during childhood, as their parents move in and out of partnerships. The latter half of this chapter describes the trends in children's family structure and stability, emphasizing how and why these patterns are related to child outcomes. Much like the growing divide observed for the family patterns of adults, so too are children experiencing diverging destinies.[6] Children in highly educated, financially advantaged families have reaped considerable gains, whereas children in less-educated families are falling further behind. These differentials emerge not just in the living arrangements of children but also in the ways in which parents rear their children, ultimately reinforcing the growing class divide across generations.[7]

MARITAL STATUS AND ADULT WELL-BEING

What is the secret to a long, healthy, happy, and productive life? According to some, the answer is simple: marriage. After all, the married not only live longer, they are also happier, healthier, and richer than the unmarried. In the 1990s, Linda Waite, a leading sociologist at the University of Chicago, urged her colleagues to embark on a public-health campaign to promote marriage, likening the cause to antismoking efforts that have been widely credited with reducing the prevalence of smokers in the United States. Encouraging marriage, she argued, would improve population health by enhancing individual well-being.[8]

The advantages that accrue to marrieds span multiple dimensions of well-being, including physical and mental health, longevity, and economic security. Relative to their unmarried counterparts, men tend to reap larger benefits from marriage than women. For women, the marriage advantage in well-being is smaller and sometimes negligible. Similarly, there are racial-ethnic differences in the magnitude of the marriage advantage, with the greatest benefits observed for whites. The gains from marriage for blacks and Hispanics are comparatively modest. Although there are some theoretical explanations for these gender and racial-ethnic differentials (discussed in the following section), such patterns nevertheless indicate that marginalized groups (women and racial-ethnic minorities) typically derive fewer benefits from marriage compared with white men, presaging a shaky foundation for the bold assertion that marriage could play a key role in improving population health.[9]

Indeed, the explanation for the apparent benefits linked to marriage remain hotly contested by social scientists. Does marriage actually confer improved well-being? Or, is marriage primarily a status marker, reflecting the propensity of the most advantaged to select into marriage? Some researchers share Linda's Waite's view that the benefits characterizing marriage are a direct result of marriage. From this standpoint, marriage has a causal effect on well-being. Scholars who are skeptical of this viewpoint maintain that the purported benefits are not a consequence of marriage but in fact predate marriage entry and simply are an artifact of selection. People who get (and stay) married are the most advantaged from the outset and this makes them attractive mates in the marriage market.[10]

Proponents of the social causation explanation for the marriage advantage underscore the numerous ways in which marriage provides spouses with resources and support that bolster well-being. This also is termed the relationship effect, signaling that the marital relationship positively affects health and well-being. For example, the presence of a spouse means that one has a ready source of social support to turn to in times of distress, helping to ease psychological burdens. Spouses also provide material support to one another, such as physical care during times of illness. They monitor each other's behaviors, which enhances spousal health and well-being. For instance, a wife might prepare her husband healthy meals and schedule medical checkups for him. If he was unmarried, he might have a poorer diet and not seek regular well-care services.[11] Men in particular tend to benefit from the social support and social control (or monitoring) that spouses provide.[12]

A key mechanism through which marriage confers benefits is financial well-being and this is especially true for women.[13] Marriage allows couples to pool resources, creating economies of scale that can minimize financial insecurity. Economic disadvantage is tremendously stressful and often takes a serious toll on health and well-being. Marriage operates as a buffer to economic and social adversity, which appears to have less deleterious effects for spouses than for singles.[14] Spouses increasingly collaborate not just economically but also in childrearing and housework, which may have particular benefits for women. In other words, marriage is a setting in which individuals can access a ready source of social, economic, and legal benefits that are not as easily obtained outside of marriage.

But the relationship effect is at most only part of the story. Most social scientists agree that the association between marriage and well-being is largely an artifact of selection, or the types of people who get married in the first place.[15] This is termed the selection effect. The individuals who choose to marry are an elite group, and this distinction has become more pronounced in recent years as marriage rates continue to decline. Recall that the most-educated and financially secure individuals are the ones who are most likely to get married. Those who marry are also happier and healthier prior to marriage, which makes sense considering that they would be the most attractive individuals in the marriage market. Social and economic advantage precedes marriage. In fact, a primary driver of marriage entry is advantaged status. Once we account for premarriage characteristics, the purported benefits linked to marriage are substantially reduced. Thus, what appear to be direct benefits from marriage are actually an artifact of selection.[16]

But it is not easy to tease apart the origins of the marriage advantage. Adjudicating between the social causation (or relationship effect) and selection explanations presents a tremendous challenge. The causation explanation cannot be rigorously tested. To do so would require devising an experiment in which some individuals are randomly assigned to marry whereas others are forbidden to marry. Clearly, this approach is untenable for ethical reasons. But it also is unlikely to capture the true extent of the benefits of marriage because people do not make arbitrary decisions about whether or whom to marry. Marriage is based on a love match which cannot be replicated in a social experiment. There are also limitations to our ability to fully and correctly identify the role of selection. Social scientists can only account for factors they can measure, but other unmeasured factors may shape the relationship between marriage and well-being. For this reason, it is difficult to address the selection explanation, too.

These challenges do not mean that the marriage advantage is not worth studying. But pitting the causation and selection explanations against each other is overly facile. Instead, it is more likely that some combination of causation and selection factors are operating, although it can be challenging to decipher the relative contributions of causation versus selection. According to sociologist Gary Lee's recent appraisal of the evidence, there are several reasons to be cautious.[17] First, the large literature on marriage and well-being has not yielded uniform conclusions about whether people appear to benefit from marriage. Most studies identify a marital advantage, but some do not. Second, some groups appear to benefit more from marriage than others. For example, the gains from marriage are larger for men and whites than for women and nonwhites. Men tend to benefit from the social support marriage provides whereas women accrue advantage from marriage through economic resources. Yet as women achieve economic independence, their dependence on marriage for financial security diminishes. Likewise, black women do not gain as much economically as white women do from marriage.[18] Another reason why benefits of marriage appear to be smaller for blacks than whites is because blacks tend to report more marital conflict.[19] Spouses in lower-quality marriages may not experience appreciable benefits from marriage and appear more similar to the unmarried. And the marriage advantage seems to attenuate over time. Finally, the possibility of divorce may undercut some of the benefits of marriage as those who experience marital dissolution are arguably worse off than the never married. These caveats illustrate that the relationship between marriage and well-being is actually more nuanced than proponents would have us believe. The next three sections provide an assessment of the empirical evidence on the linkages between marriage and core dimensions of well-being: psychological, physical health, and economic.

Marriage and Psychological Well-being

Researchers have tracked marital-status differentials in happiness for decades and the pattern is clear: marrieds are happier, on average, than never-marrieds. Since the early 1970s, the share of marrieds reporting that they are very happy has been roughly twice that of never-marrieds.[20] The happiness gap is not just a U.S. phenomenon; it has been documented in several European countries.[21] Similar patterns emerge for other indicators of psychological well-being such as depressive symptoms. Furthermore, depressive symptoms tend to decline following marriage entry, suggesting that marriage improves well-being.

But the story gets a little more complicated for a couple of reasons. First, the well-being gap between the married and unmarried is evident prior to marriage. That is, unmarried individuals who eventually marry exhibit fewer depressive symptoms than their counterparts who never married.[22] Second, the marriage advantage in mental health diminishes as the length of marriage increases. There is an initial bump in well-being following marriage entry, but that benefit attenuates over time.[23]

The basic comparison of the married versus the unmarried could be masking important variation among the unmarried now that cohabitation is widespread. Cohabitation offers some but not all of the benefits of marriage. Similar to marriage, cohabitation provides companionship, intimacy, social support, and the opportunity to pool resources. But unlike marriage, cohabitation is not a legally binding contract that confers rights and responsibilities. Marriage is distinctive in that it is characterized by enforceable trust, whereas cohabitation is an informal union outside the boundaries of the law. Marriage facilitates joint investments, especially in relationship-specific capital such as children, which solidifies relationship commitment. Cohabitors are viewed as less committed to their relationship, largely because they remain unmarried.[24]

In their reexamination of Waite's arguments on the case for marriage, sociologists Kelly Musick and Larry Bumpass uncovered little evidence that marriage was advantageous compared with cohabitation for psychological well-being, health, and social ties with family and friends. By accounting for preunion well-being and then following individuals as they formed (and sometimes dissolved) unions, the authors found that there were few appreciable advantages of marriage over cohabitation and they seemed to diminish over time. Musick and Bumpass concluded that cohabitors were actually largely comparable to marrieds, reflecting the growing similarity between the two union types.[25] Cohabitation has gained ground as a family form at the same time that marriage is becoming deinstitutionalized, blurring the boundaries between cohabitation and marriage.

There may be a modest relationship effect of marriage on psychological well-being, but there is also ample evidence of selection.[26] The advantages linked to marriage precede the couple's walk down the aisle and the initial psychological boost that follows marriage steadily deflates with the passage of time. Cohabitation is not so different than marriage, at least in terms of psychological outcomes and social ties, lending further support to the selection explanation. The changing institution of marriage, which itself is now more selective, may be reshaping the linkages between marriage and well-being.

Marriage and Physical Health

It is possible that the health benefits of marriage have shifted over time given the broader changes in marriage that have occurred in recent decades.[27] Marriage is more selective now than in the past, as fewer adults get and stay married. Moreover, marriage is increasingly concentrated among the most advantaged in society. A capstone event, marriage has become the province of the economic elite. Consequently, the health advantage of marriage may be magnified in our time. Alternatively, it may have diminished, as many of the benefits traditionally accessible only through marriage are now available to unmarried individuals, too. Individuals can derive social support through friends and partners. And increasingly, adults are living outside of marriage.

Since the early 1970s, the association between marital status and self-rated health (a rating of one's own health on a five-point scale from poor to excellent) has changed in ways that suggest the health benefits of marriage may be attenuating. One notable shift is that the self-rated health of never-marrieds has improved over time, converging with the married. This convergence is sharper among men than women and among blacks than whites. The explanation for this pattern is not entirely clear. It is possible that never-married individuals have greater access to social-support resources as a growing share of adults are unmarried. Or, the social meaning of never having been married may have changed such that there is less stigma associated with singlehood. Finally, the selection into remaining never-married probably has changed in recent years. Still, it is not clear why the convergence by marital status would be larger for men and blacks.[28]

At the same time, previously married adults, especially widows, have experienced a steep decline in their health since the early 1970s. Meanwhile, the self-rated health of married men has held steady since the 1970s whereas for married women it has actually improved over time. The health advantage for currently versus previously married women is larger today than it was four decades ago, which is a puzzling result. Despite being in poor health, it could be that the previously married are living longer these days that they did years ago, making the well-being gap appear larger now. Ultimately though, the health gains from marriage are more equivocal today than in decades past. Never-married men do not report better health than married men, and marrieds who experience marital disruption fare worse nowadays.[29]

The health benefits associated with marriage extend to longevity. It is well established that married men and women survive to later ages than do the unmarried. In fact, this gap appears to have widened over time, with marrieds experiencing especially rapid gains in mortality improvement in recent years.[30] Marrieds have higher family incomes, they experience fewer life stressors and have more social support, and they tend to engage in more healthy behaviors than the divorced, widowed, or never-married.

A 2012 study offered new insights on how marital status is linked to mortality by examining whether the mortality of cohabitors was comparable to that of marrieds, revealing a complex set of findings that differed by gender and race.[31] Married men and women enjoyed lower mortality than cohabiting men and women, but this advantage held only for whites. Black co-resident couples—whether married or cohabiting—experienced comparable mortality risks. The absence of a marriage advantage for blacks could reflect the unique meaning cohabitation has for blacks than whites. For blacks, cohabitation is more marriagelike whereas for whites it is more often a stepping stone to marriage. Alternatively, it may be because married blacks do not have appreciably more resources than cohabiting blacks. Nor do they differ in terms of relationship quality.[32] Relative to the unpartnered, cohabiting men (white and black alike) tended to live longer, but cohabiting women (whether white or black) did not live appreciably longer than their single counterparts. This gender differential is consistent with long-standing evidence that being in a union is more beneficial for men's than for women's health.[33] Notably, all of these patterns persisted even after adjusting for factors known to be associated with marital status and mortality, including income, health behaviors (e.g., smoking, drinking, and exercise), and psychological distress.[34]

Thus far, we have unpacked the unmarried category, differentiating among cohabitors, the never-married, and the previously married, included divorceds and widoweds. But the married is not a homogenous group. Some are happily married whereas others are in loveless marriages. Marriages can be marked by frequent conflict, tension, and even violence. The health benefits of marriage are partially a function of marital dynamics, with those in happier marriages reaping health advantages while spouses with poorer marital quality often do not realize such benefits and sometimes actually fare worse than the unmarried. For men and women alike, marital strain hastens age-related decline in self-related health, suggesting that the persistence of poor marital quality has a cumulative effect on health.[35] Marital distress is associated with worse cardiovascular health and poorer immune functioning.[36] Spouses with poor marital quality require longer periods of time for wound healing than do their counterparts in high-quality marriages, reflecting the chronic stress imposed by marital strain.[37]

The relationship between marriage and health is complex. It varies in terms of the couple's marital dynamics. It also differs by structural factors, such as race and gender, and appears to be shifting across time as broader changes occur to marriage as an institution and as alternatives to marriage, including cohabitation, become more widespread. The health of never-married individuals is looking more similar to marrieds whereas the previously married are more disadvantaged than a generation or two ago. The marital biography, which describes the trajectory of one's experiences of union formation and dissolution across the life course, is tied to health outcomes.[38] Individuals in first marriages enjoy better health at midlife than their counterparts who are remarried following divorce. In turn, the remarried are advantaged compared with those who remain divorced or widowed. The more years one has spent divorced or widowed, the more chronic conditions and mobility limitations one has at midlife. These health dimensions tend to develop slowly, which could help to explain why they are linked to duration of exposure to marital disruption. Other health indicators, such as depressive symptoms, appear more responsive to current marital status. Today's adults experience more varied and complex marital biographies that increasingly include spells of cohabitation, marriage, divorce, and repartnership. Particularly during mid- and later life, the linkages between marriage and health should be viewed within this richer and more nuanced framework of marital biographies to capture the ways in which current and prior marital experiences jointly operate to shape health and longevity.

A nascent literature examines the health and well-being of same-sex cohabitors relative to both different-sex married and unpartnered individuals. Same-sex cohabitors report poorer self-rated health than do different-sex married individuals and this differential holds net of socioeconomic status, indicating that the marriage advantage is not merely a function of economic resources. It is possible that sexual minorities experience greater stress because of their status and this undermines their overall health. Same-sex cohabitors report better health than do singles (whether divorced, widowed, or never-married), but this advantage is entirely explained by their higher economic status.[39]

Marriage and Economic Well-being

Part of the marriage advantage in health reflects the higher level of economic resources that married couples possess. The benefits of financial security are numerous. Simply put, having money means being able to live well—to readily afford not only the basic necessities of life but also occasional splurges. And to have savings to draw on when unexpected expenses arise. Couples who are comfortable financially have fewer stresses and strains because they do not have to worry about money. They pay their bills and save some of their money for a rainy day.

The median household income of married couples exceeds that of households headed by an individual. The gap has widened as the financial gains for married couples have become more pronounced in recent years. Marriage is now more selective of the most educated and economically secure individuals. Moreover, individuals increasingly choose spouses who are similar to themselves in terms of education and occupation, contributing to the larger societal trend of growing income inequality.[40] A generation or two ago, a doctor married a nurse. Now, a doctor marries a doctor, which is a tremendous boost to family income. In fact, wives earned more their husbands in nearly 30 percent of all dual-earner marriages as of 2015. By comparison, only 21 percent earned more than their husbands in 1991.[41]

Beyond the rise in assortative mating, which has helped to close the gender gap in earnings for husbands and wives, a primary reason why married couples enjoy greater financial security compared with single individuals is simply because there are two earners who pool resources and take advantage of the economies of scale that come from co-residence.

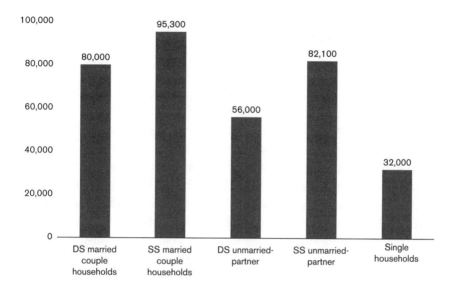

Figure 14. Median Household Income by Householder Couple Status, 2014. Source: Ruggles et al. 2015.

But selection also plays a big role because unmarried cohabiting couples do not have comparable levels of economic resources. Rather, cohabiting households have incomes that fall in between married-couple and single-person households. Recall that many couples cohabit precisely because they are not economically prepared for marriage. Until they achieve a modicum of financial stability, which includes the completion of their education, stable employment, and no debts, couples are reluctant to tie the knot.[42] The economic prerequisites for marriage these days effectively shut out those with more precarious finances, leaving them to cohabit unmarried. In contrast, same-sex couple households are quite well off, on average, enjoying higher median incomes than their different-sex married counterparts. This in part reflects the high average level of education of same-sex co-resident couples relative to different-sex married or cohabiting couples. As shown in figure 14, different-sex and same-sex married couples report the highest median household incomes at $80,000 and $95,300, respectively. For their respective cohabiting couple households, the figures are a bit lower with a median household income of $56,000 for different-sex cohabiting households and $82,100 for same-sex cohabiting households. Single (i.e., noncouple) households have a median household income of only $32,000.

CHILDREN'S FAMILY LIVING ARRANGEMENTS

The traditional nuclear family composed of a breadwinner-homemaker married couple and their shared children is a relic of the past. Just 20 percent of children live in this family form nowadays.[43] Typically, children in married-parent families have mothers who are employed. Today's children reside in a diverse array of family types. According to sociologist Philip Cohen, when it comes to family structure "different is the new normal."[44] The term *family structure* describes a child's relationship to his or her parent(s) in the household. Most children reside in married-parent families, but a sizeable minority lives in unmarried families, as depicted in figure 15. In 2013, 59 percent of children lived with two biological married parents. Another 5 percent resided in a married stepfamily. Roughly one in five children were in a single-mother family whereas just 3 percent lived in a single-father family. Nearly one in ten children resided with cohabiting parents: about 3 percent of children lived in a two biological cohabiting parent family and another 5 percent were in a cohabiting stepfamily. A small share of children (4 percent) lived with no biological parents. Many of these children resided with other relatives, such as grandparents.

The family living arrangements of children have shifted dramatically over time, with a marked decrease in the share of children in the traditional two-biological-married-parent family. Historically, most children resided in this family form. In 1970, 84 percent of children lived in this family type. Only about 10 percent of children were in single-mother families.[45] But rising levels of divorce and repartnering in recent decades coupled with rapid growth in nonmarital childbearing contributed to the diversification of children's living arrangements. These changes have been especially pronounced among racial and ethnic minorities and the less-educated, contributing to the emergence of diverging destinies for chil-

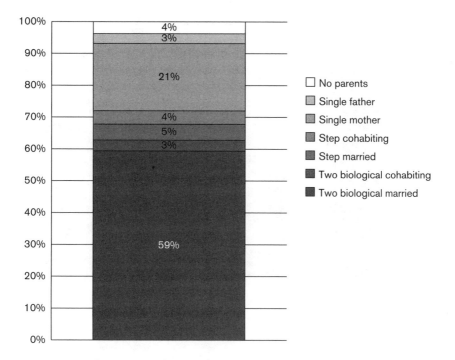

Figure 15. Family Structure of Minor Children, 2013. Source: Payne 2013a, figure 1.

dren. Economic and social inequality has widened the gap between the most and least advantaged children.[46]

Nearly all (89 percent) children of college-educated mothers live with a married mother, as illustrated in figure 16a–c. This pattern has persisted in recent decades, remaining essentially unchanged since 1980. In contrast, for children of moderately or less-educated mothers, the share with married mothers has steadily declined as the proportions cohabiting increased considerably. Among children living with mothers who did not have a high school diploma, the share of mothers who were married fell from 73 percent in 1980 to 66 percent in 2010. The drop for mothers with a high school degree or some postsecondary schooling was even more precipitous, falling from 85 percent to 70 percent. This group also experienced a notable increase in single parenthood, which rose from 14 percent to 22 percent over the forty-year time period. Whereas these moderately educated mothers more closely resembled the college-graduate mothers

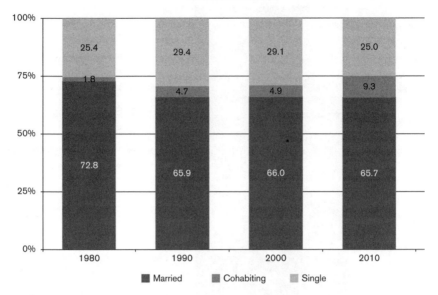

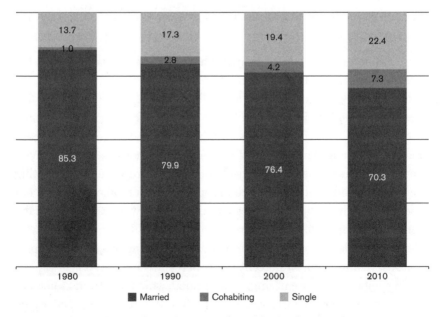

Figure 16a–c. Mother's Relationship Status by Mother's Educational Attainment.
Source: Stykes and Williams 2013, figure 3.

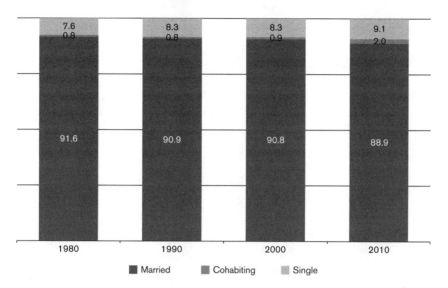

Figure 16c. (continued)

in 1980, today they are more similar to less-educated mothers who did not finish high school, giving rise to the bifurcation of children's family experiences.

Stated differently, married mothers are disproportionately highly educated compared with cohabiting and single mothers. Whereas over 40 percent of married mothers have a college degree, just 13 percent and 17 percent of cohabiting and single mothers, respectively, have completed college. The racial and ethnic composition of mothers also differs by union status. More than two-thirds of married mothers are white, whereas less than one-half of single mothers are white. Fewer than 10 percent of married mothers are black whereas over 30 percent of single mothers are black.[47]

As illustrated in figure 17, children's family structure differs by racial and ethnic group. For white children, most reside in two-biological-married-parent families (69 percent) or single-mother families (13 percent). About 6 percent are in married stepfamilies and another 6 percent are in cohabiting families. For black children, nearly one-half reside in a

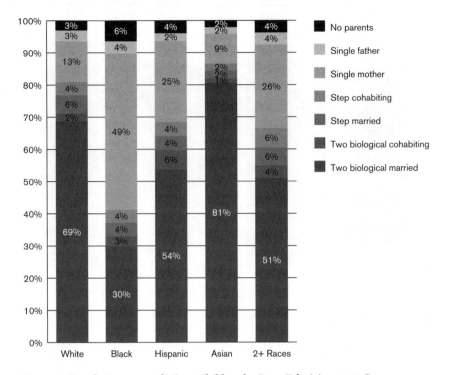

Figure 17. Family Structure of Minor Children by Race-Ethnicity, 2013. Source: Payne 2013a, figure 2.

single-mother family. Only 30 percent live in two-biological-married-parent families, and 4 percent are in married stepfamilies. About 7 percent live in cohabiting families. Hispanic children are in between with 54 percent in two-biological-married-parent families, 4 percent in married stepfamilies, and 10 percent in cohabiting families. Another one-quarter reside in single-mother families. Four out of five Asian children live in two-biological-married-parent families and just 9 percent are in single-mother families. A mere 3 percent live in cohabiting families. Many children are multiracial and their living arrangements appear most similar to those of Hispanic children. About half of multiracial children live in two-biological-married-parent families, 10 percent are in cohabiting families, and one-quarter are in single-mother families.

Measuring Children's Living Arrangements

The diversity of children's living arrangements presents important measurement challenges. As families become more varied, the measures we use to capture children's family lives must be adaptable. New approaches to gauging children's living arrangements may be necessary to reflect the full range of children's experiences.[48]

For example, the conventional measure of family structure captures a child's relationships to parents in the household, obscuring children's ties to resident siblings, who may be either full biological, half, or step. A newer term, *family complexity*, describes a child's sibling relationships. Family complexity emerges when children reside with either half- or step-siblings.[49] By restricting the focus to parents when we measure family structure, we may be underestimating the share of children in step-families. A child residing with two biological married parents, for instance, may reside with a half-sibling from a parent's prior union. Or, children living with a single mother may not all share the same biological father. Both of these are examples of complex families. Family complexity occurs for about 12 percent of children. Although it is most common in married and cohabiting stepfamilies, it also occurs in other family forms, including two-biological-married-parent families and single-mother families. Roughly one-half of married stepfamilies and more than one-quarter of cohabiting stepfamilies are characterized by family complexity.[50] Family complexity matters for children because it is often reflective of differential distribution of resources within the family. Children may be treated differently depending on who their parents are and this could alter the family environment for all children in a household.

Another measurement challenge is family-boundary ambiguity. Family structure is treated like an objective fact, but actually it can be rather subjective. The measurement of family structure relies on self-reports from individuals, who appraise family membership. The boundaries demarcating who is in and out of the family are blurrier in our time because families are so diverse. When asked to report members of their family, married and cohabiting parents often disregard stepchildren but nearly always report the presence of biological children.[51] Similarly, stepsiblings tend to be underreported in comparison with biological siblings.[52] The fuzziness surrounding family structure is especially pronounced for emerging family forms such as cohabiting stepfamilies.

A comparison of family-structure reports by mother-adolescent pairs underscores the role of subjectivity in reports. Comparing the adolescent's report to that of the mother, nearly all (99 percent) agreed when they resided in two-biological-married-parent families and concordance was also quite high in single-mother families (88 percent). But only 70 percent of adolescents agreed with their mothers' reports of living in a married stepfamily. And, for mothers who reported that the child lived in a cohabiting stepfamily, a mere one-third of adolescents agreed. Parents and their children were more likely to disagree than agree about living in a cohabiting stepfamily. Children often ignored the cohabiting partner, reporting that they lived in a single-mother family.[53] These differentials elucidate the difficulty involved in measuring children's living arrangements. Family structure is as much a social construction as an objective fact.

Boundary ambiguity will only intensify as more families are formed outside of marriage. And, it has notable ramifications for population estimates of the distribution of children's family structure. Depending on whether adolescent or mother reports of family structure are used, the estimated share of teens living in cohabiting stepfamilies varies by nearly 100 percent. Family boundary ambiguity is likely to become increasingly significant over time as more children experience less traditional family living arrangements, further compromising estimates of children's family structure. This is of concern not just from a measurement standpoint, but also for family dynamics, as research indicates boundary ambiguity is linked to poorer family functioning, including weaker family ties and less closeness.[54]

Family Structure and Child Well-being

As children's living arrangements have become more diverse in recent decades, researchers have extensively studied how children's family structure is related to well-being. The dramatic rise in divorce during the 1970s and early 1980s prompted scholars to investigate how children raised by a single mother fare compared with children reared in a traditional, two-biological-married-parent family. As many single mothers remarried, researchers broadened their focus to include children in married step-families. Did outcomes improve for children whose mothers remarried? More recently, the growth in unmarried childbearing has led researchers to consider various pathways to single-parent families: some children are born to a single mother and never reside with their biological father whereas others are born to married parents who eventually divorce. And, children increasingly reside in cohabiting families, whether because they are born to two biological cohabiting parents or their biological parent (typically a mother) forms a cohabiting union. In short, children reside in a range of family structures and these living arrangements are related to child well-being.[55]

Despite the proliferation of family forms, the basic conclusions about the relationship between family structure and child well-being are straight-forward: children residing in two-biological-married-parent families tend to fare better, on average, across numerous domains of well-being, than their counterparts residing outside of this family form. This differential is modest in magnitude, but has been documented consistently across stud-ies. Children who live with two biological married parents enjoy better cog-nitive, education, behavioral, emotional, and social outcomes than other children, on average.[56] The well-being of children who do not live with two biological married parents varies relatively little by family structure. The outcomes of children residing with a single parent, in a married stepfamily, or a cohabiting family are largely similar.[57] Children residing with two same-sex parents tend to have outcomes comparable to their counterparts in two-biological-married-parent families.[58]

The association between family structure and child well-being varies by race and ethnicity. For black and Hispanic children, family structure appears to have weaker or even negligible effects on child outcomes.[59] By comparison, family structure differentials in child well-being are larger among white children. These patterns may emerge because diverse family forms are more common among racial and ethnic minorities and there-fore may be more widely accepted and normative, resulting in less stigma and stress for minority children than for white children. At the same time, it appears blacks and Hispanics derive fewer benefits from marriage which may also contribute to the narrower gap in child well-being across family structures.

Theoretical Explanations

Family structure is not deterministic. Living with two biological married parents does not ensure a privileged, carefree upbringing that culminates in a successful adulthood, nor does parental divorce ruin a child's future. Rather, the linkage between family structure and child outcomes is mediated by key intervening factors, namely economic resources and parental socialization, which in turn are likely to shape children's development and well-being.[60] Family structure provides a social address of sorts, serving as a marker for family resources and processes that are more closely tied to child outcomes.

Economic resources, including parental education and income, are critical to child well-being.[61] Financial security enables parents to purchase housing in safe neighborhoods with high-quality schools. It also allows parents not just to meet but to exceed children's material needs, purchasing additional advantages for children, such as tutoring or private-school tuition. Apart from these direct effects, parental resources operate indirectly by enhancing the well-being of parents.[62] Parents who do not have to worry about financial resources are able to focus their efforts on parenting and the well-being of their children. Those whose economic situation is more precarious are often distracted by worries about money, undermining their ability to effectively parent their child.[63] Children living in married-parent families tend to have more educated parents who likely enjoy higher family incomes than children living in single-parent families. Family structure is related to child poverty, ranging from less than 10 percent for children in two-biological-married-parent families to nearly 50 percent for children in single-mother families.[64] Economic disadvantage is the largest predictor of child well-being and accounts for about half of the family structure variation in child outcomes.[65]

Parental socialization describes how parents rear their children. Effective parenting is marked by high levels of parental warmth and support. Children benefit from parental acceptance, engagement, and involvement. Effective parents also consistently enforce rules through moderate control or discipline.[66] Neither harsh nor permissive parenting is advantageous for children. Children are most likely to thrive when parents combine high warmth with moderate control. This parenting style is termed authoritative parenting. Parental socialization is often impeded when parents are dealing with other relationship challenges, such as marital conflict or adjustment to a new stepfamily, which may hinder a parent's ability to engage in consistent, effective parenting.[67] Single parents can be at a disadvantage because there is no second parent to provide additional support and control. Parental involvement and monitoring may be limited in single-parent families, jeopardizing their ability to parent effectively.[68] Mothers tend to be highly involved parents regardless of family structure, but fathering is more variable largely because of residential status.[69] Nonresident fathers tend to spend much less time with their children than resident fathers. Both resident fathering and nonresident fathering are linked to child well-being.[70]

A Note about Selection

Family structure operates largely through the mediating influences of economic resources and parental socialization. The correlation between family structure and child well-being is considerably reduced after accounting for these factors.[71] But uncertainty remains about the roles of selection versus causation. Are the benefits that typically accrue to children in two-biological-married-parent families primarily an artifact of selection? If so, this would mean that the most well-adjusted, stable, and resource-rich couples marry and rear children within marriage. It is not parental marriage per se that advantages children but rather that marriage is selective of the best kinds of parents, on average.

Alternatively, family structure could have a direct, causal effect on child well-being. Perhaps marriage itself nudges parents to behave in ways that are especially advantageous for children. It is nearly impossible to fully adjudicate between selection and causation because children cannot be randomly assigned to be reared by married versus single parents, for example.

Nonetheless, there is substantial evidence for selection because controlling for parent characteristics and the family environment greatly diminishes family-structure variation in child well-being.[72] Of course, evidence of selection does not negate the possibility of a causal effect of parental marriage.[73] Recent efforts to address causation have yielded conflicting conclusions. It is unlikely that the contentious policy debate over whether parental marriage can enhance child well-being will be resolved any time soon.

One approach to this issue is to consider variation among two-parent family forms. If children in two-biological-married-parent families enjoy the best outcomes, is it because there are two biological parents, the parents are married, or both? Their advantage does not appear to accrue solely from having two biological parents. Children who reside with two biological cohabiting parents tend to fare worse than their counterparts with married parents, signaling that marriage is more than "just a piece of paper." Despite the presence of two biological parents, couples who have a child in cohabitation are different from those whose child is born within marriage. Children living with two biological cohabiting parents appear more similar to children in cohabiting stepfamilies, underscoring the role of selection into family structure.[74] Similarly, the advantage is not merely a function of marriage because children residing in married stepfamilies have worse outcomes, on average, than their counterparts in two-biological-married-parent families.[75] These patterns indicate that living with two biological married parents is associated with unique advantages for children. Both biological status and marital status play a role.[76]

Family Instability

Family structure is a static measure, capturing living arrangements at a particular point in time. But this measurement approach obscures movement from one family structure to another, an increasingly common occurrence. Moreover, family structure is confounded with family stability. To a large extent, the purported benefits of two-biological-married-parent families for children actually could be due to stability. These families are stable essentially by definition. Is the advantage associated with this family type a result of stability? This seems plausible given that children benefit from consistency in their daily routines. Still, children in two-biological-cohabiting-parent families, which presumably are indicative of family stability, are not as advantageous for children.

Family instability, which describes transitions into and out of various family structures, is now recognized as a critical element of children's family life course.[77] Children who reside in a stable single-mother family, for example, tend to have better outcomes than children who experience what Andrew Cherlin termed "the marriage-go-round," which describes parents who form and dissolve multiple partnerships.[78] Family stability has enduring benefits for children, which persist into adulthood.[79] Similar to the pattern observed for family structure, the linkages between family instability and well-being are more modest for racial-ethnic minorities than for white children.[80]

Much like family structure, family instability also presents measurement challenges. Family instability has been conceptualized and measured in various ways. Perhaps the most common approach has been to tally the number of living-arrangement transitions a child has experienced, with the expectation that each additional transition is related to worse child outcomes. There is some evidence to support a linear association, although other studies indicate one transition is less harmful than two or more transitions.[81] Regardless, this approach ignores the types of family transitions children experience. For example, parental divorce would count the same as parental remarriage, but the two types of transitions may have unique effects on child well-being. This appears to be the case for marital versus cohabiting transitions. It is well established that parental divorce is detrimental for child well-being. But transitioning out of a cohabiting family and into a single-mother family has no appreciable downsides and actually is related to gains in children's academic performance.[82]

If family instability undermines child well-being, then presumably family stability is beneficial for child outcomes. But not all stable family forms are similarly benign. In particular, children in stable cohabiting families fare worse than their counterparts in stable remarried or single-mother families.[83] Family scholars recognize that family instability is an important component of child well-being, but there is not yet consensus on how to conceptualize and measure instability.[84] Children's family trajectories are increasingly complex, and it is possible that multiple dimensions of instability contribute to children's well-being. Both the number and type of transitions were discussed here, but other dimensions that have been studied include the duration of time spent in a particular family form and the developmental timing of family transitions. Early childhood transitions appear to have enduring consequences for child outcomes.[85]

Children in Same-sex Families

Recent legal struggles over same-sex marriage as well as adoption and parenting rights for same-sex couples has brought to the foreground another family type: same-sex two-parent families. Over the past few decades, there has been increasing attention to the well-being of children living in same-sex-parent families and this research has been integral in shaping the shifting legal terrain for same-sex couples.[86] For example, proponents of same-sex marriage pointed to the benefits of parental marriage for the well-being of children, whereas opponents indicated that marriage is for procreation and a same-sex couple cannot reproduce together. Of course, not all different-sex married couples choose to have children or are capable of reproduction. Moreover, roughly 225,000 children were residing in a same-sex-couple household in 2013, with nearly three-quarters living with female-female same sex couples and the remainder with male-male same sex couples.[87] In 2010, about one in six same-sex-couple households included children versus roughly two in five different-sex-couple households.[88]

Still, children in same-sex-parent families constitute a very small fraction of all children. Even among children who live with their biological or adoptive mother in a two-parent family, less than 0.5 percent are in a female-female same-sex family.[89] The rarity of this family form makes it challenging to study because it is difficult to obtain a sufficient number of cases for analyses even in a very large representative sample. For this reason, many of the studies to date have relied on nonrepresentative samples to assess child outcomes, although there are notable exceptions.

Despite the methodological challenges inherent in the study of this population, a strong consensus has emerged that children in same-sex-parent families have outcomes that are comparable to those of children living with two biological married parents. In an exhaustive assessment of the social science research, sociologist Wendy Manning and her team of graduate student researchers combed through every study published in the past decade on the topic. They concluded that children in same-sex parent families do not appreciably differ from their counterparts in different-sex-parent families across numerous outcomes, including cognition and academic achievement, social competence, psychological well-being, sexual activity, substance use, and delinquency.[90] This conclusion is corroborated by other recent assessments of the research.[91]

The research conducted by Manning and her team formed the basis of an amicus brief sponsored by the American Sociological Association that was submitted as evidence in a case brought against the state of Michigan by April DeBoer and Jayne Rowse, a lesbian couple who had each adopted children but could not legally adopt them together as a couple without being married. Social science evidence on the outcomes of children reared in same-sex-parent families was central to the decision by federal judge Bernard Friedman to overturn the state of Michigan's constitutional amendment banning same-sex marriage. The state contended that children suffer in same-sex-parent families, pointing to a study funded by conservatives to support its assertions.[92] The federal judge found the study leader Mark Regnerus's "testimony entirely unbelievable and not worthy of serious consideration."[93] Instead, the judge was convinced by the broad consensus in both the social science and medical fields that children in same-sex families do just as well as children in different-sex families.

There is still much to learn about same-sex families. In particular, the work to date largely has examined lesbian-couple families with children. Less is known about children living with gay male parents. The emphasis on same-sex-couple families ignores variation among single parents, some of whom are presumably gay, lesbian, or bisexual. Children in same-sex-parent families are typically compared with children in two-biological-married-parent families, but perhaps different-sex-cohabiting-parent families would be more appropriate because until 2015 same-sex couples could not legally marry in many states. Moreover, some same-sex families may be stepfamilies in which only one member of the couple has been a parent to the child since birth.

Diverging Destinies for Children

The experience of childhood has changed in recent decades, and the shift is not merely due to the diversification of family structures and the growth in family instability. Nowadays, children are bifurcated according to social class, resulting in what Sara McLanahan termed "diverging destinies."[94] Just as rising inequality has altered the family formation and dissolution patterns adults experience, as described in chapters 2 and 3, so too have these shifts altered the contours of childhood. With the hollowing out of the middle class, children are more concentrated at the two extremes of poverty and wealth. Children with advantaged parents enjoy more resources today than did previous generations. In contrast, children at the other extreme are experiencing sharper disadvantage than their predecessors. At the upper end of the spectrum, children reap the benefits of residing in more stable family forms that often are composed of two biological married parents. Both parents are college-educated, gainfully employed, and actively involved in childrearing. Children on the low end of the spectrum typically live with single mothers who have comparatively few resources. Fathers may be an intermittent presence in these children's lives, contributing to the instability they experience. They often provide few economic resources, compounding the financial challenges faced by many single mothers, who tend to be less educated and work only part-time. Furthermore, the public safety net for economically disadvantaged children has shrunk in recent decades as welfare programs now have time limits and work requirements. The value of welfare benefits today, after adjusting for inflation, is less than it was in the 1970s.[95] This has direct implications for the well-being of children, exacerbating the precarious position of those on the bottom rungs of the ladder.

McLanahan has documented the increasing prominence of social class in shaping childhood experiences by illustrating how family resources have diverged in recent decades according to the mother's position in the education distribution. She classified mothers into three groups, with the high group composed of mothers in the top education quartile, the low group containing mothers in the bottom education quartile, and the middle group with mothers in one of the two middle quartiles. This measure effectively nets out the overall rise in women's education over time by classifying women's position relative to their peers. She showed widening outcomes according to maternal education position, as the middle group skews increasingly toward the least-educated group and the highly educated diverges from the other two groups. One example she provided was trends in single motherhood. In 1960, the levels of single motherhood were low regardless of maternal education, ranging from about 5 percent for the most educated to over 10 percent for the least educated. By 2000,

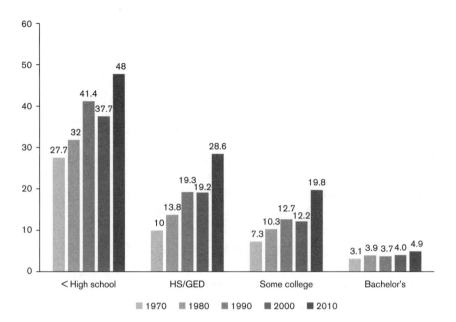

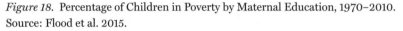

Figure 18. Percentage of Children in Poverty by Maternal Education, 1970–2010.
Source: Flood et al. 2015.

the gap was much more pronounced. The level of single motherhood remained modest for the most educated, at less than 10 percent. But it exceeded 40 percent for the least educated and was nearly 30 percent among the moderately educated. During this same forty-year timespan, family incomes were stubbornly flat for middle- and low-educated mothers, yet climbed precipitously for highly educated mothers.[96]

Child poverty tracks closely with maternal education, as shown in figure 18. Whereas nearly one-half of children whose mothers did not finish high school were living in poverty, just 5 percent of children of college-educated mothers were poor in 2010. By comparison, the distribution of child poverty according to maternal education was much flatter in 1970. Only 28 percent of children whose mothers had not completed high school lived in poverty, compared with about 3 percent of children with college-educated mothers. Across all maternal-education groups, child poverty has risen since 1970, with the most growth among those with lower levels of education. For example, for mothers with a high school diploma, child poverty was about 10 percent in 1970 versus nearly 30 percent in 2010. A similar pattern obtained among mothers with some college: child poverty climbed from 7 percent in 1970 to 20 percent in 2010.

The diverging destinies structuring contemporary childhood extend to how parents rear their children. In her acclaimed book *Unequal Childhoods: Class, Race, and Family Life,* sociologist Annette Lareau describes how parenting differs by social class.[97] Middle-class parents tend to be highly involved in their children's lives, scheduling a full slate of formal activities for their children to enhance the development of their skills and talents. She terms this parenting style *concerted cultivation* because it is a time- and resource-intensive approach to childrearing that requires sustained parental involvement and investment. This approach is akin to "helicopter parenting" of the overscheduled child. A core feature of concerted cultivation is the willingness of middle-class parents to reason with their children, actively engaging them to enhance their assertiveness and comfort level around adults by honing their logic and negotiating skills. Middle-class children's regular involvement in organized activities provides structured opportunities for them to learn how to interact with both peers and unrelated adults, valuable skills for adulthood.

For example, Lareau describes ten-year-old Garrett, whose scheduled activities for the month of May include "baseball, Forest soccer (a private soccer club), Intercounty soccer (an all-star, elite team of boys drawn from various soccer clubs), swim team practice, piano lessons, and saxophone. Only the saxophone lessons take place at school; all the rest are extracurriculars."[98] Garrett is one of three children in the Tallinger family. His parents are both employed and, as the oldest and busiest child, Garrett's schedule "set[s] the pace of life for all family members."[99] Their hectic schedules are worth it, according to middle-class parents, because their children benefit in the long run. Alexander Williams's mother maintains "sports provide great opportunities to learn how to be competitive. Learn how to accept defeat. Learn how to accept winning, in a gracious way. Also it gives him the opportunity to learn leadership skills and how to be a team player. Those . . . sports really provide a lot of really great opportunities."[100] Alexander's activities are not limited to sports. His father articulates the benefits of his son's music lessons this way: "I don't know baroque from classical—but he does. How can that not be a benefit in later life? I'm convinced that this rich experience will make him a better person, a better citizen, a better husband, a better father—certainly a better student."[101]

Working-class parents take a less intensive approach to childrearing, which Lareau characterizes as the accomplishment of *natural growth*. Children's time is relatively unstructured and marked by few if any formal activities. Lareau describes the experience of Tyrec, a fifth-grader and son of a working-class single mother. He played organized football during the summer, but the schedule was time-consuming so he did not continue the sport during the school year. Lareau writes: "Although Ms. Taylor seemed genuinely pleased that her son had enjoyed being on the football team, she saw no reason for him to repeat the experience. . . . Since simply stepping out the front door and joining his neighborhood friends for informal play obviously gave Tyrec much pleasure, his mother felt that was preferable to having him involved in an activity that required extensive involvement on her part. For her, as with other working-class and poor mothers, being a good mother did not include an obligation to cultivate her children's various interests, particularly if doing so would require radically rearranging her own life."[102]

Working-class children are more autonomous and thus their activities are often self-directed, typically involving informal play with neighborhood kids, siblings, or cousins. Unlike middle-class children, who spend a lot of time in the company of unrelated adults through their participation in scheduled extracurricular and academic activities, working-class children's interactions with other adults is largely confined to extended family members. There is also a clearer dividing line between working-class parents and children. Parents less often engage in extensive reasoning with their children. Instead, they offer more directives.

These distinct approaches to childrearing persist through adolescence and into early adulthood. In fact, Lareau finds that the gap between middle- and working-class children widens with age as the social-class differences in parenting become even more pronounced. Parents play a leading role as middle-class children prepare for and enter college, ensuring they successfully navigate the complex college-admissions process and adjust to campus life both socially and academically. Middle-class children are equipped to advocate for themselves, but their parents are always at the ready to quickly intervene when children have difficulties. In contrast, working-class parents are unlikely to steer their children's educational careers. Working-class children are less likely than their middle-class counterparts to pursue higher education, and those who do have less familial support to draw on than do the middle class, which can be a significant impediment to college persistence and graduation. College-educated parents have both firsthand experience and the social and material resources to adroitly steer their children through the complicated maze of higher education.

Lareau points to strengths and weaknesses of both parenting approaches. Concerted cultivation provides children with specialized training (e.g., sports, music lessons, tutoring) that teaches children how to perform, what it means to win or lose, and how to work as a team. They also learn how to interact with adults in an assertive manner that prepares them for adult roles. And their intensive, highly communicative relationships with their parents build their vocabularies and their reasoning skills. Yet the frenetic pace of life for middle-class children wears them down and is disruptive for families. Natural growth proceeds at a slower, more relaxed pace and these children are both more energetic and less often bored than their middle-class counterparts. But working-class children are not being trained by their parents and other adults to be assertive and to expect social institutions to be responsive to them. Instead, their lives are marked by constraint and powerlessness.[103]

CONCLUSION

The linkages between family living arrangements and individual well-being are not as straightforward as they initially appear. For adults, marriage is related to health and well-being. The married are happier, healthier, and richer than the unmarried, but this relationship is larger for some groups (e.g., men or whites) than others and the advantage tends to diminish over time. Meanwhile, unmarried adults are a heterogeneous group, with those who experience a marital dissolution through either divorce or widowhood worse off, on average, than their never-married counterparts. Cohabitation is less advantageous than marriage for health and well-being among whites, but the two union types are more comparable for blacks. Static indicators of marital status are of limited utility though because they only provide a snapshot of one's experiences. The marital biography, which encompasses union formation and dissolution experiences across the life course, structures well-being pathways. For example, remarriage following divorce does not entirely undo the negative effects of marital disruption on health.

The picture is also complicated for children. True, there is ample evidence that children fare better in two-biological-married-parent families than in other family forms. The variation in well-being among children in a single-parent versus a married stepfamily, for instance, is negligible. But echoing the importance of the marital biography for adults, family instability is a critical determinant of child outcomes. Family transitions are stressful and disruptive, upsetting family routines that are beneficial to children's development. Family structure is perhaps less important than family stability over the course of childhood. Indeed, part of the reason why children fare so well in two-biological-married-parent families is because they are by definition stable.

Another layer of complexity surrounds selection versus causation. Broad conclusions about family living arrangements and well-being must be tempered to acknowledge this uncertainty. Just because we can identify a marriage advantage does not mean that marriage is causally related to well-being. Rather, selection drives much of the observed associations between marital status (or family structure) and outcomes. Individuals are not randomly sorted into families but instead actively select into and remain in or exit from family types with different frequencies according to various characteristics or factors (such as education) that are in turn also associated with well-being.

Even in the face of these complexities, it is clear that growing family inequality is leading to bifurcated outcomes, especially for children. As family patterns change, we can expect that how they are related to health and well-being might be altered, too. This is particularly likely to occur when family patterns shift in different ways for particular subgroups, such as subgroups distinguished by levels of education. As marriage becomes more restricted to those with a college degree, it might appear that marriage is especially protective of health and well-being. In fact, this association is an artifact of the composition of the married population. Were marriage to become as common among those with lower levels of education, its apparent benefits would presumably diminish.

Essentially, we are chasing a moving target. Family change continues apace, and thus the ways in which living arrangements are tied to well-being is also shifting. One of the main reasons why policymakers and scholars are interested in family change is because family living arrangements are closely linked to individual well-being. Some may believe it is worthwhile either to facilitate or to deter certain types of families, perhaps through social policy incentives. Another way of approaching this issue though is to enact social policies that ease the strains individuals and their families face. For instance, the social safety net is designed to alleviate the burdens confronting economically disadvantaged families. Access to parental or family leave, sick leave, and vacation time can help families balance competing demands from home and work. These topics are explored in the next chapter on family policy issues.

5 Family Policy Issues

DOMESTIC AND INTERNATIONAL PERSPECTIVES

Family change has long spurred debate in the policy arena. Reformers and politicians aim to refashion family life in response to perceived threats to family stability. For instance, the emergence of companionate marriage during the early twentieth century prompted worries about promiscuity and divorce. Judge Ben B. Lindsey coauthored a book to justify the emergence of modern marriage. He opened the preface of his book this way: "Companionate marriage is legal marriage, with legalized Birth Control, and with the right to divorce by mutual consent for childless couples, usually without payment of alimony. Companionate marriage is an already established social fact in this country. It is conventionally respectable. Sophisticated people, are without incurring social reproach, everywhere practicing Birth Control and also obtaining collusive divorce, outside the law, whenever they want it. They will continue the practice, and no amount of prohibitive legislation can stop them."[1]

His message is that detractors can try all they want to put the brakes on companionate marriage, but Americans have already embraced it. There is no turning back. Attempts to beat back modern marriage, birth control, and divorce through legislation simply will not work, according to Lindsey.

141

The theme of his argument is remarkably contemporary. Just a few short years ago, the same logic was applied to the issue of same-sex marriage. Detractors were increasingly outnumbered by swelling support among the public. The dramatic shift in public attitudes and the swift actions occurring at the state level to extend marriage to same-sex couples signaled a sea-change.[2] It culminated in the U.S. Supreme Court decision that made marriage among same-sex couples legal across the nation. There are reports of lingering pockets of resistance, but same-sex marriage is here to stay.

At the heart of family policy debates are moral struggles about who deserves rights, protections, or assistance. As discussed in the introduction, this is one of the main reasons why it matters how we define a family. What types of living arrangements do we as a society want to encourage, and what types should we discourage? When do purportedly private family problems become of concern to the broader public and merit a response from the state? Recall the discussion from chapter 1 of the Social Security Act of 1935. This landmark legislation resulted from the recognition that families could not weather significant economic downturns without assistance from the federal government. Yet, there was apprehension about who was deserving of support and concern that individual responsibility could be undermined by readily available government-sponsored assistance.[3] These same tensions continue to characterize contemporary debates about family policy.

This chapter examines three pivotal family policy issues, assessing how social institutions and the government have responded to widespread, persistent challenges facing families. International comparisons provide additional context for understanding alternative approaches to these fundamental issues. First, we trace efforts to reduce poverty and single motherhood through welfare and marriage policy. Second, we address the growing problem of how to combine family and work as individuals and couples struggle to balance the competing demands of parenthood and employment with few if any institutional supports. Third, we consider the ramifications of population aging in an era of family upheaval for elder caregiving, an issue that is arguably still at the margins of family policy.

WELFARE AND MARRIAGE POLICY

In 1965, Assistant Secretary of Labor Daniel Patrick Moynihan, who went on to be a four-term U.S. senator (D-New York), published *The Negro Family: The Case for National Action,* a treatise on the "tangle of pathology" associated with the high level of single-mother families among blacks relative to whites. Moynihan asserted that the economic disadvantage of blacks stemmed primarily from family breakdown: "At the heart of the deterioration of the fabric of Negro society is the deterioration of the Negro family. It is the fundamental source of the weakness of the Negro community at the present time.... There is one truly great discontinuity in family structure in the United States at the present time: that between the white world in general and that of the Negro American. The white family has achieved a high degree of stability and is maintaining that stability. *By contrast, the family structure of lower class Negroes is highly unstable, and in many urban centers is approaching complete breakdown.*"[4]

Although Moynihan acknowledged that slavery and Jim Crow had shaped contemporary black-family patterns, he did not grapple with the roles of institutional racism and discrimination. For this reason, many critics said he blamed the victim. Critics also charged that despite his acknowledgment in his treatise that he was describing lower- not middle-class blacks, the empirical evidence he provided did not differentiate blacks (or whites) by social class. He also spoke of "the Negro family," implying a monolithic group.[5]

According to Moynihan, "at the center of the tangle of pathology is the weakness of family structure ... [which] now serves to perpetuate the cycle of poverty and deprivation."[6] In other words, he viewed the rise of single-mother families among blacks, which he described as "a matriarchal arrangement," as the primary driver of the disadvantaged position of blacks in American society because "it seriously retards the progress of the group [blacks] as a whole."[7] These bold claims prompted conservatives and liberals alike to think about the linkages between family structure and economic well-being. Conservatives emphasized the role of cultural factors (e.g., acceptance of nonmarital childbearing), whereas liberals pointed to structural conditions (e.g., male unemployment) to account for economic disadvantage among blacks. His treatise was also a springboard for extensive research on the relationship between the family environment and children's outcomes, particularly their academic achievement.[8]

The Moynihan Report has had an enduring influence on the debate over single motherhood, marriage, and poverty. Scholars and policymakers continue to discuss whether poverty causes single motherhood or single motherhood leads to poverty. Sociologist Sara McLanahan has concluded that we do not have a definitive answer; there is evidence to support both assertions.[9] Looking back on Moynihan's treatise, sociologist Frank Furstenberg has maintained that the policy implications might have been different if Moynihan had recognized that the family patterns he uncovered for blacks were characteristic of low-income populations across racial and ethnic groups.[10] Fifty years after its publication, it continues to figure prominently in both academic and policy discussions about racial and ethnic variation in poverty.

The Moynihan Report has shaped the discourse on the U.S. welfare system. Critics drew on Moynihan's work to buttress their calls to "end welfare as we know it." By providing single mothers with cash benefits and a host of in-kind benefits including food stamps, Medicaid, and housing subsidies, critics maintained that the federal government served as a better "husband" than poor men could, diminishing the attractiveness of marriage among low-income women. Government support was reliable and steady. Mothers could support themselves economically without having to rely on a man. Furthermore, critics argued, cash benefits not only deterred marriage, they also reduced the incentive for mothers to work. As the share of middle-class mothers in the labor force climbed, attitudes toward low-income mothers shifted accordingly. The new norm was that most mothers were working outside the home and therefore poor mothers should get jobs to support their families. This viewpoint relies on an equity argument, but ignores the fact that the cost of staying out of the labor force is much smaller for disadvantaged women, who are not qualified for high-paying positions. Low-income mothers earn paltry wages that may barely net any gains after covering the child care and transportation costs associated with employment.[11]

Welfare, according to its detractors, was the linchpin in the cycle of poverty, perpetuating generation after generation of government dependence by an underclass that was disproportionately a minority. Politicians talked about "welfare queens driving Cadillacs" and single mothers having babies to increase their monthly welfare checks.[12] Even though welfare played a critical role in the well-being of mothers and their children, and welfare benefits were only weakly correlated with nonmarital childbearing rates, these negative stereotypes fostered resentment among Americans that culminated in a dramatic upheaval in the welfare system.[13]

Welfare Reform

In 1996, Democratic President Bill Clinton authorized welfare reform by signing into law the Personal Responsibility and Work Opportunity Reconciliation Act (PRWORA). The overarching goal was to end welfare as we knew it. The bill replaced the existing welfare program, Aid to Families with Dependent Children (AFDC), with Temporary Assistance to Needy Families (TANF). The changes were far-reaching, fundamentally altering the structure and rules governing the welfare system.[14] Perhaps the most remarkable change was the shift away from welfare as an entitlement. Previously, individuals who met the economic threshold could receive welfare benefits, including a monthly check, for life. The new rules stipulated that cash assistance was temporary. Regardless of economic need, individuals could not receive benefits for more than five years in a lifetime. Moreover, recipients had to be able to demonstrate they were pursuing employment opportunities or were gainfully employed. The aim was to move people from welfare to work, underscoring the notion that single mothers should be economic providers for themselves and their children. TANF came into effect during the economic boom of the late 1990s, when the technology bubble emerged. The strong economy buoyed expectations for self-sufficiency. Welfare rolls shrunk by 50 percent and politicians declared it a great success.[15]

Participation in welfare programs has declined dramatically over time. As of 2012, only 32 percent of those eligible for cash benefits through the TANF program actually receive them. By comparison, when welfare reform was enacted in 1996, the participation rate in AFDC hovered around 80 percent. Participation in food stamps (SNAP) is much higher with nearly 90 percent of those eligible enrolled in the program. This high participation

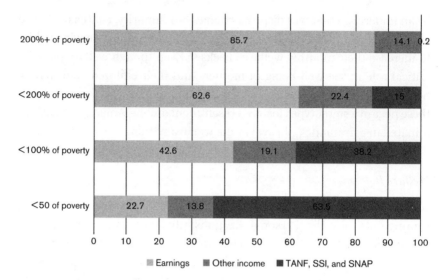

Figure 19. Percentage of Total Income from Earnings, Other Income, and Public Assistance by Poverty Status, 2012. Source: U.S. Department of Health and Human Services, 2015, figure IND 1b.

rate is a recent phenomenon. In the mid-1990s only about 60 percent of those eligible received food stamps. Supplemental Security Income (SSI), which is cash-based support for low-income disabled or aged individuals, is received by about two-thirds of the adults eligible for it.[16]

A key goal of the TANF program was to move families from dependency and self-sufficiency. Earned income constitutes a nontrivial share of total income for all groups, including those living in poverty, as shown in figure 19. For poor individuals, more than 40 percent of their income is derived from earnings. Almost 40 percent is from welfare benefits and the remaining share is from other income, which includes non-means-tested, nonearnings such as child support. Even among those in deep poverty (defined as having an income less than one-half of the poverty line), close to one-quarter of their income comes from earnings. Nearly two-thirds is from welfare benefits. The remainder is from other income.[17]

But a growing share of low income (defined as 200 percent of the poverty line) single mothers are "disconnected," meaning they are neither working nor receiving benefits. Scholars at the Urban Institute estimated that this share grew from less than 10 percent in 1996 to over 20 percent in 2010.[18] The drop in participation in TANF among eligible families is especially concerning given the rise in disconnected single mothers. Indeed, poverty remains stubbornly high among children in single-mother families, with roughly one in two children residing in a single-mother family living in poverty.[19]

Marriage Promotion as an Antipoverty Strategy

PRWORA was more than an overhaul of the welfare system. It also established the preeminence of marriage. The U.S. Congress stipulated that "(1) marriage is the foundation of a successful society and (2) marriage is an essential institution of a successful society which promotes interests of children."[20] A key component of welfare reform was the promotion and maintenance of two-parent, married families. Since 2001, the federal government has spent more than $600 million to support marriage promotion and responsible fatherhood through the Healthy Marriage Initiative. The monies have funded several types of activities, including marriage-skills training, marriage education (including at the high school level), marriage-mentoring programs, and public advertising campaigns to promote marriage.

The government supported three large demonstration projects to test whether relationship skills programs could improve couple relationship stability (and, by extension, child well-being). These large, multiyear studies uncovered no significant gains in relationship stability. In fact, a troubling finding emerged: participation in some of the relationship-skills classes was associated with increases in interpersonal violence.[21] By asking couples to engage in discussions about their relationship, relationship tension and conflict was stoked, which sometimes erupted into violence outside the classroom. This pattern indicates that some forms of relationship-skills training may be detrimental to individual health and well-being, particularly for couples with a history of interpersonal violence. Thus, the measurable benefits of marriage promotion efforts for individuals appears to be negligible at best, and in some cases, negative. Spending on marriage promotion also has had no real effects. Specifically, state-level expenditures on healthy-marriage programming do not correspond with either higher state-level marriage rates or lower state-level divorce rates.[22] In short, the considerable federal investment in marriage promotion has netted no appreciable gains.

Perhaps the lack of tangible evidence to support the effectiveness of marriage-promotion activities is not so surprising when we consider that nearly all Americans, including those who are economically disadvantaged, want to get married. The retreat from marriage does not reflect a waning interest in or appreciation for marriage; the United States remains very enthusiastic about matrimony. Instead, marriage is now beyond the reach of many Americans. As described in detail in chapter 2, a growing share lacks the economic stability that is a prerequisite for marriage nowadays. Relationship skills per se are thus unlikely to nudge many couples into marriage. Until they achieve financial security, couples are not going to tie the knot.[23]

One of the goals of welfare reform was to discourage single motherhood and nonmarital childbearing in the first place. The logic was that by reducing the economic benefits available to single mothers, women would be less likely to have children outside of marriage. Indirectly, these economic disincentives were designed to make marriage a more attractive alternative. The effectiveness of this approach is difficult to assess, though, because we do not know what would have happened to marriage and nonmarital birth rates were these disincentives not in place. Still, it seems reasonable to conclude that the effects are modest at best. Nonmarital childbearing continues to climb across all demographic subgroups. More than two of every five children are born to unmarried parents in the United States. And the single-mother family is the second most common living arrangement for children, eclipsed only by the two-biological-married-parent family.

Although part of the reason why welfare reform was enacted was to help poor mothers transition from welfare to work, parents and their children continue to struggle economically. Edin and Shaefer have uncovered a startling trend: the share of households living on two dollars per person per day in the United States has more than doubled in the past 15 years. As of 2011, there were more than 3 million children in roughly 1.5 million households surviving on this meager amount, representing about 4 percent of all children and one in five of those living in poverty. This trend signals the absence of an adequate cash safety net. Many families resort to selling their SNAP (food stamp) benefits for cash. According to Edin and Schaefer, "even for those who receive TANF, its cash value, though never high, is now very, very low—so low that it doesn't bring a family's income even to half of the poverty line in any state."[24] It appears that many families do not even realize that TANF is available.

Indeed, welfare rolls continue to shrink, yet a large majority (70 percent) of Americans believe that "poor people have become too dependent on government programs," according to a report released by the Pew Research Center in 2012. Prior to welfare reform, about 85 percent of the public held this belief.[25] The plight of the poor persists as a major social problem in the United States, particularly among children. The child poverty rate has fluctuated somewhat since 1996 but ultimately has changed very little. More than one in five children lives in poverty. Among black and Hispanic children, the proportions are even higher, at roughly 37 percent and 31 percent, respectively.[26] More than one-quarter of immigrant children live in poverty. Since welfare reform was enacted in 1996, the population of immigrant children and children with a foreign-born parent has risen by 50 percent and they now account for one in four U.S. children.[27] Welfare reform blocked access to many forms of public support that had been available to legal U.S. immigrants. The United States is on a trajectory to become a majority-minority society in another few decades, meaning that whites will constitute less than one-half of the population. This population shift is occurring most rapidly among children, and it is minority and immigrant children who face the highest levels of poverty and economic deprivation.[28] Public assistance is a critical mechanism for alleviating child poverty and enhancing child well-being. Despite sweeping welfare-reform changes and a huge investment in marriage promotion (which was conceived as an antipoverty measure), many children in the United States are struggling.[29]

The severity of child economic disadvantage in the United States is particularly striking when considered in comparison to other rich, developed countries. Using a measure of relative poverty, defined as living in a household with an income that is less than 50 percent of the median income, the United States fares worst among twenty OECD countries. As shown in figure 20, 23 percent of children in the United States in 2012 experienced

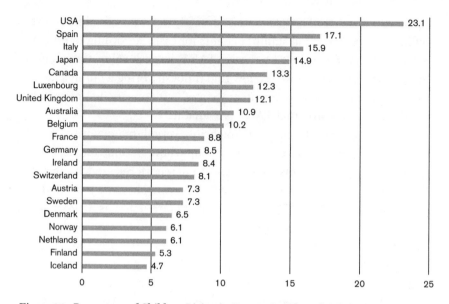

Figure 20. Percentage of Children Living in Poverty in Selected OECD Countries.
Note: Child poverty reflects the share of children living in households with income
less than 50 percent of the national median. Source: UNICEF 2012.

relative poverty. Levels were lowest in Iceland and the Nordic countries,
ranging from less than 5 percent to about 7 percent.[30]

As we might expect, poverty is related to child well-being. An examination of UNICEF's rankings of developed countries on the overall well-
being of children revealed that the United States was lagging behind
its European counterparts. On a composite measure of overall well-
being that encompassed multiple indicators of material well-being (health
and safety, education, behaviors and risks, and housing and environment)
the United States was in twenty-sixth place out of twenty-nine countries.
Children were faring worse only in Lithuania, Latvia, and Romania.
Child well-being was higher not just in Nordic and Western European
countries, but also in Canada, Poland, Estonia, and Slovakia. The low
position of the United States has been persistent over time. A comparison
of overall child well-being in twenty-one OECD countries in the early
versus the late 2000s ranked the United States last at both points in
time.[31]

FAMILY LEAVE / WORK FAMILY POLICY

Americans work long hours. We average about 1,789 hours per year, which is more than thirty-four hours per week. By comparison, in France, workers average just 1,473 hours per year or twenty-eight hours each week. Germans work even less at 1,371 annual hours or twenty-six hours weekly. The gap between European countries and the United States has widened in recent years, as Americans spend more and more time on the job.[32] Hours spent working leave less time for family labor, contributing to work-family imbalance. Nowadays, both parents are working full-time in nearly one-half of two-parent families (another one-quarter have one parent employed full-time and the other part-time).[33] The rapid increase in this employment configuration does not mean that dual-earner parents find it easier today to balance work and family. Instead, achieving balance is elusive to most parents, who face persistent challenges as they attempt to juggle the competing demands of work and family. Dual-earner couples report considerable stress in their daily lives. This strain is felt by husbands and wives alike, but is particularly acute for wives, who perform a disproportionate share of the household labor and day-to-day management of family members' schedules.[34]

Within the United States there is a growing class divide in work-family balance. White-collar, professional workers are disproportionately employed by large corporations, which tend to offer more family-friendly benefits. For this class of workers, work-family imbalance emerges from working long hours and being constantly "on-call" to respond to work-related issues (email) around the clock. The boundaries of work and family have blurred in our 24/7 economy, where employees feel compelled to respond immediately to emails and other work-related communications, regardless of the time of day.[35]

Low-wage workers are being pushed out of the labor market.[36] It is not highly educated, advantaged women dropping out of the labor force in record numbers. They are actually the most likely to be working. Instead, women with the lowest education levels are the least likely to work. The employment barriers they confront are significant. Simply put, it often doesn't pay for them to work. Minimum wage has not kept pace with inflation. And low-wage workers face considerable uncertainty in the labor market. Their work hours are highly variable and they do not have access to benefits that most of their middle-class counterparts enjoy. Hourly employees often have no benefits. If they call in sick, they risk losing their jobs. Their work hours vary as employers bend employee schedules in response to the vagaries of consumer demand. An employee may be scheduled to work, but if customers are scarce, employees get sent home, without pay. Low-wage workers face schedules that are unpredictable and hastily announced, leaving them to sort out the logistics of transportation, child care, and other family obligations.[37] Disproportionately women, these low-wage workers are being left behind.

Regardless of social class, American workers are feeling the squeeze as they attempt to mesh their work and family lives. A 2015 study by Pew Research Center showed that 60 percent of working mothers and just over half of working fathers characterized their ability to balance job and family responsibilities as either somewhat or very difficult.[38] Consider the experience of a thirty-one-year-old mother and her thirty-three-year-old partner and father of her fifteen-month-old child, who both work in state government. The mother summed up her experience straddling work and family this way: "You basically just always feel like you're doing a horrible job at everything. You're not spending as much time with your baby as you want, you're not doing the job you want to be doing at work, you're not seeing your friends hardly ever."[39]

This mother speaks for many in her shoes. About 40 percent of full-time working mothers report always feeling rushed and another 50 percent sometimes feel rushed. One-half of full-time working mothers believe they do not spend enough time with their children. For full-time working fathers, the share is 58 percent. And a majority of full-time working mothers and fathers indicate they do not have enough leisure time away from their children.[40] Mothers are not the only ones feeling the pressure to perform in their roles as parents. Fathers, too, are responding to new norms of shared parenting and involved fatherhood. A physician with three children, Dustin Baylor, was quoted in a Today.com story on the challenges he faces combining work and family: "I often feel overwhelmed trying to do it all. I love my wife, my job and my family. But whereas men in past generations emphasized being a provider first and foremost, I think modern fathers take on many more roles."[41]

Nevertheless, the division of labor remains gendered, even when both parents work full-time. Mothers are disproportionately responsible for managing children's schedules and activities and taking care of them when they are sick. Most mothers contend that they perform the majority of the household chores, but only about one-third of fathers agree. Fathers are more likely to report that housework is shared equally.[42]

In the late 1980s, sociologist Arlie Hochschild determined that wives in dual-earner couples performed what she termed a "second shift." After working in the paid labor force each day, wives came home and worked an additional shift of housework and child care. By Hochschild's estimate, employed wives put in an extra month of twenty-four-hour days each year doing unpaid care work: household management and childrearing. This additional work left them exhausted and frequently ill. It contributed to poorer marital quality and reduced sexual activity. Sure, husbands were spending more time on household tasks and child care than their fathers had a generation earlier, but their contributions were still modest compared to the intensive time commitment wives made to these activities. In essence, this created a leisure gap, with husbands enjoying more time to relax, unwind, and pursue hobbies. Although wives were achieving greater parity in the workforce, equality on the home front was lagging. Indeed, Hochschild concluded that despite the change in wives' behavior, husbands and employers were not keeping pace, which resulted in a "stalled revolution." Women had embraced paid employment, but husbands were not significantly altering their daily lives to accommodate this change in women's time use. Nor were employers particularly responsive.[43]

The situation described by Hochschild still rings true today. Working parents, particularly mothers, are harried as they spend more time on paid labor and child care. According to a recent time-use study, mothers in dual-earner two-parent families spent about sixteen hours each week on housework and twelve hours per week on child care. By comparison, fathers report spending nine hours on housework and seven hours on child care each week. Fathers spend about forty-two hours on paid labor versus thirty-one hours among mothers.[44]

Time-use studies permit us to compare time spent by mothers and fathers (regardless of employment and marital status) on housework,

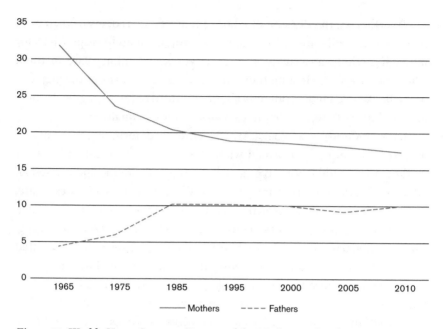

Figure 21. Weekly Hours Spent on Housework by Mothers and Fathers, 1965–2010. Source: Pew Research Center, n. d.

child care, and paid labor from 1965 to 2010. As shown in figure 21, the time mothers and fathers spent performing housework had converged over the decades, as women's time fell from thirty-two hours per week in 1965 to about seventeen hours in 2010. Meanwhile, men's time had increased from about four to ten hours weekly. Ultimately though, parents were spending less time on household chores because the decline in mothers' housework was not fully offset by fathers' rise. Gender similarity was also on the rise for paid employment, as illustrated in figure 22. Fathers' time had fallen modestly (from about forty-two to thirty-seven hours) whereas mothers' time had risen from about eight to more than twenty hours per week. The pattern for child care was distinctive, as mothers and fathers alike had increased their efforts in this domain. The patterns are shown in figure 23. Mothers' time spent on child care grew from about ten to fourteen hours per week. Fathers' rose from close to three to about seven hours per week. Thus, mothers continued to spend nearly twice as much time on child care and housework as fathers did.[45]

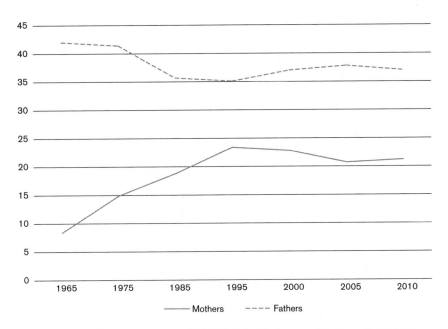

Figure 22. Weekly Hours Spent on Paid Work by Mothers and Fathers, 1965–2010.
Source: Pew Research Center, n. d.

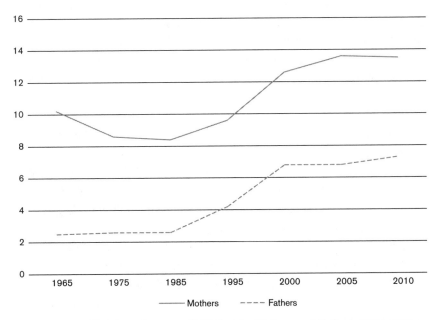

Figure 23. Weekly Hours Spent on Child Care by Mothers and Fathers, 1965–2010.
Source: Pew Research Center, n. d.

The daily lives of mothers and fathers unfold within a broader social context. Hochschild and others maintain that the burdens felt by working parents are exacerbated by the enduring rigidity of the U.S. workplace, which has been largely resistant to the fundamental changes in parental-employment patterns that have unfolded over several decades. Sociologist Mary Blair-Loy told the *New York Times* that the difficulty parents have balancing work and family "is not an individual problem, it is a social problem. This is creating a stress for working parents that is affecting life at home and for children, and we need a societal-wide response."[46]

In June 2014, the federal government convened the first White House Summit on Working Families. A few days before the summit, in his weekly radio address, President Obama bemoaned the dearth of family-friendly policies in U.S. workplaces: "Take paid family leave. Many jobs don't offer adequate leave to care for a new baby or an ailing parent, so workers can't afford to be there when their family needs them the most. That's wrong. And it puts us way behind the times. Only three countries in the world report that they don't offer paid maternity leave. . . . And the United States is one of them. It's time to change that."[47]

Family-friendly policies that provide paid parental leave, affordable, high-quality child care, and job flexibility would benefit working parents by reducing work to family spillover and bolstering psychological well-being. These policies would help to alleviate the strains involved in juggling work and family obligations. When parents are less stressed, children benefit. Parents need to be able to take care of their children when they get sick. Without access to leave, they are much less likely to take time off. Similarly, early-childhood education pays substantial dividends in the long run as these children grow up to be successful, productive adults. Family policies enhance child health and well-being. They are also good for business. In our global economy, employers compete for the most qualified and talented workers. A comprehensive benefits package helps to attract and retain the best employees.[48]

Family policies are sorely lacking in the United States.[49] Federal legislation, enacted in 1993 as part of the Family and Medical Leave Act (FMLA), requires that employers offer unpaid maternity leave to U.S. women for up to twelve weeks, provided women had worked at least 1,250 hours the previous year and the employer has at least fifty employees. In

2014, these stipulations meant that roughly 40 percent of working women were ineligible for this benefit. Additionally, about 20 percent of employers failed to comply with FMLA.[50]

As President Obama noted, the United States is one of just three countries in the world that does not offer paid maternity leave for women. Large corporations are leading the way by offering a growing range of family benefits to their employees. According to the Families and Work Institute's 2014 National Study of Employers, about 58 percent of employers offer some paid maternity leave, but of these fewer than one in ten offer full pay. Full-time workers now have more flexibility over their work schedules, yet flexibility for reduced hours is actually declining.[51]

The family policy landscape is very different in other countries. European and other industrialized nations offer employees numerous benefits that help them to successfully combine work and family. Many of these benefits are sponsored by the government, not employers, which eases the economic burdens for employers. In the United States, benefits cost employers an extra 30 percent of salary. All European countries offer long-term, paid maternity leaves and many offer paid paternity leaves, too. In some Nordic countries, parents can work reduced hours until children are eight years old. Many countries mandate vacation time and do not permit overtime work. They provide early childhood education through universal schooling at young ages. In France, children start school at age two.[52] These countries view parental leave as a key component of early childhood policy. For example, Denmark offers both paid maternity (eighteen weeks) and paternity (two weeks) leaves followed by parental leave (thirty-two weeks) and a child-care entitlement that begins when children are six months old.[53]

Numerous scholars have called on the United States to adopt some of the family policies that our European counterparts take for granted.[54] The provision of paid leave, affordable child care, and flexibility should enhance economic productivity. Women possess considerable human capital—they are now more educated, on average, than men—yet their labor-force participation rate lags behind men. Family supports would help us to move toward greater gender equality at the same time that it more fully exploits available human capital. Countries that have family policies have higher labor-force participation rates. Policies that ease the burdens mothers and fathers confront in juggling work and family contribute to a vibrant, more productive work force and enhance children's well-being.

AGING FAMILIES AND CAREGIVING

Work-family balance issues are not confined to parents of young children. Increasingly, midlife adults are caring for their children and their aging parents. These midlife adults are termed the sandwich generation, trapped between younger and older dependents. In 2015 there were 40 million unpaid elder caregivers in the United States,[55] yet the national dialogue on this topic pales in comparison to the attention devoted to issues of parental leave and child care. As Liz O'Donnell, writing in the *Atlantic*, has stated, "Elder caregivers are all but absent from the conversation. Sure, paid family leave is starting to be framed as both a childcare and eldercare issue, but many policies only address the working parent, not the worker with parents."[56]

This policy gap is troubling in light of the demographic trends. The United States is an aging society, which means that the older adult population is growing at a faster rate than younger age groups. In 2013, there were 44.7 million adults aged sixty-five and older in the United States, which represented a 25 percent increase just in the past decade. Roughly 14 percent of Americans are older adults and by 2050 this share is predicted to be at 20 percent as the Baby Boomers (born 1946–64) age into later life. People who survive to age sixty-five can expect to live nearly another two decades.[57]

Lengthening life expectancies have been accompanied by a rise in chronic diseases. Most Americans want to die peacefully in their sleep, but few do. Instead, they face a slow decline that unfolds over a period of months or years. Leading causes of death include heart disease, cancer, and Alzheimer's disease, illnesses that ravage the body and spirit and often require intensive care.[58] Even those who are fortunate enough to avoid chronic disease often experience limitations in their activities of daily living (ADLs), which describes difficulties performing basic self-care tasks such as dressing, bathing, toileting, and walking short distances. As we age, our ability to function independently often diminishes, requiring intervention and assistance from others.

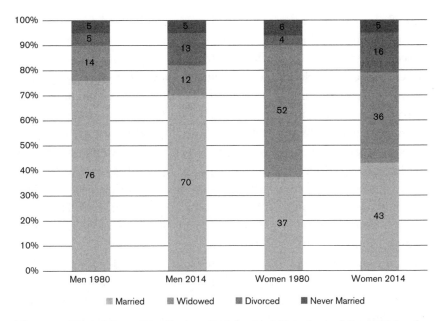

Figure 24. Marital Status Distribution of Adults Aged Sixty-five and Over, 1980 and 2014. Source: Ruggles et al. 2015.

Historically, spouses have been the first line of defense, providing care to one another. Caregiving is more often performed by wives than husbands because husbands tend to be older than wives and men live fewer years, on average, than do women. But the dramatic changes in family living arrangements documented in chapters 2 and 3 are evident among older adults, too. A shrinking share of older men are married today compared with a generation ago, as illustrated in figure 24. In 1980, 76 percent of older men were married versus 70 percent in 2014. Older women were only slightly more likely to live with a spouse in 2014 than a few decades earlier, reflecting lengthening life expectancies particularly for men. Whereas 37 percent of older women were married in 1980, the figure in 2014 stood at 43 percent. Meanwhile, the proportion widowed had dropped from 52 percent to just 36 percent. For men, widowhood remained unusual. In 1980, 14 percent of men were widowers versus 12 percent in 2014. The growth in older adult divorce over this time period was striking. Between 1980 and 2014, the percentage of men aged sixty-five and older who were divorced more than doubled, from 5 percent to 13 percent, and quadrupled among older women, from 4 percent to 16 percent. There was no appreciable change in the share of older adults who never had been married, which continued to hover at about 5 percent.

And the composition of older adults will shift more profoundly as the Baby Boomers transition into older adulthood. One in three Baby Boomers is unmarried, and already in midlife these single Boomers are disadvantaged compared with married Boomers. Relative to married Boomers, single Boomers are four times as likely to live in poverty, twice as likely to report having a disability, and less often have health insurance.[59] Baby Boomers are at the vanguard of the gray-divorce phenomenon. The rate of divorce among married individuals aged fifty to sixty-four doubled between 1990 and 2010. For those aged sixty-five and older, the rate tripled, although the overall risk of divorce was considerably lower for older than for midlife adults.[60] Repartnership is uncommon. Whether marital dissolution occurs through gray divorce or widowhood, most older adults do not form a new union. The vast majority remains single. The minority who do repartner increasingly choose cohabitation over remarriage, precisely because the expectations for these informal unions are weaker.[61] Women in particular express a reluctance to remarry because they do not want to serve as caregivers for an aging husband.[62] And cohabiting partners are less likely to provide care than are spouses.[63]

The traditional pathway of continuous marriage followed by widowhood is characteristic of a diminishing share of today's older adults. Family experiences are more varied and complex, reflecting transitions that occurred earlier in the life course. For example, a key reason why gray divorce is on the rise is because more of today's older adults are in remarriages, which are at greater risk of divorce than first marriages. As described in chapter 4, the marital biography is consequential for health and well-being in mid- and later life. It also has ramifications for caregiving.

As fewer older adults are married in the coming decades, the burden of care for frail elders will fall to other family members. The feasibility of relying on adult children and other relatives to provide care is uncertain. One reason why some elders may not be able to count on receiving assistance from their adult children is that they lack strong relationship ties. This is of particular concern for divorced fathers.[64] Following parental divorce, children typically live with their mothers. The relationships that nonresident fathers have with their children are often weaker, punctuated by less frequent interaction and lower levels of involvement and closeness. By later life, adult children whose parents divorced when they were young feel less of an obligation to assist their aging fathers. The likelihood that adult children will provide assistance to their mothers does not differ for married and single mothers.[65]

Apart from the enduring consequences of divorce, today's older adults have raised smaller families, meaning there are fewer children per family to provide care. In our mobile society, adult children often reside far away from their aging parents, limiting the amount and types of assistance they can provide. Adult daughters are usually employed, which could constrain their ability to provide care. Still, a majority of caregivers are women and over half are employed.[66]

Other aging adults have no children. Childlessness nearly doubled among midlife married adults between 1992 and 2012. However, never-married midlife adults aged fifty-one to sixty-one were less likely to be childless than twenty years earlier, reflecting the rise in nonmarital child-bearing. Whereas 81 percent of never-married midlife adults were childless in 1992, just 63 percent were in 2012.[67] Although they do not have a spouse to draw on for assistance, a sizeable minority of never-married adults now have children who could provide help.

A majority of adult children in the United States report feeling an obligation to help their aging parent. Among those with at least one parent aged sixty-five or older, 58 percent provided help with errands, house-work, or home repairs, 28 percent gave financial assistance, and 14 percent performed personal care in the previous year, according to a Pew Research Center report.[68] Caregiving is stressful and costly for adult children. They report poorer health than their counterparts who are not providing care. A thirty-five-year-old woman who had been living in her parents' home for the previous five years with her husband to take care of her sixty-five-year-old mother and eight-one-year-old father, both of whom had Alzheimer's, shared her story with a *New York Times* reporter. She described the round-the-clock care she provided, which included getting up multiple times in the night to assist her parents. Even though she had paid caregivers to assist her, "most of the caregivers [weren't] able to handle my mom in the bathroom or bathe her." Her sacrifices for her parents were significant: "[My husband] and I decided not to have children, but I feel like a mother to my parents."[69]

Caregiving also results in significant earnings loss, especially for women, jeopardizing the security of their own retirement. One estimate revealed women caregivers forgo over $324,000 in lost wages and Social Security benefits.[70] After reducing her work hours, a middle-aged business owner caring for her mother who had Alzheimer's disease worried about the economic fallout: "The biggest issue is I am now living hand-to-mouth. I am just getting by and I am not able to put money away for a rainy day. A lot of the stress is thinking about when my mom dies, what will my life look like?"[71]

Most Americans believe family members should provide care for their aging members, but recent changes in the composition of U.S. families make this less feasible going forward, especially given the acceleration in the aging population. Over ten thousand Baby Boomers are turning sixty-five each day and many are caring for aged parents. The costs for midlife caregivers are staggering, totaling nearly $3 trillion in lost wages, pension, and Social Security benefits for the nearly 10 million individuals aged fifty and older providing parental care.[72] Who will be there for the caregivers in their old age?

As a society, we are ill-prepared to take care of our aging population. Our reliance on family members to provide care to frail elders comes at a considerable cost. Caregiving takes a toll on mental and physical health and can be financially devastating. Hiring professional caregivers is expensive and out of reach for many families. Institutional supports are slim; Medicare does not cover custodial care, leaving many older adults who require assistance without access to home health aides or other support staff that would enable them to age in place at home. Instead, Medicare is designed to cover medical procedures. This means individual families are bearing the brunt of the costs associated with caregiving, a situation that is likely to become untenable in the future with rapid population aging.

The rising costs of Medicare and social security have been the subject of considerable debate by Congress, policymakers, and the public. But less attention is being paid to how society will respond to the needs of an aging population in an era of rapid family change. Efforts to secure parental leave for mothers and fathers of young children could be expanded to encompass family leave to allow adults to care for aging parents. Reimagining Medicare also might be necessary to ensure older adults are getting the day-to-day care they need, particularly as the availability of family caregivers declines. In the United States and other developed nations, the dependency ratios, which tell us the number of working age adults twenty to sixty-four to older adults aged sixty-five and older, are precariously low right now and expected to plummet in the future. The U.S. older dependency ratio stands at nearly 5 to 1, and is predicted to fall to about 2.6 by 2050.

Population aging is not unique to the United States but is a global phenomenon. Table 1 shows the old-age dependency ratios for selected OECD countries in 2010 and the estimated ratios for 2050. On average, OECD countries have a current ratio of roughly 4.2 working age adults for every older adult and this is predicted to be cut in half by 2050, when the ratio will be about 2.1. The lowest old-age dependency ratio is in Japan, where there are fewer than three working age adults for each elder. In Italy and Germany, the ratios stand at 3. Japan's level in 2050 is estimated to be 1.2 compared with 1.5 and 1.6 for Italy and Germany, respectively in 2050. Korea is expected to confront a huge decline with the ratio dropping from over 6 to just 1.5 in 2050.

Record long-life expectancies coupled with very low fertility rates combine to produce significant population aging. Table 2 depicts the share of the population that was sixty-five and older in 2013 and projections for 2050 across several OECD countries. A whopping 39 percent, or about two out of every five people, will be 65 or older in 2050 in Japan. Currently, nearly one-quarter (23 percent) are in this age group. Korea will see its share of older adults more than triple from 11 percent in 2010 to 37 percent in 2050. Germany, Italy, and Greece can all expect to have about one-third of their population aged sixty-five and older in 2050. Currently, the share hovers around 20 percent. In the United States, about 13 percent of the population is older adults, and this share is projected to rise to 21 percent in 2050. The OECD average percentage aged sixty-five and older stands at about 15 percent and will climb to 27 percent by 2050.

A comparison of family support in Italy, Germany, and the United States reveals that Italians and Germans believe the state should shoulder

Table 1   Old-Age Dependency Ratios for Selected OECD
Countries, 2010 and 2050

Country	2010	2050
Japan	2.8	1.2
Korea	6.3	1.5
Germany	3.0	1.6
Italy	3.0	1.5
Greece	3.4	1.6
Czech Republic	4.4	1.9
Poland	4.8	1.8
Estonia	3.6	2.2
Austria	3.6	1.8
Switzerland	3.7	2.0
Hungary	3.9	2.1
Finland	3.7	2.0
OECD average	4.2	2.1
Netherlands	4.2	2.1
France	3.5	1.9
New Zealand	4.7	2.4
Ireland	5.6	2.2
Belgium	3.5	2.0
Canada	4.6	2.1
Sweden	3.3	2.2
Denmark	3.7	2.3
United Kingdom	3.7	2.4
China	7.9	2.4
Norway	4.1	2.3
Iceland	5.1	2.0
Chile	6.8	2.5
Brazil	8.9	2.6
Australia	4.5	2.3
Russian Federation	4.9	2.4
United States	4.7	2.6

SOURCE: OECD Pensions at a Glance 2011.

Table 2 Percentage of the Population Aged Sixty-five and
Over for Selected OECD Countries, 2010 and 2050

Country	2010	2050
Japan	23	39
Korea	11	37
Germany	21	33
Italy	20	33
Greece	19	33
Czech Republic	15	32
Poland	13	30
Estonia	17	29
Austria	18	28
Switzerland	17	28
Hungary	17	28
Finland	17	27
OECD average	15	27
Netherlands	15	27
France	17	26
New Zealand	13	26
Ireland	11	26
Belgium	17	25
Canada	14	25
Sweden	18	24
Denmark	17	24
United Kingdom	16	24
China	8	24
Norway	15	23
Iceland	12	23
Chile	9	22
Brazil	7	22
Australia	14	21
Russian Federation	13	21
United States	13	21

SOURCE: OECD Historical Population Data and Projections
Database 2015.

the responsibility of ensuring the financial security of older adults. Not surprisingly, adult children in these two countries are less likely to provide financial assistance to their aging parent than are U.S. adult children. Nonfinancial forms of assistance are more comparable across the three contexts, with the highest levels in Italy, followed by Germany, and lastly the United States. Very few adults across all three countries anticipate that Social Security benefits will be available to them when they retire at a level that matches today's retirees. About 20 percent of U.S. adults and just 11 percent of Germans and 7 percent of Italians expect to receive federal benefits comparable to those disbursed currently.[73]

CONCLUSION

Ideally, social policies help individuals and their families. Welfare reform, for instance, was lauded for its incentives to transition mothers from government dependence to paid employment. Financial independence for women across the economic spectrum is a noble goal, but in reality policies are not necessarily effective and sometimes can even be detrimental. The poverty rate did not diminish in the two decades following welfare reform. Time limits on cash assistance for poor mothers and their children in an economic environment with few job opportunities for women, who face significant barriers to employment, do not diminish economic distress among the poor, but instead arguably exacerbate the vulnerability of this population. These unintended adverse outcomes are not just collateral consequences of specific policy initiatives. In fact, the absence of policy also can undermine family well-being. Until all parents have access to paid leave, for example, it will be difficult for most parents to balance the competing demands of a job and a baby. Their productivity at work is likely to suffer, which is a drag on the economy. And their parenting capacity is compromised by stress and overload, which could be harmful for their children's development. Similarly, family caregivers for the aged are operating on the fringes, without adequate institutional supports. The economic and health costs of population aging for family caregivers are enormous. Family policies could go a long way toward alleviating some of the burdens that currently rest primarily on individuals and their families.

We can look to our peers in Europe and other developed nations for viable models. International comparisons offer a picture of how other nations accommodate family change. In important regards, the United States appears to be a laggard, slow to respond to the new realities that today's families confront. Paid family leave is the law of the land in nearly all developed countries, except the United States. The social safety net is simply smaller in the United States than in many other countries, reflecting our cultural ethos of low taxes, limited governmental interference, and individual responsibility.

Caring for vulnerable members of society—young and old—is a core function of families, but families could perform this task more effectively with broader social and institutional supports. Indeed, some families do not have the resources to provide adequate care to their dependents. The changing demographics of America's families may further inhibit their ability to care for their members. An aging society, the United States is contending with shrinking family sizes and a generation of young people whose successful transition to adulthood and financial independence has been disrupted by the economic downturn. Meanwhile, Americans are living longer than ever before, placing new strains on families and society. The concluding chapter of this volume summarizes these and other recent family changes, considers how these trends are likely to unfold in the coming years, and their implications for families.

Conclusion

Family change has been profound. A quick glance at how families are depicted in popular culture underscores the scale of the change. The hit television series *Modern Family* illustrates some of the diverse types of family forms that are gaining prominence these days, such as complex remarried stepfamilies that include both joint children and children from prior unions, and a married same-sex couple with an adopted child. True, the show also includes a breadwinner-homemaker family that includes three children. But the monolithic family landscape of decades past is largely a fiction in today's society. Less than one in five children resides in a married-couple family that includes a breadwinner father and a stay-at-home mother.[1]

Despite its numeric demise, the benchmark for comparison remains this idealized 1950s suburban breadwinner-homemaker family. Many Americans venerate this family form, even though it represents an aberration in U.S. family history. For much of our nation's past, wives were producers alongside their husbands. Suburban housewifery was stifling for women, who entered the labor force after the 1950s. Now the dual-earner couple family is the norm, and the second most common living arrangement for children is single-mother families, which are formed not only through divorce but increasingly through unwed childbearing. Driven by a multitude of factors, including the shift from an agrarian to an industrial economy, urbanization, and declining fertility and mortality, family change has been pretty constant since the founding of our country.[2] Although the married breadwinner-homemaker arrangement is arguably the epitome of "the American family," it is in fact a relic of the past. The pace of family change has been swift and at times surprising, which makes it challenging to envision what will happen to families in the future.

SOCIAL RESPONSES TO FAMILY CHANGE

This uncertainty about the direction and implications of family change shapes public discourse on the state of American families. Our elected officials, pundits, and the public often wring their hands over family change, fearful of the demise of this important social institution. Divorce is commonplace, children are increasingly born outside of marriage, and young people are turning away from marriage in favor of cohabitation, cry the doomsayers. And these are just a few examples of family change that have prompted widespread concern.

Others are more accepting of family change. Recall from the introduction that nearly one-third of Americans are unfazed by the sweeping changes we have observed in contemporary family life. Another one-third are largely accepting, but express concern about the rise in single-mother families.[3] Family living arrangements that were once on the margins of society are now gaining acceptance, and a growing number of family forms are considered mainstream by the majority of Americans. The flexibility characterizing today's family pathways is unprecedented. Individuals enjoy varied options. They can marry, cohabit, or form a LAT relationship. Marriage is open to same-sex and different-sex couples alike. Partnership is optional and individuals increasingly choose to remain solo. Similarly, childbearing is a choice. It is no longer confined to marriage and is growing rapidly in cohabiting unions.

Even though families come in varied forms nowadays, they continue to perform key functions, notably rearing the next generation and taking care of aging members. The well-being of adults and children alike is shaped in part by their family experiences. Nevertheless, deciphering the extent to which variation in individual outcomes is a function of marital status or family structure per se is challenging. Much of the variation reflects differential selection into particular family types. The causation versus selection debate notwithstanding, it is essential to capture the dynamic component of our family experiences, which rarely remain constant across the life course. We move into and out of different living arrangements and these unique trajectories can alter well-being. For children in particular, mounting evidence indicates that family transitions can be detrimental to health and development.[4] One expert has cautioned parents to "slow down" and delay repartnership to avoid subsequent instability, particularly for the sake of their children.[5]

The family landscape is now bifurcated, reflecting rising social and economic inequality. The most advantaged segment of society enjoys a stable, harmonious family life that typically unfolds according to the traditional normative script of marriage followed by childbearing. Relative to their less-educated counterparts, the marriages of those with a college degree or more tend to be long-lasting and exhibit a much lower risk of divorce. Importantly, the couple dynamics characterizing these marriages is unlike that of prior generations. The gender inequality that pervaded marriages in decades past has diminished. Nowadays, lifelong, stable marriages are more egalitarian, as spouses view each other as best friends and perform similar tasks. In most marriages today, both spouses are employed and both spouses are involved parents. Especially for the most advantaged in society, marriage is perhaps better than ever, offering a supportive union that accommodates each spouse's needs and desires, typifying the individualized marriages of the contemporary era. The elite have arguably achieved a new level of stability, security, and personal satisfaction through marriage.

The less-advantaged, which encompasses not just those on the bottom but also those who a generation or two ago were in the middle, experience distinct family pathways that often do not include marriage. Individuals without a college degree are delaying marriage and are less likely ever to marry than their more educated counterparts. Rather, their family experiences increasingly unfold within cohabitation or as single parents. These diverging destinies coincide with significant economic hardship for families on much of the economic ladder.

Social policy can help to assuage the challenges confronting families. Economic security, for example, brings stability to children's lives and enhances parenting effectiveness by easing the strain that accompanies financial distress.[6] Yet family policy remains contentious as undergirding most debates is a tension between individual responsibility and collective support. Certainly this tension has informed welfare policy. Welfare reform was designed to encourage mothers to get jobs by reducing access to government assistance. In fact, the two leading words in the name of the 1996 welfare-reform bill were "personal responsibility." However, critics maintain that tightening eligibility rules led to unnecessary suffering by mothers and their children. Many insist that the support available for poor families in the post–welfare reform era is inadequate and that low-wage jobs do not pay enough for families to make ends meet.[7]

Another way in which welfare reform relied on strategies guided by individual responsibility was the encouragement of marriage (and discouragement of single motherhood) under the guise of improving the financial circumstances of those struggling economically. This feature of welfare reform is just one example of policymakers trying to put the brakes on family change instead of meeting families where they are and providing institutional supports to assist them.

Social policy has the potential to enhance or impede family functioning. Oftentimes it seems that policy is reactionary, lagging behind significant change. Our reluctance to move ahead on federal legislation to provide parental leave is a case in point. It also signals that balancing work and family conflict is an individual problem that does not merit governmental intervention.

Regardless of our family policies, the transformation of American families will persist into the future. For instance, the marriage rate continues to drop despite federal efforts to promote marriage. Likewise, the share of children born outside of marriage is still rising. Family change, as described in the preceding chapters, is a constant. It unfolds in the larger social context, reflecting economic and cultural change. Identifying the precise forms this transformation will take in the coming years could be a fool's errand. Just in the past few decades we have witnessed dramatic shifts in family patterns that are altering the demography of families and society. Delayed marriage, falling fertility, and population aging are just a few of the trends that have the potential to rewrite the family experiences of future generations. The remainder of this chapter is devoted to reflections on how contemporary shifts in family life may unspool over time.

PREDICTING THE FUTURE

Demographers have a poor track record at predicting family change. None foresaw the Baby Boom, and one eminent demographer even dismissed the onset of the rise in childbearing during the late 1940s as merely an artifact of the drop in age at marriage.[8] In 1963, William J. Goode argued in his landmark book *World Revolution and Family Patterns* that countries around the globe would exhibit a convergence in family patterns that aligned with the conjugal, nuclear family of the 1950s. Of course, this prediction did not come to pass.[9] The United States and other developed nations have been marked by a retreat from marriage. Few families are structured and function like the stereotypical breadwinner-homemaker family from a half-century ago.

By the 1960s, the second demographic transition was occurring, marking the beginning of the modern families era. Marriage was less central to family life. Cohabitation and nonmarital childbearing rose. Couples were waiting longer to marry. Married couples were no longer willing to remain in unsatisfying unions, contributing to the divorce revolution in the 1970s that dramatically altered family patterns. Although most Americans still profess an interest in getting married, Europeans are less sanguine about marriage. Cohabitation is a popular alternative to marriage and serves as a childbearing and childrearing union context in much of Europe. Cohabiting unions in some European countries are more stable and long-lasting than marriage is in the United States.[10]

Will cohabitation supplant marriage? Some scholars have proposed that cohabitation could eventually be so integrated into family life that it is indistinguishable from marriage. Although other countries may be approaching this threshold, in the United States cohabitation remains distinctive.[11] It continues to be a short-term union, operating more akin to an alternative to singlehood or prelude to marriage than a long-term marriage substitute, particularly among young adults. Even though cohabitation is the context of more than one in five births today, it is not a stable family form for children. Less than two-thirds of children born to cohabiting parents are still living with both parents by age twelve.[12]

Nonetheless, cohabitation is now a part of the family life course. It is the most common path to marriage. Unlike the median age at first marriage, which has risen in recent years, the median age at first cohabitation remains unchanged at about twenty-two for women. Young people continue to form partnerships at early ages, only they are cohabiting not marital unions.[13] There are a couple of reasons why the popularity of cohabitation has probably not peaked yet. First, there are no signs to suggest that the widening economic inequality is likely to contract anytime soon. The retreat from marriage is greatest among the less advantaged in society. If inequality worsens, marriage is likely to become even more exclusive and cohabitation will be the partnership choice of the masses. Second, there is a lot of room for growth in cohabitation during the second half of life. Baby Boomers were the first generation to cohabit in large numbers during young adulthood. Now, as they enter older adulthood, one in three Boomers is single.[14] Others will become single through gray divorce or widowhood. Baby Boomers recognize the advantages of cohabitation, which offers flexibility and financial independence for older adults.[15]

Flexibility in family life may be the watch word. According to Andrew Cherlin, sociologist and author of *The Marriage-Go-Round*, "what has happened is that marriage and family life have become matters of personal choice to an extent that would have astounded Americans in the 1950s."[16] Most people still get married, but the pathways to marriage are often circuitous, and marriages are unstable. Alternatives abound. The formation of families outside of marriage is unlikely to slow over the next few decades.

Predicting the future of marriage is perilous ground. On the one hand, we might imagine that marriage will retain it preeminent position as the preferred family status, a capstone achievement that tells our friends, family members, and coworkers that we have made it. It is a milestone aspired to by the vast majority of Americans. To the extent that marriage as an institution remains sufficiently flexible to accommodate individuals' needs and desires, it is likely to persist. In fact, marriage is a remarkably resilient institution that continues to change and evolve in response to broader social and economic changes.[17] Same-sex marriage is a case in point. The struggle over the legalization of same-sex marriage underscores the symbolic value of marriage in the United States. Marriage is a highly valued marker of social status that confers, not only numerous economic and legal benefits, but also considerable cultural cache.

On the other hand, the precipitous decline in marriage cannot be overlooked. Marriage is not only decreasing among the less-educated but also among blacks. In recent decades, the family behaviors of blacks were harbingers, of sorts, of the types of family change that eventually occurred among whites. For example, the levels of single-mother families and nonmarital childbearing were initially high among blacks but now whites are closing the racial gap as they experience more rapid increases and as the pace of growth for blacks slows. We could see a similar pattern for marriage in the coming years.

This scenario seems especially plausible for the Millennial generation, which is delaying family formation amid economic insecurity. The transition to adulthood is more circuitous for this generation as they pursue additional years of education but also accumulate education-related debt and confront a tight job market following the Great Recession. Their precarious economic situation is an impediment to family formation, particularly marriage. Financial independence is a prerequisite for marriage nowadays. Moreover, this generation is receptive to diverse family living arrangements and are likely to feel less compulsion or even inclination to marry than did previous generations. Both these economic and attitudinal trends point in the direction of a delay and perhaps even a decline in marriage in the future.

The future of childbearing is also difficult to foresee. Fertility is below replacement level right now. Despite the economic recovery following the Great Recession, there has not been a corresponding uptick in fertility. Indeed, the birth rate in other developed nations is even lower than ours, hovering at just over one child per woman. Even with economic incentives to encourage additional childbearing, these extremely low levels are largely not changing. As childbearing levels converge across racial and ethnic groups, might fertility continue its slow decline in the United

States? This seems a likely scenario, particularly as families privilege child quality, which necessitates considerable investments of money and time by parents. Yet, childbearing is now more common among highly educated women than it was a generation ago,[18] reflecting the willingness of women with high earning potential to combine work and family. As marriage has become more collaborative and women have made strides in the workplace, childlessness among college-educated women has declined. Meanwhile nonmarital fertility will probably continue to rise in the near future as all of the recent growth in this trend has occurred within cohabiting unions. With couples waiting longer to tie the knot or forgoing marriage altogether, cohabitation presumably will be the setting for an increasing share of U.S. births.

These expectations about family change center on the early-adult life course and are largely confined to patterns of family formation. Yet mounting evidence indicates that significant changes are occurring during middle and later adulthood, too, which have ramifications for older adults and their children as well as society at large. Population aging is altering the family landscape. The share of the U.S. population that is aged sixty-five and older is growing rapidly as Baby Boomers move into later life. The media and others have termed this phenomenon "the aging tsunami."[19] As older adults live longer, they face chronic diseases that decrease quality of life and often require specialized care that can be prohibitively expensive. Relying on informal family care is the preferred route but the viability of this cost-friendly alternative is becoming less certain as fewer older adults are married and thus do not have a spouse to care for them. Although many have offspring, they often live far away or have their own children and jobs to juggle, precluding full-time caregiving. The retreat from marriage and shrinking family sizes among today's middle-aged and younger adults foretell sustained challenges related to population aging in the coming decades. The more complex marital biographies experienced by older adults presage both poorer health in later life and fewer potential family caregivers to provide assistance, which could strain existing social services.[20] Family formation and dissolution patterns have enduring, rippling effects across the life course, shaping the opportunities and burdens faced by current and succeeding generations.

Indeed, one thing is for certain: families will continue to change in new and surprising ways. Just as demographers failed to see the Baby Boom coming, family scholars of the 1950s could not have imagined how contemporary families would look today. Our diverse families emerge from a confluence of historical, economic, and social factors that can be difficult to parse. The rapidity of family change reinforces the importance of documenting and deciphering family patterns.

Notes

INTRODUCTION

1. U.S. Census Bureau n.d., "Frequently Asked Questions."
2. Goode 1964.
3. Carr and Springer 2010.
4. Taylor, Morin, and Wang 2011.
5. Powell et al. 2010.
6. Powell et al. 2010.
7. Popenoe 1993.
8. Cott 2000.
9. Stewart 2007, 214.
10. Cherlin 2009.
11. Mintz and Kellogg 1988.
12. Nock 2005; Lee 2015; Waite and Gallagher 2000.
13. McLanahan and Sandefur 1994.
14. McLanahan 2004.
15. Liu and Reczek 2012.

CHAPTER 1. HISTORICAL AND CONTEMPORARY
PERSPECTIVES ON FAMILIES

1. Parsons and Bales 1956, 22.
2. Coontz 1992; Mintz and Kellogg 1988.

3. Cohn, Livingston, and Wang 2014.
4. Popenoe 1993; Waite and Gallagher 2000.
5. Gordon 1994; Lichter and Jayakody 2002.
6. Cherlin 2009.
7. Mintz and Kellogg 1988.
8. Mintz and Kellogg 1988.
9. Kerber 1988.
10. Degler 1980.
11. Mintz 2004.
12. Furstenberg and Cherlin 1986.
13. Evans 1989.
14. Casper and Bianchi 2002.
15. Demos 1970.
16. Evans 1989; Mintz 2004; Mintz and Kellogg 1988.
17. Mintz and Kellogg 1988.
18. Cott 1997; Degler 1980; Mintz and Kellogg 1988.
19. Coontz 2005.
20. Coontz 1988.
21. Coontz 2005.
22. Coontz 2005.
23. Kerber 1988.
24. Coontz 2005.
25. Mintz and Kellogg 1988.
26. Gutman 1976; Jones 1985; Mintz and Kellogg 1988.
27. Mintz and Kellogg 1988.
28. Lindsey and Evans 1929.
29. Mintz 2004.
30. Coontz 1992; Mintz and Kellogg 1988.
31. Degler 1980; Kessler-Harris 1982.
32. Lindsey and Evans 1929.
33. Mintz 1998.
34. Lynd and Lynd 1956.
35. Mintz and Kellogg 1988.
36. Mintz and Kellogg 1988.
37. Apple 1995.
38. Coontz 1992; Strasser 1982.
39. Mintz 2004.
40. Garfinkel and McLanahan 1986.
41. Mintz and Kellogg 1988.
42. Mintz and Kellogg 1988.
43. Cherlin 1992.
44. Gordon 1994; Garfinkel and McLanahan 1986.

45. Mintz and Kellogg 1988.

46. May 1988.

47. Coontz 2005; May 1988; Mintz and Kellogg 1988.

48. Coontz 1992.

49. May 1988.

50. Mintz 2004.

51. May 1988; Mintz 2004.

52. Coontz 1992.

53. Mintz and Kellogg 1988.

54. May 1988.

55. Coontz 1992.

56. Coontz 1992.

57. Cherlin 1992.

58. Glick 1957.

59. Coontz 2005.

60. Coontz 1992.

61. Mintz 1998.

62. Cherlin 2009; Coontz 1992 and 2005.

63. May 1988.

64. Coontz 2005.

65. Mintz and Kellogg 1988.

66. Friedan 1963.

67. Mintz and Kellogg 1988.

68. Mintz 2004.

69. Coontz 1992.

70. Coontz 1992.

71. McLanahan 2004.

72. Luker 1984, 118

73. Guttmacher Institute 2016; Nash et al. 2016.

74. Cherlin 1990; Newsweek Staff 2006.

75. Smock 2000.

76. Bumpass and Sweet 1989.

77. Cherlin 1992.

78. Becker, Landes, and Michael 1977.

79. Oppenheimer 1994 and 1988.

80. Garfinkel and McLanahan 1986.

81. Child Trends Databank 2015.

82. S. Williams 2012.

83. McLanahan and Sandefur 1994.

84. Popenoe 1993.

85. Popenoe 1993, 539.

86. Popenoe 1993, 540.

87. Stacey 1993, 545.
88. Cowan 1993; Stacey 1993.
89. Stacey 1993.
90. McLanahan 2004.
91. DeParle 2012.
92. DeParle 2012.
93. DeParle 2012.
94. Lesthaeghe and Neidert 2006.
95. Lesthaeghe 2010.
96. Lesthaeghe 2010.
97. Cherlin 2009.

CHAPTER 2. PATHWAYS TO FAMILY FORMATION

1. Coontz 2005, 230.
2. U.S. Census Bureau 2016a.
3. Kreider and Ellis 2011.
4. Lamidi, Manning, and Brown 2015.
5. Manning, Brown, and Stykes 2015.
6. Gibson-Davis and Rackin 2014.
7. Koenig 2016.
8. Kreider and Vespa 2014.
9. Kreider and Vespa 2014.
10. McGarry and Schoeni 2000.
11. Span 2009.
12. Klinenberg 2012.
13. Elliott et al. 2012.
14. Parker and Wang 2014.
15. Parker and Wang 2014.
16. Elliott et al. 2012.
17. Parker and Wang 2014.
18. Lichter at al. 1992; Wilson 1987.
19. Parker and Wang 2014.
20. Lamidi 2015.
21. Fry and Passel 2014.
22. Payne 2013b.
23. Davidson 2014.
24. Davidson 2014.
25. Manning, Brown, and Payne 2014.
26. Samuelson 2011.
27. Clark University Poll 2015.

28. Rosenfeld and Thomas 2012.

29. Smith and Duggan 2013.

30. Smith and Duggan 2013.

31. Slater 2013.

32. Rosenfeld and Thomas 2012; Smith and Duggan 2013.

33. Bailey 1988.

34. Bailey 1988; Mintz and Kellogg 1988.

35. Mintz and Kellogg 1988.

36. Coronet Films 1950.

37. Mintz and Kellogg 1988.

38. Coontz 1992.

39. England, Shafer, and Fogarty 2008.

40. Reid, Elliott, and Webber 2011.

41. Armstrong, England, and Fogarty 2012.

42. Giddens 1992.

43. Funk and Kobayashi 2016; Strohm et al. 2009.

44. Benson and Coleman 2016, 806.

45. Watson and Stelle 2011.

46. Benson and Coleman 2016, 803.

47. Benson and Coleman 2016.

48. Aleccia 2013.

49. Manning and Stykes 2015.

50. Eickmeyer 2015.

51. Author's calculations.

52. Brown 2005; Smock 2000.

53. Manning and Stykes 2015.

54. Lamidi 2014.

55. Manning, Brown, and Payne 2014.

56. Lamidi 2015a.

57. Lamidi et al. 2015.

58. Edin and Kefalas 2005, 115.

59. Gibson-Davis, Edin, and McLanahan 2005, 138.

60. Smock, Manning, and Porter 2005, 690.

61. Wu and Schimmele 2005.

62. Lichter, Turner, and Sassler 2010.

63. Cohen and Manning 2010; Lichter, Turner, and Sassler 2010.

64. Cohen and Manning 2010; Lichter and Qian 2008.

65. Brown 2005; Casper and Sayer 2000.

66. Brown 2000.

67. Rindfuss and VandenHeuvel 1990.

68. Lichter, Sassler, and Turner 2014.

69. Manning 2004.

70. Bumpass and Sweet 1989; Lamidi, Manning, and Brown 2015.

71. Brown, Bulanda, and Lee 2012.

72. Brown, Lee, and Bulanda 2006; Chevan 1996; Hatch 1995.

73. Brown and Wright 2016.

74. Cherlin 1978; Nock 1995.

75. Cherlin 2004, 2009.

76. Manning and Stykes 2015.

77. Brown, Manning, and Payne 2015.

78. Brown 2000.

79. Liefbroer and Dourleijn 2006.

80. Bennett, Blanc, and Bloom 1988; DeMaris and Rao 1992; Dush, Cohan, and Amato 2003; Jose, O'Leary, and Moyer 2010.

81. Liefbroer and Dourleijn 2006.

82. Manning and Cohen 2012; Reinhold 2010.

83. Smock 2000.

84. Jacobson n.d.

85. Smock, Manning, and Porter 2005, 689.

86. Cruz 2013a.

87. Cruz 2013a.

88. U.S. Census Bureau 2015b.

89. Manning, Brown, and Payne 2014.

90. Manning et al. 2014.

91. Bureau of Labor Statistics n.d.

92. Cherlin 2009.

93. Wayne 2013.

94. Center for Retirement Research 2013.

95. Bogle and Wu 2010.

96. Bogle and Wu 2010.

97. Cohn 2013.

98. Manning et al. 2014.

99. Lichter, Graefe, and Brown 2003.

100. Gibson-Davis, Edin, and McLanahan 2005, 1309.

101. Lichter et al. 1992; Wilson 1987.

102. Becker 1991.

103. Stevenson and Wolfers 2007; Sweeney 2002.

104. Cherlin 2009.

105. Oppenheimer 1988.

106. Schwartz 2013.

107. Cherlin 2015.

108. U.S. Supreme Court 2015, 28.

109. Masci and Motel 2015.

110. Masci and Motel 2015.

111. Motel and Dost 2015.

112. Cherlin 2004.

113. Child Trends 2015.

114. Martin et al. 2015.

115. Taylor, Livingston, and Motel 2011.

116. Martin et al. 2015.

117. Astone, Martin, and Peters 2015.

118. Taylor et al. 2010.

119. Centers for Disease Control 2016.

120. Martin et al. 2015, table 5.

121. Lamidi and Payne 2013.

122. Arroyo et al. 2013.

123. Hayford, Stykes, and Guzzo 2014.

124. Manning, Brown, and Stykes 2015.

125. Manning, Brown, and Stykes 2015.

126. Manning, Brown, and Stykes 2015.

127. Manning, Brown, and Stykes 2015.

128. Manning, Brown, and Stykes 2015.

129. Cruz 2013b.

130. U.S. Department of Health and Human Services 1995.

131. Nash et al. 2016.

132. U.S. Department of Health and Human Services 1995.

133. Guzzo 2014.

134. Baskin 2014.

135. Edin and Kefalas 2005, 171–72.

136. Edin and Nelson 2013, 204.

CHAPTER 3. UNION DISSOLUTION
AND REPARTNERING

1. Gibson-Davis, Edin, and McLanahan 2005; Manning and Smock 2009; Miller, Sassler, and Kusi-Appouh 2011.

2. Gibson-Davis, Edin, and McLanahan 2005, 1309.

3. Bumpass and Lu 2000; Lamidi, Manning, and Brown 2015.

4. Kennedy and Ruggles 2014.

5. Kennedy and Ruggles 2014.

6. Sweeney 2010.

7. Brown and Lin 2013.

8. Becker, Landes, and Michael 1977; Sweeney 2010; Teachman 2008.

9. Brown and Lin 2012.

10. Cherlin 1992; Kennedy and Ruggles 2014.

11. Amato 2010; Cherlin 1992; McLanahan and Sandefur 1994; Weitzman 1985.

12. Lee 2013; Sullivan and Fenelon 2014.

13. Booth and Dunn 1994.

14. Raley and Bumpass 2003; Kennedy and Ruggles 2014.

15. Gibson-Davis, Edin, and McLanahan 2005; Manning and Smock 2009; Miller, Sassler, and Kusi-Appouh 2011.

16. Holmes and Rahe 1967.

17. Preston and McDonald 1979.

18. Cherlin 1992.

19. Amato 2010; Raley and Bumpass 2003.

20. S. P. Martin 2006.

21. Kennedy and Ruggles 2014.

22. Brown and Lin 2012.

23. Karraker and Latham 2015; Lin, Brown, and Hammersmith 2017.

24. Bair 2007.

25. Bramlett and Mosher 2002; S. P. Martin 2006.

26. S. P. Martin 2006.

27. Bramlett and Mosher 2002.

28. Amato 2010; Sweeney and Phillips 2004.

29. Cherlin 1992; Stevenson and Wolfers 2007; Weitzman 1985.

30. Cherlin 2004.

31. Chesley 2011; Galinsky, Aumann, and Bond 2009.

32. Burgess and Locke 1945; Cherlin 2009; Coontz 2005.

33. Mintz and Kellogg 1988.

34. Lindsey and Evans 1929.

35. Cherlin 2009; Coontz 2005.

36. Cherlin 2009; 2004.

37. Glenn 1996.

38. Coontz 2005.

39. Thornton and Young-DeMarco 2001.

40. Weitzman 1985.

41. Mintz and Kellogg 1988.

42. Allen 1992; Coontz 2005; Friedberg 1998; Peters 1992 and 1986; Wolfers 2003.

43. Coontz 1992; May 1988; Mintz and Kellogg 1988.

44. Glick 1957.

45. Bureau of Labor Statistics n.d.

46. Bureau of Labor Statistics n.d.

47. Oppenheimer 1997; Sayer and Bianchi 2000.

48. Oppenheimer 1994.

49. Schoen et al. 2002.

50. Rogers and DeBoer 2001.

51. Cleek and Pearson 1985; Coontz 1992.

52. Friedan 1963.

53. Bumpass, Sweet, and Martin 1990.

54. Becker, Landes, and Michael 1977.

55. Cherlin 2009 and 2004.

56. Amato 2010; White 1990.

57. Raley and Bumpass 2003.

58. Teti and Lamb 1989.

59. Booth and Edwards 1985.

60. Martin and Bumpass 1989; Sweeney 2010.

61. Levinger 1965.

62. Amato 2010.

63. Amato and DeBoer 2001.

64. White, Booth, and Edwards 1986.

65. Morgan, Lye, and Condran 1988.

66. Katzev, Warner, and Acock 1994.

67. Manning and Cohen 2012.

68. S. P. Martin 2006.

69. Amato 2010.

70. Gottman and Silver 2015; Gottman 1995.

71. Amato and Hohmann-Marriott 2007.

72. Glenn 1998.

73. Whitehead 1993.

74. Amato 2010; McLanahan and Sandefur 1994.

75. Amato and Booth 1991.

76. Cherlin et al. 1991; Sun 2001; Sun and Li 2002.

77. Weiss 1976.

78. Cherlin 1992; Weiss 1979.

79. McLanahan and Sandefur 1994.

80. McLanahan and Booth 1989.

81. Hoffman and Duncan 1988; Peterson 1996.

82. Sorensen 1997.

83. Lin, Brown, and Hammersmith 2017.

84. Amato 2010; Brown 2010.

85. Amato 2010.

86. Sun and Li 2002.

87. Sun and Li 2002.

88. Strohschein 2005.

89. Amato and Booth 1991.

90. Amato and Booth 1991.

91. Lamidi, Manning, and Brown 2015.

92. Manning and Smock 1995; Rinelli and Brown 2010.
93. Kuo and Raley 2016.
94. Brown 2000; Smock and Manning 1997.
95. Lamidi, Manning, and Brown 2015.
96. Brown 2000.
97. Avellar and Smock 2005.
98. Williams, Sassler, and Nicholson 2008; Wu and Hart 2002.
99. Kim 2013.
100. Badgett and Herman 2013.
101. Manning, Brown, and Stykes 2016.
102. Manning, Brown, and Stykes 2016; Rosenfeld 2014.
103. U.S. Census Bureau 2014.
104. U.S. Census Bureau 2014.
105. Holmes and Rahe 1967.
106. Sasson and Umberson, 2014.
107. Caserta et al. 2014.
108. Carr and Springer 2010.
109. Sullivan and Fenelon 2014.
110. Sullivan and Fenelon 2014.
111. Meyer, Wolf, and Himes 2006.
112. Angel, Jimenez, and Angel 2007; Lin and Brown 2012.
113. Wu, Schimmele, and Ouellet 2015.
114. Talbott 1998; Watson and Stelle 2011.
115. Cruz 2012a.
116. Schoen and Standish 2001.
117. Sweeney 2010.
118. Brown and Lin 2013.
119. Lamidi and Cruz 2014.
120. Cruz 2012a.
121. Lamidi 2015.
122. Cherlin 2009.
123. Cherlin 2009.
124. Cherlin 2009, 194; emphasis in original.
125. Stewart 2007.
126. Hetherington and Jodl 1994.
127. Ganong et al. 2015, 228.
128. Cherlin 1978.
129. Brown 2010; McLanahan and Sandefur 1994.
130. Stewart 2007.
131. Brown and Manning 2009.
132. King 2009.

133. Brown 2006; Cavanagh 2008; Hao and Xie 2002.

134. Brown, Manning, and Payne 2016; Manning and Brown 2006.

135. Buchanan, Maccoby, and Dornbusch 1996.

136. Payne 2013a.

137. Stewart 2007.

138. Van der Pas, Tilburg, and Silverstein 2013.

139. Hughes and Waite 2009; Lin et al. 2016.

140. Kennedy and Ruggles 2014.

141. Brown and Lin 2012.

CHAPTER 4. ADULT AND CHILD WELL-BEING
IN FAMILIES

1. Lasch 1977, xiii.

2. Klinenberg 2012.

3. Lee 2015; Waite and Gallagher 2000.

4. Hughes and Waite 2009.

5. Brown 2010.

6. McLanahan 2004.

7. Lareau 2011.

8. Waite 1995.

9. Lee 2015.

10. Musick and Bumpass 2012.

11. Waite and Gallagher 2000.

12. Liu and Umberson 2008; Ross, Mirowsky, and Goldsteen 1990.

13. Liu and Umberson 2008.

14. Pearlin and Johnson 1977.

15. Lee 2015.

16. Musick and Bumpass 2012.

17. Lee 2015.

18. Farley 1988; Liu and Umberson 2008.

19. Umberson et al. 2005.

20. Lee and Bulanda 2005.

21. Soons and Kalmijn 2009.

22. Lee 2015.

23. Marks and Lambert 1998; Musick and Bumpass 2012.

24. Brown 2005.

25. Musick and Bumpass 2012.

26. Lee 2015.

27. Liu and Umberson 2008.

28. Liu and Umberson 2008.

29. Liu and Umberson 2008.

30. Liu and Umberson 2008.

31. Liu and Reczek 2012.

32. Brown 2003.

33. Gove 1973; Liu and Umberson 2008.

34. Liu and Reczek 2012.

35. Umberson et al. 2006.

36. Liu and Waite 2014.

37. Robles and Kiecolt-Glaser 2003.

38. Hughes and Waite 2009.

39. Liu, Reczek, and Brown 2013.

40. Greenwood et al. 2014; Schwartz 2013.

41. U.S. Census Bureau 2016d.

42. Smock, Manning, and Porter 2005.

43. Cohn, Livingston, and Wang 2014.

44. Schulte 2014.

45. Kreider 2007.

46. McLanahan 2004.

47. Cruz 2012b.

48. Brown 2010.

49. Gennetian 2005; Halpern-Meekin and Tach 2008.

50. Brown, Manning, and Stykes 2015.

51. Stewart 2005.

52. White 1998.

53. Brown and Manning 2009.

54. Brown and Manning 2009.

55. Brown 2010.

56. Artis 2007; Brown 2004; Carlson and Corcoran 2001; Manning and Lamb 2003; Videon 2002.

57. Artis 2007; Brown 2004; Manning and Lamb 2003.

58. Manning, Fettro, and Lamidi 2014.

59. Dunifon and Kowaleski-Jones 2002; Fomby and Estacion 2011; Heard 2007a, 2007b; Manning and Brown 2006.

60. Amato 2005; Carlson and Corcoran 2001; Demo and Fine 2010; McLanahan and Sandefur 1994; Wu and Thomson 2001.

61. McLanahan and Sandefur 1994; Thomson, Hanson, and McLanahan 1994.

62. Carlson and Corcoran 2001.

63. Demo and Fine 2010.

64. S. Williams 2012.

65. McLanahan and Sandefur 1994.

66. Thornton 2001.

67. Hetherington and Jodl 1994; Sun 2001.

68. Dunifon and Kowaleski-Jone 2002; Sandberg and Hofferth 2001.

69. Carlson 2006.

70. Day and Lamb 2004.

71. Amato 2005.

72. Hofferth 2005.

73. Amato 2005.

74. Artis 2007; Brown 2004; Brown et al. 2016; Manning and Brown 2006.

75. Brown 2004; Carlson and Corcoran 2001; Manning and Lamb 2003.

76. Brown 2010.

77. Cavanagh and Huston 2006, 2008; Cavanagh, Schiller, and Riegle-Crumb 2006; DeLeire and Kalil 2002; Fomby and Cherlin 2007; Heard 2007b.

78. Cherlin 2009.

79. Wolfinger 2000.

80. Fomby and Cherlin 2007; Heard 2007a; Wu and Thomson 2001.

81. Cavanagh and Huston 2006, 2008; Fomby and Cherlin 2007; Wu and Thomson 2001.

82. Brown 2006.

83. Brown 2006; Cavanagh 2008; Hao and Xie 2002.

84. Brown 2010.

85. Cavanagh and Huston 2008; Heard 2007b.

86. Manning, Fettro, and Lamidi 2014; Potter 2012; Rosenfeld 2010.

87. Payne and Manning 2015.

88. Burgoyne 2012.

89. Brown et al. 2016.

90. Manning et al. 2014.

91. Biblarz, Carroll, and Burke 2014; Moore and Stambolis-Ruhstorfer 2013.

92. Regnerus 2012.

93. *DeBoer v. Snyder.* 772 F.3d 388 (6th Cir. 2014).

94. McLanahan 2004.

95. Moffitt, Ribar, and Wilhelm 1998.

96. McLanahan 2004.

97. Lareau 2011.

98. Lareau 2011, 42.

99. Lareau 2011, 42.

100. Lareau 2011, 113.

101. Lareau 2011, 113.

102. Larreau 2011, 79.

103. Lareau 2011.

CHAPTER 5. FAMILY POLICY ISSUES

1. Lindsey and Evans 1929.
2. Motel and Dost 2015.
3. Gordon 1994; Garfinkel and McLanahan 1986.
4. Moynihan 1965, 5; emphasis in original.
5. Geary 2015.
6. Moynihan 1965, 30.
7. Moynihan 1965, 29.
8. Furstenberg 2009; Geary 2015.
9. McLanahan 2009.
10. Furstenberg 2009.
11. Edin and Lein 1997.
12. Levin 2013.
13. Hays 2003.
14. Moffitt 2003.
15. Semuels 2016.
16. U.S. Department of Health and Human Services 2015.
17. U.S. Department of Health and Human Services 2015.
18. Loprest and Nichols 2011.
19. S. Williams 2012.
20. Administration for Children and Families n.d.
21. Wood et al. 2012.
22. Manning et al. 2014.
23. Gibson-Davis, Edin, and McLanahan 2005.
24. Edin and Shaefer 2015, 170.
25. Parker 2012.
26. DeNavas-Walt and Proctor 2015.
27. Child Trends Databank 2014.
28. Johnson and Lichter 2010.
29. Edin and Shaefer 2015.
30. UNICEF 2012.
31. UNICEF 2013.
32. OECD 2015.
33. Pew Research Center 2015b.
34. C.C. Miller 2015.
35. C.C. Miller 2015.
36. J.C. Williams 2010.
37. Kantor 2014.
38. Pew Research Center 2015b.
39. C.C. Miller 2015.
40. Pew Research Center 2015b.

41. Linn 2012.

42. Pew Research Center 2015b.

43. Hochschild 1989.

44. Pew Research Center 2013 n. d.

45. Pew Research Center 2013 n. d.

46. C. C. Miller 2015.

47. White House 2014.

48. Gornick and Meyers 2003; J. C. Williams 2010.

49. J. C. Williams 2010.

50. Matos and Galinsky 2014.

51. Matos and Galinsky 2014.

52. Gornick and Meyers 2003.

53. Adema, Clarke, and Frey 2015.

54. Gornick and Meyers 2003; J. C. Williams 2010.

55. Bureau of Labor Statistics 2015.

56. O'Donnell 2016.

57. Administration on Aging 2014; Jacobsen et al. 2011.

58. National Center for Health Statistics 2015.

59. Lin and Brown 2012.

60. Brown and Lin 2012.

61. Brown et al. 2016.

62. Talbott 1998; Watson and Stelle 2011.

63. Noël-Miller 2011.

64. Lin 2008.

65. Lin 2008.

66. Bureau of Labor Statistics 2015.

67. Wu, Brown, and Payne 2016.

68. Pew Research Center 2015a.

69. Span 2016.

70. *MetLife Study of Caregiving Costs to Working Caregivers* 2011.

71. O'Donnell 2016.

72. *MetLife Study of Caregiving Costs to Working Caregivers* 2011.

73. Pew Research Center 2015a.

CONCLUSION

1. Cohn, Livingston, and Wang 2014.

2. Coontz 2005; Mintz and Kellogg 1988.

3. Taylor, Morin, and Wang 2011.

4. Brown 2010.

5. Cherlin 2009.

6. Mayer 1997; McLanahan and Sandefur 1994.

7. Edin and Shaefer 2015; Semuels 2016.

8. Cherlin 2012; Notestein 1950.

9. Cherlin 2012; Goode 1963.

10. Cherlin 2009.

11. Heuveline and Timberlake 2004; Kiernan 2001.

12. Brown, Stykes, and Manning 2016.

13. Manning et al. 2014.

14. Lin and Brown 2012.

15. Brown and Wright 2016.

16. Cherlin 2009, 184.

17. Cherlin 2009.

18. Lamidi and Payne 2013.

19. Barusch 2013.

20. Hughes and Waite 2009; Lin and Brown 2012.

References

Adema, Willem, Chris Clarke, and Valerie Frey. *Paid Parental Leave: Lessons from OECD Countries and Selected U.S. States.* OECD Social, Employment and Migration Working Papers 172. Paris: OECD Publishing, 2015. Available at OECD iLibrary, http://dx.doi.org/10.1787/5jrqgvqqb4vb-en (accessed December 8, 2016).

Administration on Aging. "The Older Population." U.S. Department of Health and Human Services, Administration for Community Living, last modified August 25, 2014, https://aoa.acl.gov/Aging_Statistics/Profile/2013/3.aspx (accessed January 16, 2017).

Administration for Children and Families. "The Healthy Marriage Initiative." ACF Archives, n.d., http://archive.acf.hhs.gov/healthymarriage/about /mission.html#background (accessed October 7, 2016).

Aleccia, Joe. "'The New Normal': Cohabitation on the Rise, Study Finds." NBC News, April 4, 2013, www.nbcnews.com/health/health-news/new-normal-cohabitation-rise-study-finds-f1C9208429 (accessed December 8, 2016).

Allen, Douglas A. "Marriage and Divorce: Comment." *American Economic Review* 82, no. 3 (1992): 679–85.

Amato, Paul R. "The Impact of Family Formation Change on the Cognitive, Social, and Emotional Well-being of the Next Generation." *Future of Children* 15, no. 2 (2005): 75–96.

———. "Research on Divorce: Continuing Trends and New Developments." *Journal of Marriage and Family* 72, no. 3 (2010): 650–66.

Amato, Paul R., and Alan Booth. "Consequences of Parental Divorce and Marital Unhappiness for Adult Well-being." *Social Forces* 69, no. 3 (1991): 895–914.

Amato, Paul R., and Danielle D. DeBoer. "The Transmission of Marital Instability across Generations: Relationship Skills or Commitment to Marriage?" *Journal of Marriage and Family* 63, no. 4 (2001): 1038–51.

Amato, Paul R., and Bryndl Hohmann-Marriott. "A Comparison of High- and Low-Distress Marriages That End in Divorce." *Journal of Marriage and Family* 69, no. 3 (2007): 621–38.

Angel, Jacqueline L., Maren A. Jimenez, and Ronald J. Angel. "The Economic Consequences of Widowhood for Older Minority Women." *Gerontologist* 47, no. 2 (2007): 224–34.

Apple, Rima D. "Constructing Mothers: Scientific Motherhood in the Nineteenth and Twentieth Centuries." *Social History of Medicine* 8, no. 2 (1995): 161–78.

Armstrong, Elizabeth A., Paula England, and Alison C. K. Fogarty. "Accounting for Women's Orgasm and Sexual Enjoyment in College Hookups and Relationships." *American Sociological Review* 77, no. 3 (2012): 435–62.

Arroyo, Julia, Krista K. Payne, Susan L. Brown, and Wendy D. Manning. "Crossover in Median Age at First Marriage and First Birth: Thirty Years of Change." NCFMR Family Profile FP-13-06, National Center for Family & Marriage Research, Bowling Green State University, Bowling Green, OH, 2013, www.bgsu.edu/content/dam/BGSU/college-of-arts-and-sciences /NCFMR/documents/FP/FP-13-06.pdf (accessed January 7, 2017).

Artis, Julie E. "Maternal Cohabitation and Child Well-being among Kindergarten Children." *Journal of Marriage and Family* 69, no. 1 (2007): 222–36.

Astone, Nan Marie, Steven Martin, and H. Elizabeth Peters. *Millennial Childbearing and the Recession.* Urban Institute, Washington DC, 2015, www.urban.org/sites/default/files/alfresco/publication-pdfs/2000203-Millennial-Childbearing-and-the-Recession.pdf (accessed January 7, 2017).

Avellar, Sarah, and Pamela J. Smock. "The Economic Consequences of the Dissolution of Cohabiting Unions." *Journal of Marriage and Family* 67, no. 3 (2005): 315–27.

Badgett, M. V. Lee, and Jody L. Herman. "Patterns of Relationship Recognition by Same-sex Couples in the United States." In *International Handbook on the Demography of Sexuality,* edited by Amanda K. Baule, 331–62. Springer Netherlands, 2013.

Bailey, Beth. *From Front Porch to Back Seat.* Baltimore: Johns Hopkins University Press, 1988.

Bair, Deirdre. *Calling It Quits: Late-life Divorce and Starting Over.* New York: Random House, 2007.

Barusch, Amanda S. "The Aging Tsunami: Time for a New Metaphor?" *Journal of Gerontological Social Work* 53, no. 3 (2013): 181–84.

Baskin, Kara. "With Affluent Parents, 'Four is the New Three.'" *Boston Globe,* July 2, 2014.

Becker, Gary S. *A Treatise on the Family.* Cambridge, MA: Harvard University Press, 1991.

Becker, Gary S., Elisabeth M. Landes, and Robert T. Michael. "An Economic Analysis of Marital Instability." *Journal of Political Economy* 85, no. 6 (1977): 1141–87.

Bennett, Neil G., Ann Klimas Blanc, and David E. Bloom. "Commitment and the Modern Union: Assessing the Link between Premarital Cohabitation and Subsequent Marital Stability." *American Sociological Review* 53, no. 1 (1988): 127–38.

Benson, Jacquelyn J., and Marilyn Coleman. "Older Adults Developing a Preference for Living Apart Together." *Journal of Marriage and Family* 78, no. 3 (2016): 797–812.

Bianchi, Suzanne M., Melissa A. Milkie, Liana C. Sayer, and John P. Robinson. "Is Anyone Doing the Housework? Trends in the Gender Division of Household Labor." *Social Forces* 79, no. 1 (2000): 191–228.

Bianchi, Suzanne M., Liana C. Sayer, Melissa A. Milkie, and John P. Robinson. "Housework: Who Did, Does or Will Do It, and How Much Does It Matter?" *Social Forces* 91, no. 1 (2012): 55–63.

Biblarz, Timothy J., Megan Carroll, and Nathaniel Burke. "Same-sex Families." In *The Wiley Blackwell Companion to the Sociology of Families,* edited by Judith Treas, Jacqueline Scott, and Martin Richards, 109–31. Chichester, UK: John Wiley & Sons, 2014.

Bogle, Ryan, and Hsueh-Sheng Wu. "Thirty Years of Change in Marriage and Union Formation Attitudes, 1976–2008." NCFMR Family Profile FP-10-03, National Center for Family & Marriage Research, Bowling Green State University, Bowling Green, OH, 2010, www.bgsu.edu/content/dam/BGSU/college-of-arts-and-sciences/NCFMR/documents/FP/FP-10-03.pdf (accessed January 7, 2017).

Booth, Alan, and Judy Dunn. *Stepfamilies: Who Benefits? Who Does Not?* Hillsdale, NJ: Larwence Erlbaum Associates, 1994.

Booth, Alan, and John N. Edwards. "Age at Marriage and Marital Instability." *Journal of Marriage and the Family* 47, no. 1 (1985): 67–75.

Bramlett, Matthew D., and William D. Mosher. "Cohabitation, Marriage, Divorce, and Remarriage in the United States." *Vital Health Statistics* 23, no. 22 (2002): 1–32.

Brown, Susan L. "Family Structure and Child Well-being: The Significance of Parental Cohabitation." *Journal of Marriage and Family* 66, no. 2 (2004): 351–67.

———. "Family Structure Transitions and Adolescent Well-being." *Demography* 43, no. 3 (2006): 447–61.

———. "How Cohabitation Is Reshaping American Families." *Contexts* 4, no. 3 (2005): 33–37.

———. "Marriage and Child Well-being: Research and Policy Perspectives." *Journal of Marriage and Family* 72, no. 5 (2010): 1059–77.

———. "Relationship Quality Dynamics of Cohabiting Unions." *Journal of Family Issues* 24, no. 5 (2003): 83–601.

———. "Union Transitions among Cohabitors: The Significance of Relationship Assessments and Expectations." *Journal of Marriage and Family* 62, no. 3 (2000): 833–46.

Brown, Susan L., Jennifer Roebuck Bulanda, and Gary R. Lee. "Transitions into and out of Cohabitation in Later Life." *Journal of Marriage and Family* 74, no. 4 (2012): 774–93.

Brown, Susan L., Gary R. Lee, and Jennifer Roebuck Bulanda. "Cohabitation among Older Adults: A National Portrait." *Journals of Gerontology Series B: Psychological Sciences and Social Sciences* 61, no. 2 (2006): S71-S79.

Brown, Susan L., and I-Fen Lin. "Age Variation in the Remarriage Rate, 1990–2011." NCFMR Family Profile FP-13-17, National Center for Family & Marriage Research, Bowling Green State University, Bowling Green, OH, 2013, www.bgsu.edu/content/dam/BGSU/college-of-arts-and-sciences/NCFMR/documents/FP/FP-13-17.pdf (accessed January 7, 2017).

———. "The Gray Divorce Revolution: Rising Divorce among Middle-aged and Older Adults, 1990–2010." *Journals of Gerontology Series B: Psychological Sciences and Social Sciences* 67, no. 6 (2012): 731–41.

Brown, Susan L., I-Fen Lin, Anna M. Hammersmith, and Matthew R. Wright. "Later Life Marital Dissolution and Repartnership Status: A National Portrait." *Journals of Gerontology: Social Sciences.* Published electronically April 30, 2016 https://doi.org/10.1093/geronb/gbw051 (accessed January 25, 2017).

Brown, Susan L., and Wendy D. Manning. "Family Boundary Ambiguity and the Measurement of Family Structure: The Significance of Cohabitation." *Demography* 46, no. 1 (2009): 85–101.

Brown, Susan L., Wendy D. Manning, and Krista K. Payne. "Family Structure and Children's Economic Well-being: Incorporating Same-sex Cohabiting Mother Families." *Population Research and Policy Review* 35, no. 1 (2016): 1–21.

Brown, Susan, Wendy D. Manning, and Krista K. Payne. "Relationship Quality among Cohabiting Versus Married Couples." *Journal of Family Issues.* Available electronically at http://link.springer.com/article/10.1007/s11113-015-9375-8 (accessed January 25, 2017).

Brown, Susan L., Wendy D. Manning, and J. Bart Stykes. "Family Structure and Child Well-being: Integrating Family Complexity." *Journal of Marriage and Family* 77, no. 1 (2015): 177–90.

Brown, Susan L., J. Bart Stykes, and Wendy D. Manning. "Trends in Children's Family Instability, 1995–2010." *Journal of Marriage and Family* 78, no. 5 (2016): 1173–83.

Brown, Susan L., and Matthew R. Wright. "Older Adults' Attitudes toward Cohabitation: Two Decades of Change." *Journals of Gerontology Series B: Psychological Sciences and Social Sciences* 71, no. 4 (2016): 755–64.

Buchanan, Christy M., Eleanor E. Maccoby, and Sanford M. Dornbusch. *Adolescents after Divorce.* Cambridge, MA: Harvard University Press, 1996.

Bumpass, Larry, and Hsien-Hen Lu. "Trends in Cohabitation and Implications for Children's Family Contexts in the United States." *Population Studies* 54, no. 1 (2000): 29–41.

Bumpass, Larry L., and James A. Sweet. "National Estimates of Cohabitation." *Demography* 26, no. 4 (1989): 615–25.

Bumpass, Larry, James A. Sweet, and Teresa Castro Martin. "Changing Patterns of Remarriage." *Journal of Marriage and the Family* 52, no. 3 (1990): 747–56.

Bureau of Labor Statistics. "Mothers and Families." Women's Bureau, n.d., www.dol.gov/wb/stats/mother_families.htm#chart2 (accessed January 14, 2017).

———. "Unpaid Eldercare in the United States—2013-14 Summary." Economic News Release, September 23, 2015, www.bls.gov/news.release/elcare.nr0 .htm (accessed January 16, 2017).

Burgess, Ernest Watson, and Harvey James Locke. *The Family: From Institution to Companionship.* New York: American Book Company, 1945.

Burgoyne, Sarah. 2012. "Demographic Profile of Same-sex Parents." NCFMR Family Profile FP-12-15, National Center for Family & Marriage Research, Bowling Green State University, Bowling Green, OH, 2012, www.bgsu.edu /content/dam/BGSU/college-of-arts-and-sciences/NCFMR/documents/FP /FP-12-15.pdf (accessed January 25, 2017).

Carlson, Marcia J. "Family Structure, Father Involvement, and Adolescent Behavioral Outcomes." *Journal of Marriage and Family* 68, no. 1 (2006): 137–54.

Carlson, Marcia J., and Mary E. Corcoran. "Family Structure and Children's Behavioral and Cognitive Outcomes." *Journal of Marriage and Family* 63, no. 3 (2001): 779–92.

Carr, Deborah, and Kristen W. Springer. "Advances in Families and Health Research in the 21st Century." *Journal of Marriage and Family* 72, no. 3 (2010): 743–61.

Caserta, Michael, Rebecca Utz, Dale Lund, Kristin Lee Swenson, and Brian de Vries. "Coping Processes among Bereaved Spouses." *Death Studies* 38, no. 3 (2014): 145–55.

Casper, Lynne M., and Suzanne M. Bianchi. *Continuity and Change in the American Family.* Thousand Oaks, CA: Sage Publications, 2002.

Casper, Lynne M., and Liana C. Sayer. "Cohabitation Transitions: Different Attitudes and Purposes, Different Paths." Paper presented at the Annual Meeting of the Population Association of America, Los Angeles, 2000.

Cavanagh, Shannon E. "Family Structure History and Adolescent Adjustment." *Journal of Family Issues* 29, no. 7 (2008): 944–80.

Cavanagh, Shannon E., and Aletha C. Huston. "Family Instability and Children's Early Problem Behavior." *Social Forces* 85, no. 1 (2006): 551–81.

———. "The Timing of Family Instability and Children's Social Development." *Journal of Marriage and Family* 70, no. 5 (2008): 1258–70.

Cavanagh, Shannon E., Kathryn S. Schiller, and Catherine Riegle-Crumb. "Marital Transitions, Parenting, and Schooling: Exploring the Link between Family-Structure History and Adolescents' Academic Status." *Sociology of Education* 79, no. 4 (2006): 329–54.

Center for Retirement Research. "Student Loans = No House, No New Car." Squared Away Blog, May 23, 2013, http://squaredawayblog.bc.edu/squared-away/student-loans-no-house-no-new-car/attachment/student-debt (accessed January 25, 2017).

Centers for Disease Control. "About Teen Pregnancy." Last modified April 26, 2016, www.cdc.gov/teenpregnancy/about/index.htm (accessed January 25, 2017).

Cherlin, Andrew. "The Deinstitutionalization of American Marriage." *Journal of Marriage and Family* 66, no. 4 (2004): 848–61.

———. "Goode's World Revolution and Family Patterns: A Reconsideration at Fifty Years." *Population and Development Review* (2012): 577–607.

———. "Remarriage as an Incomplete Institution." *American Journal of Sociology* 84, no. 3 (1978): 634–50.

———. "A Review: The Strange Career of the 'Harvard-Yale Study.'" *Public Opinion Quarterly* 54, no. 1 (1990): 117–24.

———. *Labor's Love Lost: The Rise and Fall of the Working-Class Family in America.* New York: Russell Sage Foundation, 2014.

———. *Marriage, Divorce, and Remarriage.* Cambridge, MA: Harvard University Press, 1992.

———. *The Marriage-Go-Round.* New York: Vintage Books, 2009.

———. "The Triumph of Family Diversity." Contexts Blog, July 7, 2015, https://contexts.org/blog/the-triumph-of-family-diversity (accessed January 25, 2017).

Cherlin, Andrew J., Frank F. Furstenberg, Lindsay Chase-Lansdale, Kathleen E. Kiernan, Philip K. Robins, Donna Ruane Morrison, and Julien O. Teitler. "Longitudinal Studies of Effects of Divorce on Children in Great Britain and the United States." *Science* 252, no. 5011 (1991): 1386–89.

Chesley, Noelle. "Stay-at-Home Fathers and Breadwinning Mothers: Gender, Couple Dynamics, and Social Change." *Gender and Society* 25, no. 5 (2011): 642–64.

Chevan, Albert. "As Cheaply as One: Cohabitation in the Older Population." *Journal of Marriage and the Family* 58, no. 3 (1996): 656–67.

Child Trends Databank. "Births to Unmarried Women." Last modified December 2015, www.childtrends.org/wp-content/uploads/2015/03/75_Births_to_Unmarried_Women.pdf (accessed January 25, 2017).

———. "Immigrant Children." Last modified October 2014, www.childtrends.org/wp-content/uploads/2012/07/110_Immigrant_Children.pdf (accessed January 25, 2017).

Clark University Poll. *Clark University Poll of Emerging Adults: Work, Education, and Identity,* 2015. Clark University website, www2.clarku.edu/clark-poll-emerging-adults/pdfs/2015-clark-poll-report.pdf (accessed January 25, 2017).

Cleek, Margaret Guminski, and T. Allan Pearson. "Perceived Causes of Divorce: An Analysis of Interrelationships." *Journal of Marriage and the Family* 47, no. 1 (1985): 179–83.

Cohen, Jessica, and Wendy Manning. "The Relationship Context of Premarital Serial Cohabitation." *Social Science Research* 39, no. 5 (2010): 766–76.

Cohn, D'Vera. "Love and Marriage." Pew Research Center, February 13, 2013, www.pewsocialtrends.org/2013/02/13/love-and-marriage (accessed January 25, 2017).

Cohn, D'Vera, Gretchen Livingston, and Wendy Wang. "After Decades of Decline, a Rise in Stay-at-Home Mothers." Washington, DC: Pew Research Center's Social and Demographic Trends Project, April 8, 2014, www.pewsocialtrends.org/files/2014/04/Moms-At-Home_04-08-2014.pdf (accessed January 25, 2017).

Coontz, Stephanie. *Marriage, a History: How Love Conquered Marriage.* New York: Viking Books, 2005.

———. *Social Origins of Private Life.* London: Verso, 1988.

———. *The Way We Never Were: American Families and the Nostalgia Trap.* New York: Basic Books, 1992.

———. "The World Historical Transformation of Marriage." *Journal of Marriage and Family* 66, no. 4 (2004): 974–79.

Coronet Films. *What to Do on a Date.* Instructional film, 1950, YouTube video, 10:51. Posted by "Motion Vault," October 9, 2013, https://youtu.be/LGXwN-bJPzOA (accessed January 25, 2017).

Cott, Nancy F. *The Bonds of Womanhood: "Woman's Sphere" in New England, 1780–1835.* New Haven, CT: Yale University Press, 1997.

———. *Public Vows: A History of Marriage and the Nation.* Cambridge, MA: Harvard University Press, 2000.

Cowan, Philip A. "The Sky Is Falling, but Popenoe's Analysis Won't Help Us Do Anything about It." *Journal of Marriage and Family* 55, no. 3 (1993): 548–53.

Cruz, Julissa. "First Marriage vs. Remarriage in the U.S., 2010." NCFMR Family Profile FP-12–21, National Center for Family & Marriage Research, Bowling Green State University, Bowling Green, OH, 2012a, www.bgsu.edu/content/dam/BGSU/college-of-arts-and-sciences/NCFMR/documents/FP/FP-12-21.pdf (accessed January 25, 2017).

———. "Marriage: More than a Century of Change." NCMFR Family Profile FP-13–13, National Center for Family & Marriage Research, Bowling Green State University, Bowling Green, OH, 2013a, www.bgsu.edu/content/dam/BGSU/college-of-arts-and-sciences/NCFMR/documents/FP/FP-13-13.pdf (accessed January 25, 2017).

———. "Single, Cohabiting, and Married Mothers in the U.S., 2011." NCFMR Family Profile FP-12–23, National Center for & Marriage Research, Bowling Green State University, Bowling Green, OH, 2012b, www.bgsu.edu/content/dam/BGSU/college-of-arts-and-sciences/NCFMR/documents/FP/FP-12-23.pdf (accessed January 25, 2017).

———. "Women Who Gave Birth within the Past 12 Months, 2011." NCFMR Family Profile FP-13–10, National Center for Family & Marriage Research, Bowling Green State University, Bowling Green, OH, 2013b, www.bgsu.edu/content/dam/BGSU/college-of-arts-and-sciences/NCFMR/documents/FP/FP-13-10.pdf (accessed January 25, 2017).

Davidson, Adam. "It's Official: The Boomerang Kids Won't Leave." *New York Times Magazine*, June 20, 2014.

Day, Randal D., and Michael E. Lamb, eds. *Conceptualizing and Measuring Father Involvement*. Mahwah, NJ: Lawrence Erlbaum Associates, 2004.

DeBoer v. Snyder. 772 F.3d 388 (6th Cir. 2014).

Degler, Carl. *At Odds: Women and the Family in America from the Revolution to the Present*. New York: Oxford University Press, 1980.

DeLeire, Thomas, and Ariel Kalil. "Good Things Come in Threes: Single-Parent Multigenerational Family Structure and Adolescent Adjustment." *Demography* 39, no. 2 (2002): 393–413.

DeMaris, Alfred, and K. Vaninadha Rao. "Premarital Cohabitation and Subsequent Marital Stability in the United States: A Reassessment." *Journal of Marriage and the Family* 54, no. 1 (1992): 178–90.

Demo, David H., and Mark A. Fine. *Beyond the Average Divorce*. Thousand Oaks, CA: Sage, 2010.

Demos, John. *A Little Commonwealth: Family Life in Plymouth Colony*. New York: Oxford University Press, 1970.

DeNavas-Walt, Carmen, and Bernadette D. Proctor. Current Population Reports, P60–252, *Income and Poverty in the United States: 2014*. Washington, DC: U.S. Government Printing Office, 2015.

DeParle, Jason. "Two Classes, Divided by 'I Do.'" *New York Times,* July 14, 2012.

Dunifon, Rachel, and Lori Kowaleski–Jones. "Who's in the House? Race Differences in Cohabitation, Single Parenthood, and Child Development." *Child Development* 73, no. 4 (2002): 1249–64.

Dush, Claire M. Kamp, Catherine L. Cohan, and Paul R. Amato. "The Relationship between Cohabitation and Marital Quality and Stability: Change across Cohorts?" *Journal of Marriage and Family* 65, no. 3 (2003): 539–49.

Edin, Kathryn, and Maria Kefalas. *Promises I Can Keep: Why Poor Women Put Motherhood before Marriage.* Berkeley, CA: University of California Press, 2005.

Edin, Kathryn, and Laura Lein. *Making Ends Meet: How Single Mothers Survive Welfare and Low-wage Work: How Single Mothers Survive Welfare and Low-wage Work.* New York: Russell Sage Foundation, 1997.

Edin, Kathryn, and Timothy Jon Nelson. *Doing the Best I Can: Fatherhood in the Inner City.* Berkeley, CA: University of California Press, 2013.

Edin, Kathryn J., and H. Luke Shaefer. *$2.00 a Day: Living on Almost Nothing in America.* Boston: Houghton Mifflin Harcourt, 2015.

Eickmeyer, Kasey J. "Generation X and Millenials: Attitudes Toward Marriage & Divorce." NCFMR Family Profile FP-15-12, National Center for Family & Marriage Research, Bowling Green State University, Bowling Green, OH, 2015, www.bgsu.edu/ncfmr/resources/data/family-profiles/eickmeyer-gen-x-millennials-fp-15-12.html (accessed January 25, 2017).

Elliott, Diana, Kristy Krivicas, Matthew W. Brault, and Rose M. Kreider. "Historical Marriage Trends from 1980–2010: A Focus on Race Differences." SEHSD Working Paper Number 2012-12. Paper presented at the Annual Meeting of the Population Association of America, San Francisco, May 2012.

England, Paula, Emily Fitzgibbons Shafer, and Alison C. K. Fogarty. "Hooking Up and Forming Romantic Relationships on Today's College Campuses." *Gendered Society Reader* 3 (2008): 531–93.

Evans, Sara M. *Born for Liberty: A History of Women in America.* New York: Free Press, 1989.

Farley, Reynolds. "After the Starting Line: Blacks and Women in an Uphill Race." *Demography* 25, no. 4 (1988): 477–95.

Flood, Sarah, Miriam King, Steven Ruggles, and J. Robert Warren. *Integrated Public Use Microdata Series, Current Population Survey: Version 4.0.* [dataset]. Minneapolis: University of Minnesota, 2015, available at http://doi.org/10.18128/D030.V4.0 (accessed January 30, 2017).

Fomby, Paula, and Andrew J. Cherlin. "Family Instability and Child Well-being." *American Sociological Review* 72, no. 2 (2007): 181–204.

Fomby, Paula, and Angela Estacion. "Cohabitation and Children's Externalizing Behavior in Low-income Latino Families." *Journal of Marriage and Family* 73, no. 1 (2011): 46–66.

Friedan, Betty.*The Feminine Mystique.* New York: W. W. Norton, 1963.

Friedberg, Leora. "Did Unilateral Divorce Raise Divorce Rates? Evidence from Panel Data." *American Economic Review* 88 (1998): 608–27.

Fry, Richard, and Jeffrey S. Passel. "In Post-recession Era, Young Adults Drive Continuing Rise in Multi-generational Living." Washington, DC: Pew Research Center's Social and Demographic Trends project, July 17, 2014, www.pewsocialtrends.org/files/2014/07/ST-2014-07-17-multigen-households-report.pdf (accessed January 25, 2017).

Funk, Laura M., and Karen M. Kobayashi. "From Motivations to Accounts: An Interpretive Analysis of 'Living Apart Together' Relationships in Mid- to Later-life Couples." *Journal of Family Issues* 37, no. 8 (2016): 1–22.

Furstenberg, Frank F. "If Moynihan Had Only Known: Race, Class, and Family Change in the Late Twentieth Century." annals *of the American Academy of Political and Social Science* 621, no. 1 (2009): 94–110.

Furstenberg, Frank F., and Andrew J. Cherlin. *The New American Grandparent: A Place in the Family, A Life Apart.* New York: Basic Books, 1986.

Galinsky, Ellen, Kerstin Aumann, and James T. Bond. *Times Are Changing: Gender and Generation at Work and at Home.* New York: Families and Work Institute, 2009.

Ganong, Lawrence, Marilyn Coleman, Tyler Jamison, and Richard Feistman. "Divorced Mothers' Coparental Boundary Maintenance after Parents Repartner." *Journal of Family Psychology* 29, no. 2 (2015): 221–31.

Garfinkel, Irwin, and Sara S. McLanahan. *Single Mothers and Their Children.* Washington, DC: Urban Institute Press, 1986.

Geary, Daniel. "The Moynihan Report: An Annotated Edition." *Atlantic,* September 14, 2015.

Gennetian, Lisa A. "One or Two Parents? Half or Step Siblings? The Effect of Family Structure on Young Children's Achievement." *Journal of Population Economics* 18, no. 3 (2005): 415–36.

Gibson-Davis, Christina M., Kathryn Edin, and Sara S. McLanahan. "High Hopes but Even Higher Expectations: The Retreat from Marriage among Low-income Couples." *Journal of Marriage and Family* 67, no. 5 (2005): 1301–12.

Gibson-Davis, Christina M., and Heather Rackin. "Marriage or Carriage? Trends in Union Context and Birth Type by Education." *Journal of Marriage and Family* 76, no. 3, (2014): 506–19.

Giddens, Anthony. *The Transformation of Intimacy: Sexuality, Love, and Eroticism in Modern Societies.* Cambridge: Polity Press, 1992.

Glenn, Norval D. "The Course of Marital Success and Failure in Five American 10-year Marriage Cohorts." *Journal of Marriage and the Family* 60, no. 3 (1998): 569–76.

———. "Values, Attitudes, and the State of American Marriage." In *Promises to Keep: Decline and Renewal of Marriage in America,* edited by David

Popenoe, Jean Bethke Elshtain, and David Blankenhorn, 15–33. Lanham, MD: Rowman and Littlefield Publishers, 1996.

Glick, Paul C. *American Families*. New York: John Wiley & Sons, 1957.

Goode, William J. *The Family*. Englewood Cliffs, NJ: Prentice-Hall, 1964.

———. *World Revolution and Family Patterns*. Glencoe, IL: Free Press, 1963.

Gordon, Linda. *Pitied but Not Entitled: Single Mothers and the History of Welfare, 1890–1935*. Cambridge, MA: Harvard University Press, 1994.

Gornick, Janet C., and Marcia K. Meyers. *Families That Work: Policies for Reconciling Parenthood and Employment*. New York: Russell Sage Foundation, 2003.

Gottman, John. *Why Marriages Succeed or Fail*. New York: Simon & Schuster, 1995.

Gottman, John, and Nan Silver. *The Seven Principles for Making Marriage Work: A Practical Guide from the Country's Foremost Relationship Expert*. New York: Harmony Books, 2015.

Gove, Walter R. "Sex, Marital Status, and Mortality." *American Journal of Sociology* 79, no. 1 (1973): 45–67.

Greenwood, Jeremy, Nezih Guner, Georgi Kocharkov, and Cezar Santos. "Marry Your Like: Assortative Mating and Income Inequality." *American Economic Review* 104, no. 5 (2014): 348–53.

Gutman, Herbert George. *Black Family in Slavery and Freedom, 1750–1925*. New York: Pantheon Books, 1976.

Guttmacher Institute. *Induced Abortion in the United States: Fact Sheet*. September 2016, www.guttmacher.org/fact-sheet/induced-abortion-united-states (January 7, 2017).

Guzzo, Karen Benjamin. "New Partners, More Kids Multiple-partner Fertility in the United States." *annals of the American Academy of Political and Social Science* 654, no. 1 (2014): 66–86.

Halpern-Meekin, Sarah, and Laura Tach. "Heterogeneity in Two-parent Families and Adolescent Well-being." *Journal of Marriage and Family* 70, no. 1 (2008): 435–51.

Hao, Lingxin, and Guihua Xie. "The Complexity and Endogeneity of Family Structure in Explaining Children's Misbehavior." *Social Science Research* 31, no. 1 (2002): 1–28.

Hatch, Rebecca. *Aging and Cohabitation*. New York: Garland Press, 1995.

Hayford, Sarah R., Bart Stykes, and Karen Benjamin Guzzo. "Trends in Motherhood before First Marriage." NCFMR Family Profile FP-14-04, National Center for Family & Marriage Research, Bowling Green State University, Bowling Green, OH, 2014, www.bgsu.edu/content/dam/BGSU /college-of-arts-and-sciences/NCFMR/documents/FP/FP-14-04_ TrendsInMotherhood.pdf (January 25, 2017).

Hays, Sharon. *Flat Broke with Children: Women in the Age of Welfare Reform.* New York: Oxford University Press, 2003.

Heard, Holly E. "The Family Structure Trajectory and Adolescent School Performance Differential Effects by Race and Ethnicity." *Journal of Family Issues* 28, no. 3 (2007a): 319–54.

———. "Fathers, Mothers, and Family Structure: Family Trajectories, Parent Gender, and Adolescent Schooling." *Journal of Marriage and Family* 69, no. 2 (2007b): 435–50.

Hetherington, E. Mavis, and Kathleen M. Jodl. "Stepfamilies as Settings for Child Development." In *Stepfamilies: Who Benefits? Who Does Not?* edited by Alan Booth and Judy Dunn, 55–79. Hillsdale, NJ: Lawrence Erlbaum Associates, 1994.

Heuveline, Patrick, and Jeffrey M. Timberlake. "The Role of Cohabitation in Family Formation: The United States in Comparative Perspective." *Journal of Marriage and Family* 66, no. 5 (2004): 1214–30.

Hochschild, Arlie. *The Second Shift: Working Parents and the Revolution at Home.* New York: Avon, 1989.

Hofferth, Sandra L. "Secondary Data Analysis in Family Research." *Journal of Marriage and Family* 67, no. 4 (2005): 891–907.

Hoffman, Saul D., and Greg J. Duncan. "What Are the Economic Consequences of Divorce?" *Demography* 25, no. 4 (1988): 641–45.

Holmes, Thomas H., and Richard H. Rahe. "The Social Readjustment Rating Scale." *Journal of Psychosomatic Research* 11, no. 2 (1967): 213–18.

Hughes, Mary Elizabeth, and Linda J. Waite. "Marital Biography and Health at Mid-life." *Journal of Health and Social Behavior* 50, no. 3 (2009): 344–58.

Jacobsen, Linda A., Mary Kent, Marlene Lee, and Mark Mather. "America's Aging Population." *Population Bulletin* 66, no. 1 (2011): 1–20.

Jacobson, Ivy. "Average Wedding Cost Hits National All-time High." The Knot. com, n.d., www.theknot.com/content/average-wedding-cost (accessed October 3, 2016).

Johnson, Kenneth M., and Daniel T. Lichter. "Growing Diversity among America's Children and Youth: Spatial and Temporal Dimensions." *Population and Development Review* 36, no. 1 (2010): 151–76.

Jones, Jacqueline. *Labor of Love, Labor of Sorrow: Black Women, Work and the Family, from Slavery to the Present.* New York: Basic Books, 1985.

Jose, Anita, K. Daniel O'Leary, and Anne Moyer. "Does Premarital Cohabitation Predict Subsequent Marital Stability and Marital Quality? A Meta-analysis." *Journal of Marriage and Family* 72, no. 1 (2010): 105–16.

Kantor, Jodi. "Working Anything but 9 to 5." *New York Times,* August 13, 2014.

Karraker, Amelia, and Kenzie Latham. "In Sickness and in Health? Physical Illness as a Risk Factor for Marital Dissolution in Later Life." *Journal of Health and Social Behavior* 56, no. 3 (2015): 420–35.

Katzev, Aphra R., Rebecca L. Warner, and Alan C. Acock. "Girls or Boys? Relationship of Child Gender to Marital Instability." *Journal of Marriage and the Family* 56, no. 1 (1994): 89–100.

Kennedy, Sheela, and Steven Ruggles. "Breaking Up Is Hard to Count: The Rise of Divorce in the United States, 1980–2010." *Demography* 51, no. 2 (2014): 587–98.

Kerber, Linda K. "Separate Spheres, Female Worlds, Woman's Place: The Rhetoric of Women's History." *Journal of American History* 75, no. 1 (1988): 9–39.

Kessler-Harris, Alice. *Out to Work: A History of Wage-earning Women in the United States.* New York: Oxford University Press, 1982.

Kiernan, Kathleen. "The Rise of Cohabitation and Childbearing Outside Marriage in Western Europe." *International Journal of Law, Policy, and the Family* 15, no. 1 (2001): 1–21.

Kim, Eun Kyung. "For Gay Couples, Divorce Comes with Extra Costs." *Today News,* August 6, 2013.

King, Valarie. "Stepfamily Formation: Implications for Adolescent Ties to Mothers, Nonresident Fathers, and Stepfathers." *Journal of Marriage and Family* 71, no. 4 (2009): 954–68.

Kirk, Dudley. "Demographic Transition Theory." *Population Studies* 50 (2010): 361–87.

Klinenberg, Eric. *Going Solo: The Extraordinary Rise and Surprising Appeal of Living Alone.* New York: Penguin Books, 2012.

Koenig, Ronnie. "Divorced Parents, Living Close for the Children's Sake." *New York Times,* January 15, 2016.

Kreider, Rose M. *Living Arrangements of Children: 2004.* Current Population Reports P70–114. Washington, DC: U.S. Census Bureau, 2007.

Kreider, Rose M., and Renee Ellis. *Number, Timing, and Duration of Marriages and Divorces: 2009.* Current Population Reports P70–125. Washington, DC: U.S. Census Bureau, 2011.

Kreider, Rose M., and Jonathan Vespa. *The Historic Rise of One-Person Households, 1850–2010.* SEHSD Working Paper no. 2014–19. Washington, DC: U.S. Census Bureau, 2014.

Kuo, Janet Chen-Lan, and R. Kelly Raley. "Diverging Patterns of Union Transition among Cohabitors by Race/Ethnicity and Education: Trends and Marital Intentions in the United States." *Demography* 53, no. 4 (2016): 921–35.

Lamidi, Esther. "Single, Cohabiting, and Married Households, 1995–2012." NCFMR Family Profile FP-14–1, National Center for Family & Marriage Research, Bowling Green State University, Bowling Green, OH, 2014, www.bgsu.edu/content/dam/BGSU/college-of-arts-and-sciences/NCFMR/documents/FP/FP-14-01.pdf (accessed January 25, 2017).

———. "Trends in Cohabitation: The Never Married and Previously Married, 1995–2014." NCFMR Family Profile FP-15–21, National Center for Family & Marriage Research, Bowling Green State University, Bowling Green, OH, 2015, www.bgsu.edu/ncfmr/resources/data/family-profiles/lamidi-cohab-trends-never-previously-married-fp-15-21.html (accessed January 25, 2017).

Lamidi, Esther, and Julissa Cruz. "Remarriage Rate in the U.S., 2012." NCFMR Family Profile FP-14–10, National Center for Family & Marriage Research, Bowling Green State University, Bowling Green, OH, 2014, www.bgsu.edu /content/dam/BGSU/college-of-arts-and-sciences/NCFMR/documents/FP /FP-14-10-remarriage-rate-2012.pdf (accessed January 25, 2017).

Lamidi, Esther, Wendy D. Manning, and Susan L. Brown. "Change in the Stability of First Premarital Cohabitation, 1980–2009." CFDR Working Paper Series no. 2015–26, Center for Family and Demographic Research, Bowling Green State University, Bowling Green, OH, 2015, www.bgsu.edu /content/dam/BGSU/college-of-arts-and-sciences/center-for-family-and-demographic-research/documents/working-papers/2015/WP-2015-26-Lamidi-Change-in-Stability-of-First-Premarital-Cohabitation.pdf (accessed January 25, 2017).

Lamidi, Esther, and Krista K. Payne. "Change in Proportion of Childless Women, 1995–2010. NCFMR Family Profile FP-13–20, National Center for Family & Marriage Research, Bowling Green State University, Bowling Green, OH, 2013, www.bgsu.edu/content/dam/BGSU/college-of-arts-and-sciences/NCFMR/documents/FP/FP-13-20.pdf (accessed January 25, 2017).

Lareau, Annette. *Unequal Childhoods: Class, Race, and Family Life.* Berkeley: University of California Press, 2011.

Lasch, Christopher. *Haven in a Heartless World: The Family Besieged.* New York: Basic Books, 1977.

Lee, Gary R. "Current Research on Widowhood: Devastation and Human Resilience." *Journals of Gerontology Series B: Psychological Sciences and Social Sciences* 69B, no. 1 (2013): 2–3.

———. *The Limits of Marriage: Why Getting Everyone Married Won't Solve All Our Problems.* Lanham, MD: Lexington Books, 2015.

Lee, Gary R., and Jennifer Roebuck Bulanda. "Change and Consistency in the Relation of Marital Status to Personal Happiness." *Marriage and Family Review* 38, no. 1 (2005): 69–84.

Lesthaeghe, Ron J. "The Unfolding Story of the Second Demographic Transition." *Population and Development Review* 36, no. 2 (2010): 211–51.

Lesthaeghe, Ron J., and Lisa Neidert. "The Second Demographic Transition in the United States: Exception or Textbook Example?" *Population and Development Review* 32, no. 4 (2006): 669–98.

Levin, Josh. "The Welfare Queen." *Slate,* December 19, 2013.

Levinger, George. "Marital Cohesiveness and Dissolution: An Integrative Review." *Journal of Marriage and the Family* 27, no. 1 (1965): 19–28.

Lichter, Daniel T., Deborah Roempke Graefe, and J. Brian Brown. "Is Marriage a Panacea? Union Formation among Economically Disadvantaged Unwed Mothers." *Social Problems* 50, no. 1 (2003): 60–86.

Lichter, Daniel T., and Rukamalie Jayakody. "Welfare Reform: How Do We Measure Success?" *Annual Review of Sociology* 28 (2002): 117–41.

Lichter, Daniel T., Diane K. McLaughlin, George Kephart, and David J. Landry. "Race and the Retreat from Marriage: A Shortage of Marriageable Men?" *American Sociological Review* 57, no. 6 (1992): 781–99.

Lichter, Daniel T., and Zhenchao Qian. "Serial Cohabitation and the Marital Life Course." *Journal of Marriage and Family* 70, no. 4 (2008): 861–78.

Lichter, Daniel T., Sharon Sassler, and Richard N. Turner. "Cohabitation, Post-conception Unions, and the Rise in Nonmarital Fertility." *Social Science Research* 47 (2014): 134–47.

Lichter, Daniel T., Richard N. Turner, and Sharon Sassler. "National Estimates of the Rise in Serial Cohabitation." *Social Science Research* 39, no. 5 (2010): 754–65.

Liefbroer, Aart C., and Edith Dourleijn. "Unmarried Cohabitation and Union Stability: Testing the Role of Diffusion Using Data from 16 European Countries." *Demography* 43, no. 2 (2006): 203–21.

Lin, I-Fen. "Consequences of Parental Divorce for Adult Children's Support of Their Frail Parents." *Journal of Marriage and Family* 70, no. 1 (2008): 113–28.

Lin, I-Fen, and Susan L. Brown. "Unmarried Boomers Confront Old Age: A National Portrait." *Gerontologist* 52, no. 2 (2012): 153–65.

Lin, I-Fen, Susan L. Brown, and Anna M. Hammersmith. "Marital Biography, Social Security Receipt, and Poverty." *Research on Aging* 39, no. 1 (2017): 86–110.

Lindsey, Judge Ben B., and Wainwright Evans. *The Companionate Marriage.* Garden City, NY: Garden City Publishing, 1929.

Linn, Allison. "Many Dads Struggle to 'Have It All,' Balancing Work, Family." Today.com, June 13, 2012, www.today.com/money/many-dads-struggle-have-it-all-balancing-work-family-826045 (accessed January 25, 2017).

Liu, Hui, and Corinne Reczek. "Cohabitation and US Adult Mortality: An Examination by Gender and Race." *Journal of Marriage and Family* 74, no. 4 (2012): 794–811.

Liu, Hui, Corinne Reczek, and Dustin Brown. "Same-sex Cohabitors and Health: The Role of Race-Ethnicity, Gender, and Socioeconomic Status." *Journal of Health and Social Behavior* 54, no. 1 (2013): 25–45.

Liu, Hui, and Debra J. Umberson. "The Times They Are a Changin': Marital Status and Health Differentials from 1972 to 2003." *Journal of Health and Social Behavior* 49, no. 3 (2008): 239–53.

Loprest, Pamela, and Austin Nichols. *Dynamics of Being Disconnected from Work and TANF*. Washington, DC: Urban Institute, 2011.

Luker, Kristin. *Abortion and the Politics of Motherhood*. Berkeley: University of California Press, 1984.

Lynd, Robert S., and Helen Merrell Lynd. *Middletown: A Study in American Culture*. New York: Harcourt Brace Jovanovich, 1956.

Manning, Wendy D. "Children and the Stability of Cohabiting Couples." *Journal of Marriage and Family* 66, no. 3 (2004): 674–89.

Manning, Wendy D., and Susan L. Brown. "Children's Economic Well-being in Married and Cohabiting Parent Families." *Journal of Marriage and Family* 68, no. 2 (2006): 345–62.

———. "The Demography of Unions among Older Americans, 1980-Present: A Family Change Approach." In *Handbook of Sociology of Aging*, edited by Richard A. Settersten, Jr., and Jacqueline L. Angel, 193–210. New York: Springer.

Manning, Wendy D., Susan L. Brown, and Krista K. Payne. "Two Decades of Stability and Change in Age at First Union Formation." *Journal of Marriage and Family* 76, no. 2 (2014): 247–60.

Manning, Wendy D., Susan L. Brown, Krista K. Payne, and Hsueh-Sheng Wu. "Health Marriage Initiative Spending and U.S. Marriage & Divorce Rates, a State-level Analysis." NCFMR Family Profile FP-14–02, National Center for Family and Marriage Research, Bowling Green State University, Bowling Green, OH, 2014, www.bgsu.edu/content/dam/BGSU/college-of-arts-and-sciences/NCFMR/documents/FP/FP-14-02_HMIInitiative.pdf (accessed January 25, 2017).

Manning, Wendy D., Susan L. Brown, and Bart Stykes. "Same-sex and Different-sex Cohabiting Couple Relationship Stability." *Demography* 53, no. 4 (2016): 937–53.

———. "Trends in Births to Single and Cohabiting Mothers, 1980–2013." NCFMR Family Profile FP-15–03, National Center for Family & Marriage Research, Bowling Green State University, Bowling Green, OH, 2015, www .bgsu.edu/content/dam/BGSU/college-of-arts-and-sciences/NCFMR /documents/FP/FP-15-03-birth-trends-single-cohabiting-moms.pdf (accessed January 25, 2017).

Manning, Wendy D., and Jessica A. Cohen. "Premarital Cohabitation and Marital Dissolution: An Examination of Recent Marriages." *Journal of Marriage and Family* 74, no. 2 (2012): 377–87.

Manning, Wendy D., Marshal Neal Fettro, and Esther Lamidi. "Child Well-being in Same-sex Parent Families: Review of Research Prepared for American Sociological Association Amicus Brief." *Population Research and Policy Review* 33, no. 4 (2014): 485–502.

Manning, Wendy D., and Kathleen A. Lamb. "Adolescent Well-being in Cohabiting, Married, and Single-parent Families." *Journal of Marriage and Family* 65, no. 4 (2003): 876–93.

Manning, Wendy D., and Pamela J. Smock. "Divorce-proofing Marriage: Young Adults' Views on the Connection between Cohabitation and Marital Longevity." *NCFR Report* 54 (2009): F13–F15.

———. "Why Marry? Race and the Transition to Marriage among Cohabitors." *Demography* 32, no. 4 (1995): 509–20.

Manning, Wendy D., and Bart Stykes. "Twenty-five Years of Change in Cohabitation in the U.S., 1987–2013." NCFMR Family Profile FP-15–01, National Center for Family & Marriage Research, Bowling Green State University, Bowling Green, OH, 2015, www.bgsu.edu/content/dam/BGSU/college-of-arts-and-sciences/NCFMR/documents/FP/FP-15-01-twenty-five-yrs-cohab-us.pdf (accessed January 25, 2017).

Marks, Nadine F., and James David Lambert. "Marital Status Continuity and Change among Young and Midlife Adults Longitudinal Effects on Psychological Well-being." *Journal of Family Issues* 19, no. 6 (1998): 652–86.

Martin, Joyce A., Brady E. Hamilton, and Michelle J. K. Osterman. *Births in the United States, 2014.* NCHS data brief no. 216. Hyattsville, MD: National Center for Health Statistics, 2014.

Martin, Joyce A., Brady E. Hamilton, Michelle J. K. Osterman, Sally C. Curtin, and T. J. Matthews. "Births: Final Data for 2013." *National Vital Statistics Reports* 64/1. Hyattsville, MD: National Center for Health Statistics, 2015.

Martin, Steven P. "Trends in Marital Dissolution by Women's Education in the United States." *Demographic Research* 15 (2006): 537–60.

Martin, Teresa Castro, and Larry L. Bumpass. "Recent Trends in Marital Disruption." *Demography* 26, no. 1 (1989): 37–51.

Masci, David, and Seth Motel. "5 Facts about Same-sex Marriage." Pew Research Center, last modified June 26, 2015, www.pewresearch.org/fact-tank/2015/06/26/same-sex-marriage (accessed January 25, 2017).

Matos, Kenneth, and Ellen Galinsky. *2014 National Study of Employers.* New York: Family and Work Institute, 2014. Available at Families and Work Institute website, http://familiesandwork.org/downloads/2014NationalStudyOfEmployers.pdf (accessed January 25, 2017).

May, Elaine Tyler. *Homeward Bound: American Families in the Cold War Era.* New York: Basic Books, 1988.

Mayer, Susan E. *What Money Can't Buy: Family Income and Children's Life Chances.* Cambridge, MA: Harvard University Press, 1997.

McGarry, Kathleen, and Robert F. Schoeni. "Social Security, Economic Growth, and the Rise in Elderly Widows' Independence in the Twentieth Century." *Demography* 37, no. 2 (2000): 221–36.

McLanahan, Sara S. "Diverging Destinies: How Children Are Faring under the Second Demographic Transition." *Demography* 41, no. 4 (2004): 607–27.

———. "Fragile Families and the Reproduction of Poverty." annals *of the American Academy of Political and Social Science* 621, no. 1 (2009): 111–31.

McLanahan, Sara S., and Karen Booth. "Mother-only Families: Problems, Prospects, and Politics." *Journal of Marriage and the Family* 51, no. 3 (1989): 557–80.

McLanahan, Sara S., and Gary Sandefur. *Growing Up with a Single Parent: What Hurts, What Helps.* Cambridge, MA: Harvard University Press, 1994.

McNamee, Catherine B., and R. Kelly Raley. "A Note on Race, Ethnicity, and Nativity Differentials in Remarriage in the United States." *Demographic Research* 24 (2011): 293.

MetLife Study of Caregiving Costs to Working Caregivers: Double Jeopardy for Baby Boomers Caring for Their Parents. Dated June 2011, www.metlife.com /mmi/research/caregiving-cost-working-caregivers.html (accessed January 16, 2017).

Meyer, Madonna Harrington, Douglas A. Wolf, and Christine L. Himes. "Declining Eligibility for Social Security Spouse and Widow Benefits in the United States?" *Research on Aging* 28, no. 2 (2006): 240–60.

Miller, Amanda J., Sharon Sassler, and Dela Kusi-Appouh. "The Specter of Divorce: Views From Working- and Middle-class Cohabitors." *Family Relations* 60, no. 5 (2011): 602–16.

Miller, Claire Cain. "Stressed, Tired, Rushed: A Portrait of the Modern Family." *New York Times*, November 4, 2015.

Mintz, Steven. "From Patriarchy to Androgyny and Other Myths: Placing Men's Family Roles in Historical Perspective." In *Men in Families: When Do They Get Involved? What Difference Does It Make?* edited by Alan Booth and Ann C. Crouter, 3–30. Mahwah, NJ: Lawrence Erlbaum Associates, 1998.

———. *Huck's Raft: A History of American Childhood.* Cambridge, MA: Belknap Press of Harvard University Press, 2004.

Mintz, Steven, and Susan Kellogg. *Domestic Revolutions: A Social History of American Family Life.* New York: Free Press, 1988.

Moffitt, Robert A. "The Temporary Assistance for Needy Families Program." In *Means-tested Transfer Programs in the United States*, edited by Robert A. Moffitt, 291–364. Chicago: University of Chicago Press, 2003.

Moffitt, Robert, David Ribar, and Mark Wilhelm. "The Decline of Welfare Benefits in the U.S.: The Role of Wage Inequality." *Journal of Public Economics* 68, no. 3 (1998): 421–52.

Moore, Mignon R., and Michael Stambolis-Ruhstorfer. "LGBT Sexuality and Families at the Start of the Twenty-first Century." *Annual Review of Sociology* 39 (2013): 491–507.

Morgan, S. Philip, Diane N. Lye, and Gretchen A. Condran. "Sons, Daughters, and the Risk of Marital Disruption." *American Journal of Sociology* 94, no. 1 (1988): 110–29.

Motel, Seth, and Meredith Dost. "Half of Unmarried LGBT Americans Say They Would Like to Wed." Pew Research Center, last modified June 26, 2015, www.pewresearch.org/fact-tank/2015/06/26/half-of-unmarried-lgbt-americans-say-they-would-like-to-wed (accessed January 25, 2017).

Moynihan, Daniel Patrick. *The Negro Family: The Case for National Action.* Office of Policy Planning and Research. Washington, DC: U.S. Department of Labor, 1965.

Musick, Kelly, and Larry Bumpass. "Reexamining the Case for Marriage: Union Formation and Changes in Well-being." *Journal of Marriage and Family* 74, no. 1 (2012): 1–18.

Nash, Elizabeth, Rachel Benson Gold, Zohra Ansari-Thomas, Olivia Cappello, and Lizamarie Mohammed. "Laws Affecting Reproductive Health and Rights: State Trends at Midyear, 2016." Guttmacher Institute, last modified July 21, 2016, www.guttmacher.org/article/2016/07/laws-affecting-reproductive-health-and-rights-state-trends-midyear-2016 (accessed January 25, 2017).

National Center for Health Statistics. *Health, United States, 2014: With Special Features on Adults Aged 55–64.* Hyattsville, MD, 2015.

Newsweek Staff. "Marriage by the Numbers." *Newsweek,* June 4, 2006.

Nock, Steven L. "A Comparison of Marriages and Cohabiting Relationships." *Journal of Family Issues* 16, no. 1 (1995): 53–76.

———. "Marriage as a Public Issue." *Future of Children* 15, no. 2 (2005): 13–32.

Noël-Miller, Claire M. "Partner Caregiving in Older Cohabiting Couples." *Journals of Gerontology Series B: Psychological Sciences and Social Sciences* 66B, no. 3 (2011): 341–33.

Notestein, Frank W. "The Population of the World in the Year 2000." *Journal of the American Statistical Association* 45, no. 251 (1950): 335–45.

Obergefell v. Hodges 576 U.S. (2015).

O'Donnell, Liz. "The Crisis Facing America's Working Daughters." *Atlantic,* February 9, 2016.

OECD. OECD Historical Population Data and Projections Database, 2015, last modified October 9, 2015, http://dx.doi.org/10.1787/888933281371 (accessed January 25, 2017).

———. *Pensions at a Glance.* Paris: OECD Publishing, last modified April 4, 2011, http://dx.doi.org/10.1787/888932381760 (accessed January 25, 2017).

Oppenheimer, Valerie Kincade. "A Theory of Marriage Timing." *American Journal of Sociology* 94, no. 3 (1988): 563–91.

———. "Women's Employment and the Gain to Marriage: The Specialization and Trading Model." *Annual Review of Sociology* 23 (1997): 431–53.

———. "Women's Rising Employment and the Future of the Family in Industrial Societies." *Population and Development Review* 20, no. 2 (1994): 293–342.

Parker, Kim. "Where the Public Stands on Government Assistance, Taxes, and the Presidential Candidates." Pew Research Center, last modified September 20, 2012, www.pewsocialtrends.org/2012/09/20/where-the-public-stands-on-government-assistance-taxes-and-the-presidential-candidates (accessed January 25, 2017).

Parker, Kim, and Wendy Wang. "Record Share of American Have Never Married." Washington, DC: Pew Research Center's Social and Demographic Trends Project, September 24, 2014, www.pewsocialtrends.org/files/2014/09/2014-09-24_Never-Married-Americans.pdf (accessed January 25, 2017).

Parsons, Talcott, and Robert F. Bales. *Family Socialization and Interaction Process.* London: Routledge, 1956.

Payne, Krista K. "Children's Family Structure, 2013." NCFMR Family Profile FP-13-19, National Center for Family & Marriage Research, Bowling Green State University, Bowling Green, OH, 2013a, www.bgsu.edu/content/dam/BGSU/college-of-arts-and-sciences/NCFMR/documents/FP/FP-13-19.pdf (accessed January 25, 2017).

———. "Coresident vs. Non-coresident Young Adults, 2011." NCFMR Family Profile FP-13-01, National Center for Family & Marriage Research, Bowling Green State University, Bowling Green, OH, 2013b, www.bgsu.edu/content/dam/BGSU/college-of-arts-and-sciences/NCFMR/documents/FP/FP-13-01.pdf (accessed January 25, 2017).

———. "Sequencing of Family Experiences." NCFMR Family Profile FP-11-11, National Center for Family & Marriage Research, Bowling Green State University, Bowling Green, OH, 2011, www.bgsu.edu/content/dam/BGSU/college-of-arts-and-sciences/NCFMR/documents/FP/FP-11-11.pdf (accessed January 25, 2017).

———. "Young Adults in the Parental Home, 1940–2010." NCFMR Family Profile FP-12-22, National Center for Family & Marriage Research, Bowling Green State University, Bowling Green, OH, 2012, www.bgsu.edu/content/dam/BGSU/college-of-arts-and-sciences/NCFMR/documents/FP/FP-12-22.pdf (accessed January 25, 2017).

Payne, Krista K., and Jennifer Copp. "Young Adults in the Parental Home and the Great Recession." NCFMR Family Profile FP-13-07, National Center for Family & Marriage Research, Bowling Green State University, Bowling Green, OH, 2013, www.bgsu.edu/content/dam/BGSU/college-of-arts-and-sciences/NCFMR/documents/FP/FP-13-07.pdf (accessed January 25, 2017).

Payne, Krista K., and Wendy D. Manning. "Number of Children Living in Same-sex Couple Households, 2013." NCFMR Family Profile FP-15-04, National Center for Family & Marriage Research, Bowling Green State

University, Bowling Green, OH, 2015, www.bgsu.edu/ncfmr/resources/data
/family-profiles/number-of-children-living-in-same-sex-couple-house-
holds--2013.html (accessed January 25, 2017).

Pearlin, Leonard I., and Joyce S. Johnson. "Marital Status, Life-strains, and
Depression." *American Sociological Review* 42, no. 5 (1977): 704–15.

Peters, H. Elizabeth. "Marriage and Divorce: Informational Constraints and
Private Contracting." *American Economic Review* 76, no. 10 (1986):
437–54.

———. "Marriage and Divorce: Reply." *American Economic Review* 82, no. 3
(1992): 686–93.

Peterson, Richard R. "A Re-evaluation of the Economic Consequences of
Divorce." *American Sociological Review* 61, no. 3 (1996): 528–36.

Pew Research Center. "Family Support in Graying Societies: How Americans,
Germans, and Italians Are Coping with an Aging Population." Pew
Research Center, May, 21, 2015a, www.pewsocialtrends.org/files
/2015/05/2015-05-21_family-support-relations_FINAL.pdf (accessed
January 25, 2017).

———. "Modern Parenthood: Roles of Moms and Dads Converge as They
Balance Work and Family." Pew Research Center, March 14, 2013, www
.pewsocialtrends.org/files/2013/03/FINAL_modern_parenthood_03-2013
.pdf (accessed January 25, 2017).

———. "Parental Time Use." Data Trend, Pew Research Center, n. d., www.
pewresearch.org/data-trend/society-and-demographics/parental-time-use/
(accessed January 28, 2017).

———. "Raising Kids and Running a Household: How Working Parents Share
the Load." Pew Research Center, November 4, 2015b, www.pewsocialtrends
.org/2015/11/04/raising-kids-and-running-a-household-how-working-parents-
share-the-load/ (accessed January 25, 2017).

Popenoe, David. "American Family Decline, 1960–1990: A Review and
Appraisal." *Journal of Marriage and the Family* 55, no. 3 (1993): 527–42.

Potter, Daniel. "Same-Sex Parent Families and Children's Academic Achievement." *Journal of Marriage and Family* 74, no. 3 (2012): 556–71.

Powell, Brian, Catherine Blozendahl, Claudia Geist, and Lala Carr Steelman.
*Counted Out: Same-sex Relations and Americans' Definitions of Family;
Same-sex Relations and Americans' Definitions of Family.* New York:
Russell Sage Foundation, 2010.

Preston, Samuel H., and John McDonald. "The Incidence of Divorce within
Cohorts of American Marriages Contracted since the Civil War." *Demography* 16, no. 1 (1979): 1–25.

Raley, R. Kelly, and Larry L. Bumpass. "The Topography of the Divorce Plateau:
Levels and Trends in Union Stability in the United States after 1980."
Demographic Research 8 (2003): 245–60.

Reid, Julie A., Sinikka Elliott, and Gretchen R. Webber. "Casual Hookups to Formal Dates: Refining the Boundaries of the Sexual Double Standard." *Gender and Society* 25, no. 5 (2011): 545–68.

Reinhold, Steffen. "Reassessing the Link between Premarital Cohabitation and Marital Instability." *Demography* 47, no. 3 (2010): 719–33.

Regnerus, Mark. "How Different Are the Adult Children of Parents Who Have Same-sex Relationships? Findings from the New Family Structures Study." *Social Science Research* 41, no. 4 (2012): 752–70.

Rindfuss, Ronald R., and Audrey VandenHeuvel. "Cohabitation: A Precursor to Marriage or an Alternative to Being Single?" *Population and Development Review* 16, no. 4 (1990): 703–26.

Rinelli, Lauren N., and Susan L. Brown. "Race Differences in Union Transitions among Cohabitors: The Role of Relationship Features." *Marriage and Family Review* 46, nos. 1–2 (2010): 22–40.

Robles, Theodore F., and Janice K. Kiecolt-Glaser. "The Physiology of Marriage: Pathways to Health." *Physiology and Behavior* 79, no. 3 (2003): 409–16.

Rogers, Stacy J., and Danelle D. DeBoer. "Changes in Wives' Income: Effects on Marital Happiness, Psychological Well-being, and the Risk of Divorce." *Journal of Marriage and Family* 63, no. 2 (2001): 458–72.

Rosenfeld, Michael J. "Couple Longevity in the Era of Same-sex Marriage in the United States." *Journal of Marriage and Family* 76, no. 5 (2014): 905–18.

———. "Nontraditional Families and Childhood Progress through School." *Demography* 47, no. 3 (2010): 755–75.

Ross, Catherine E., John Mirowsky, and Karen Goldsteen. "The Impact of the Family on Health: The Decade in Review." *Journal of Marriage and the Family* 52, no. 4 (1990): 1059–78.

Ruggles, Steven, Katie Genadek, Ronald Goeken, Joasiah Grover, and Matthew Sobek. *Integrated Public Use Microdata Series: Version 6.0* [dataset]. Minneapolis: University of Minnesota, 2015, available at: http://doi.org /10.18128/D010.V6.0 (accessed January 30, 2017).

Samuelson, Robert J. "Why Our Children's Future No Longer Looks So Bright." *Washington Post*, October 16, 2011.

Sandberg, John F., and Sandra L. Hofferth. "Changes in Children's Time with Parents: United States, 1981–1997." *Demography* 38, no. 3 (2001): 423–36.

Sasson, Isaac, and Debra J. Umberson. "Widowhood and Depression: New Light on Gender Differences, Selection, and Psychological Adjustment." *Journals of Gerontology Series B: Psychological Sciences and Social Sciences* 69, no. 1 (2014): 135–45.

Sayer, Liana C., and Suzanne M. Bianchi. "Women's Economic Independence and the Probability of Divorce: A Review and Reexamination." *Journal of Family Issues* 21, no. 7 (2000): 906–43.

Schoen, Robert, Nan Marie Astone, Young J. Kim, Kendra Rothert, and Nicola J. Standish. "Women's Employment, Marital Happiness, and Divorce." *Social Forces* 81, no. 2 (2002): 643–62.

Schoen, Robert, and Nicola Standish. "The Retrenchment of Marriage: Results from Marital Status Life Tables for the United States, 1995." *Population and Development Review* 27, no. 3 (2001): 553–63.

Schulte, Brigid. "Unlike in the 1950s, there is No 'Typical' U.S. Family Today." *Washington Post*, September 4, 2014.

Schwartz, Christine R. "Trends and Variation in Assortative Mating: Causes and Consequences." *Annual Review of Sociology* 39 (2013): 451–70.

Semuels, Alana. "The End of Welfare as We Know It." *Atlantic*, April 1, 2016.

Slater, Dan. "A Million First Dates." *Atlantic*, January–February 2013.

Smith, Aaron, and Maeve Duggan. "Online Dating & Relationships." Pew Research Center, October 21, 2013, www.pewinternet.org/~/media//Files/Reports/2013/PIP_Online%20Dating%202013.pdf (accessed January 25, 2017).

Smock, Pamela J. "Cohabitation in the United States: An Appraisal of Research Themes, Findings, and Implications." *Annual Review of Sociology* 26 (2000): 1–20.

Smock, Pamela J., and Wendy D. Manning. "Cohabiting Partners' Economic Circumstances and Marriage." *Demography* 34, no. 3 (1997): 331–41.

Smock, Pamela J., Wendy D. Manning, and Meredith Porter. "'Everything's There Except Money': How Money Shapes Decisions to Marry among Cohabitors." *Journal of Marriage and Family* 67, no. 3 (2005): 680–96.

Soons, Judith P. M., and Matthijs Kalmijn. "Is Marriage More Than Cohabitation? Well-being Differences in 30 European Countries." *Journal of Marriage and Family* 71, no. 5 (2009): 1141–57.

Sorensen, Elaine. "A National Profile of Nonresident Fathers and Their Ability to Pay Child Support." *Journal of Marriage and the Family* 59, no. 4 (1997): 785–97.

Span, Paula. "Living with the Parents I'm Losing to Alzheimer's." *New York Times*, March 4, 2016.

———. "They Don't Want to Live with You, Either." *New York Times*, March 24, 2009.

Stacey, Judith. "Good Riddance to 'the Family': A Response to David Popenoe." *Journal of Marriage and Family* 55, no. 3 (1993): 545–47.

Stevenson, Betsey, and Justin Wolfers. *Marriage and Divorce: Changes and Their Driving Forces.* No. w12944. Washington, DC: National Bureau of Economic Research, 2007.

Stewart, Susan D. "Boundary Ambiguity in Stepfamilies." *Journal of Family Issues* 26, no. 7 (2005): 1002–29.

———. *Brave New Stepfamilies: Diverse Paths toward Stepfamily Living.* Thousand Oaks, CA: Sage Publications, 2007.

Strasser, Susan. *Never Done: A History of American Housework.* New York: Pantheon Books, 1982.

Strohm, Charles Q., Judith A. Seltzer, Susan D. Cochran, and Vickie M. Mays. "'Living Apart Together' Relationships in the United States." *Demographic Research* 21 (2009): 177–214.

Strohschein, Lisa. "Parental Divorce and Child Mental Health Trajectories." *Journal of Marriage and Family* 67, no. 5 (2005): 1286–1300.

Stykes, J. Bart, and Seth Williams. "Diverging Destinies: Children's Family Structure Variation by Maternal Education." NCFMR Family Profile FP-13-16, National Center for Family & Marriage Research, Bowling Green State University, Bowling Green, OH, 2013, www.bgsu.edu/content/dam /BGSU/college-of-arts-and-sciences/NCFMR/documents/FP/FP-13-16.pdf (accessed January 25, 2017).

Sullivan, Allison R., and Andrew Fenelon. "Patterns of Widowhood Mortality." *Journals of Gerontology Series B: Psychological Sciences and Social Sciences* 69b, no. 1 (2014): 53–62.

Sun, Yongmin. "Family Environment and Adolescents' Well-being before and after Parents' Marital Disruption: A Longitudinal Analysis." *Journal of Marriage and Family* 63, no. 3 (2001): 697–713.

Sun, Yongmin, and Yuanzhang Li. "Children's Well-being during Parents' Marital Disruption Process: A Pooled Time-series Analysis." *Journal of Marriage and Family* 64, no. 2 (2002): 472–88.

———. "Marital Disruption, Parental Investment, and Children's Academic Achievement: A Prospective Analysis." *Journal of Family Issues* 22, no. 1 (2001): 27–62.

Sweeney, Megan M. "Remarriage and Stepfamilies: Strategic Sites for Family Scholarship in the 21st Century." *Journal of Marriage and Family* 72, no. 3 (2010): 667–84.

———. "Two Decades of Family Change: The Shifting Economic Foundations of Marriage." *American Sociological Review* 67, no. 1 (2002): 132–47.

Sweeney, Megan M., and Julie A. Phillips. "Understanding Racial Differences in Marital Disruption: Recent Trends and Explanations." *Journal of Marriage and Family* 66, no. 3 (2004): 639–50.

Talbott, Maria M. "Older Widows' Attitudes Towards Men and Remarriage." *Journal of Aging Studies* 12, no. 4 (1998): 429–49.

Taylor, Paul, D'Vera Cohn, Gretchen Livingston, Wendy Wang, and Daniel Dockterman. "The New Demography of American Motherhood." Washington, DC: Pew Research Center, Social and Demography Trends Report, August 19, 2010, www.pewsocialtrends.org/files/2010/10/754-new-demography-of-motherhood.pdf (accessed January 25, 2017).

Taylor, Paul, Gretchen Livingston, and Seth Motel. 2011. "In a Down Economy, Fewer Births." Washington, DC: Pew Research Center Social and Demographic Trends, October 12, 2011, www.pewsocialtrends.org/files/2011/10 /REVISITING-FERTILITY-AND-THE-RECESSION-FINAL.pdf (accessed January 25, 2017).

Taylor, Paul, Rich Morin, and Wendy Wang. "The Public Renders a Split Verdict on Changes in Family Structure." Washington, DC: Pew Research Center Social and Demographic Trends, February 16, 2011, www.pewsocialtrends .org/files/2011/02/Pew-Social-Trends-Changes-In-Family-Structure.pdf (accessed January 25, 2017).

Teachman, Jay. "Complex Life Course Patterns and the Risk of Divorce in Second Marriages." *Journal of Marriage and Family* 70, no. 2 (2008): 294–305.

Teti, Douglas M., and Michael E. Lamb. "Socioeconomic and Marital Outcomes of Adolescent Marriage, Adolescent Childbirth, and Their Co-occurrence." *Journal of Marriage and the Family* 51, no. 1 (1989): 203–12.

Thomson, Elizabeth, Thomas L. Hanson, and Sara S. McLanahan. "Family Structure and Child Well-being: Economic Resources vs. Parental Behaviors." *Social Forces* 73, no. 1 (1994): 221–42.

Thornton, Arland. *The Well-being of Children and Families: Research and Data Needs.* Ann Arbor: University of Michigan Press, 2001.

Thornton, Arland, and Linda Young-DeMarco. "Four Decades of Trends in Attitudes toward Family Issues in the United States: The 1960s through the 1990s." *Journal of Marriage and Family* 63, no. 4 (2001): 1009–37.

Umberson, Debra, Kristi Williams, Daniel A. Powers, Meichu D. Chen, and Anna M. Campbell. "As Good as It Gets? A Life Course Perspective on Marital Quality." *Social Forces* 84, no. 1 (2005): 493–511.

Umberson, Debra, Kristi Williams, Daniel A. Powers, Hui Liu, and Belinda Needham. "You Make Me Sick: Marital Quality and Health over the Life Course." *Journal of Health and Social Behavior* 47, no. 1 (2006): 1–16.

UNICEF. "Child Well-being in Rich Countries: A Comparative Overview." *Innocenti Report Card 11.* Florence, Italy: UNICEF Office of Research, 2013.

———. "Measuring Child Poverty: New League Tables of Child Poverty in the World's Rich Countries." *Innocenti Report Card 10.* Florence, Italy: UNICEF Innocenti Research Centre, 2012.

U.S. Census Bureau. "Frequently Asked Questions." See www.census.gov/topics /income-poverty/income/about/faqs.html (accessed October 8, 2016).

———. *65+ in the United States: 2010,* P23–212. Washington, DC: Government Printing Office, 2014.

———. "Table F-22. Married-Couple Families with Wives' Earnings Greater Than Husbands' Earnings, 1981 to 2015." Last modified September 2016d, www2.census.gov/programs-surveys/cps/tables/time-series/historical-income-families/f22.xls (accessed January 16, 2017).

———. "Table HH-1: Households by Type, 1940–Present." Last modified November 2016a, www.census.gov/hhes/families/files/hh1.xls (accessed January 7, 2017).

———. "Table MS-2: Estimated Median Age at First Marriage, by Sex, 1890 to Present." Last modified November 2016b, www.census.gov/hhes/families /files/ms2.xls (accessed January 7, 2017).

———. "Table UC-1: Unmarried Couples of the Opposite Sex, by Presence of Children, 1960 to Present." Last modified November 2016c, www.census .gov/hhes/families/files/uc1.xls (accessed January 7, 2017).

U.S. Department of Health and Human Services. *Report to Congress on Out-of-wedlock Childbearing.* Washington, DC: Government Printing Office, 1995.

———. *Welfare Indicators and Risk Factors: Fourteenth Report to Congress.* Washington, DC: Government Printing Office, 2015.

van der Pas, Suzan, Theo G. van Tilburg, and Merril Silverstein. "Stepfamilies in Later Life." *Journal of Marriage and Family* 75, no. 5 (2013): 1065–69.

Videon, Tami M. "The Effects of Parent-Adolescent Relationships and Parental Separation on Adolescent Well-being." *Journal of Marriage and Family* 64, no. 2 (2002): 489–503.

Waite, Linda J. "Does Marriage Matter?" *Demography* 32, no. 4 (1995): 483–507.

Waite, Linda J., and Maggie Gallagher. *The Case for Marriage: Why Married People Are Happier, Healthier, and Better Off Financially.* New York: Doubleday, 2000.

Watson, Wendy K., and Charlie Stelle. "Dating for Older Women: Experiences and Meanings of Dating in Later Life." *Journal of Women and Aging* 23, no. 3 (2011): 263–75.

Wayne, Teddy. "The No-Limits Job." *New York Times,* March 1, 2013.

Weiss, Robert S. "The Emotional Impact of Marital Separation." *Journal of Social Issues* 32, no. 1 (1976): 135–45.

———. *Going it Alone: The Family Life and Social Situation of the Single Parent.* New York: Basic Books, 1979.

Weitzman, Lenore J. *The Divorce Revolution.* New York: Free Press, 1985.

White House. "Weekly Address: Bringing our Workplace Policies into the 21st Century." June 21, 2014, www.whitehouse.gov/the-press-office/2014/06/21 /weekly-address-bringing-our-workplace-policies-21st-century (accessed January 25, 2017).

White, Lynn K. "Determinants of Divorce: A Review of Research in the Eighties." *Journal of Marriage and the Family* 52, no. 4 (1990): 904–12.

———. "Who's Counting? Quasi-facts and Stepfamilies in Reports of Number of Siblings." *Journal of Marriage and the Family* 60, no. 3 (1998): 725–33.

White, Lynn K., Alan Booth, and John N. Edwards. "Children and Marital

Happiness Why the Negative Correlation?" *Journal of Family Issues* 7, no. 1 (1986): 131–47.

Whitehead, Barbara Dafoe. "Dan Quayle Was Right." *Atlantic Monthly*, April 1993, 47–84.

Williams, Joan C. *Reshaping the Work-Family Debate: Why Men and Class Matter*. Cambridge, MA: Harvard University Press, 2010.

Williams, Kristi, Sharon Sassler, and Lisa M. Nicholson. "For Better or for Worse? The Consequences of Marriage and Cohabitation for Single Mothers." *Social Forces* 86, no. 4 (2008): 1481–1511.

Williams, Seth. "Child Poverty in the United States, 2010." NCFMR Family Profile FP-12-17, National Center for Family & Marriage Research, Bowling Green State University, Bowling Green, OH, 2012, www.bgsu.edu/content /dam/BGSU/college-of-arts-and-sciences/NCFMR/documents/FP/FP-12-17. pdf (accessed January 25, 2017).

Wilson, William Julius. *The Truly Disadvantaged: The Inner City, the Underclass, and Public Policy*. Chicago: University of Chicago Press, 1987.

Wolfers, Justin. "Did Unilateral Divorce Laws Raise Divorce Rates? A Reconciliation and New Results." NBER Working Paper no. 10014, National Bureau of Economic Research, Cambridge, MA, 2003, www.nber.org /papers/w10014.pdf (accessed January 25, 2017).

Wolfinger, Nicholas H. "Beyond the Intergenerational Transmission of Divorce Do People Replicate the Patterns of Marital Instability They Grew Up With?" *Journal of Family Issues* 21, no. 8 (2000): 1061–86.

Wood, Robert G., Quinn Moore, Andrew Clarkwest, Alexandra Killewald, and Shannon Monahan. *The Long-term Effects of Building Strong Families: A Relationship Skills Education Program for Unmarried Parents*. OPRE Report no. 2012–28A. Washington, DC: Office of Planning, Research and Evaluation, Administration for Children and Families, U.S. Department of Health and Human Services (OPRE), 2012.

Wu, Huijing, Susan L. Brown, and Krista K Payne. "Childlessness and Marital Status among Middle-aged Adults, 1992-2012." NCFMR Family Profile FP-16–02, National Center for Family & Marriage Research, Bowling Green State University, Bowling Green, OH, 2016, www.bgsu.edu/content/dam /BGSU/college-of-arts-and-sciences/NCFMR/documents/FP/wu-brown-payne-childlessness-marital-middle-age-fp-16-02.pdf (accessed January 16, 2017).

Wu, Lawrence L., and Elizabeth Thomson. "Race Differences in Family Experience and Early Sexual Initiation: Dynamic Models of Family Structure and Family Change." *Journal of Marriage and Family* 63, no. 3 (2001): 682–96.

Wu, Zheng, and Randy Hart. "The Effects of Marital and Nonmarital Union Transition on Health." *Journal of Marriage and Family* 64, no. 2 (2002): 420–32.

Wu, Zheng, and Christoph M. Schimmele. "Repartnering after First Union Disruption." *Journal of Marriage and Family* 67, no. 1 (2005): 27–36.

Wu, Zheng, Christoph M. Schimmele, and Nadia Ouellet. "Repartnering after Widowhood." *Journals of Gerontology Series B: Psychological Sciences and Social Sciences* 70, no. 3 (2015): 496–507.

Index

abortion, 18, 28, 74
activities of daily living (ADLs), 158
ADC (Aid to Dependent Children), 21
ADLs (activities of daily living), 158
adolescents. *See* teens; young adults
adoption, 2, 5, 74, 132
adult well-being, 110–20, 170–71; caregiving
 for elders and, 161–62; economic
 resources and, 118–20, 128; marriage
 advantage and, 109, 110–14; physical
 health and, 115–18; psychogical health
 and, 97–98, 113–14; spousal loss and, 91,
 97–99. *See also* population aging; psychological well-being
AFDC (Aid to Families with Dependent
 Children), 145
African Americans: childbearing and, 33,
 68–69, 70*fig.;* child well-being and, 127;
 divorce rate and, 81, 94; marriage advantage and, 9, 110–11, 113, 115, 116; Moynihan report and, 143–44; nonmarital
 births and, 33, 71, 72–73, 123–24, 124*fig.,*
 143; in post-slavery period, 16–17; remarriage rate and, 100, 102*fig.;* retreat from
 marriage and, 39, 60, 61, 63, 70, 175;
 stepfamily living in, 105; welfare policy
 and, 143–44, 149. *See also* racial and
 ethnic groups

age level: cohabitation and, 53, 56–57, 160;
 divorce rate and, 80–81, 106; LATs and,
 50–51; online dating and, 46; population
 aging trends and, 163, 164*fig.,* 165*fig.;*
 reasons for retreat from marriage and,
 39; remarriage rate and, 100, 101; risk of
 divorce and, 87–88; stepfamily formation
 and, 105–6. *See also* Baby Boomers;
 population aging; teens; young adults
Aid to Dependent Children (ADC), 21
Aid to Families with Dependent Children
 (AFDC), 145
Allotment Annies, 22
alternatives to marriage: child well-being
 and, 127; health benefits of marriage and,
 115–18, 138–39; retreat from marriage
 and, 29, 39–40; second demographic
 transition and, 34. *See also* cohabitation;
 divorce; family formation paths; living
 apart together relationships; marriage;
 nonmarital childbearing; singlehood;
 single-mother families; union dissolution
Asians: children's family structure and,
 124*fig.;* marriage patterns among, 39,
 60, 102*fig.;* stepfamilies and, 105. *See
 also* racial and ethnic groups
assortative mating, rise in, 118
The Atlantic (magazine), 89, 158

O'Donnell, Liz, 158
OECD countries: aging statistics in, 163, 164*fig.*, 165*fig.*; support for families in, 163, 166. *See also* global comparisons
old-age dependency ratios, in compared OECD countries, 163, 164*fig.*
online dating, 45–46, 47–48
Oppenheimer, Valerie, 30

parental leave. *See* family leave
parenting: child well-being and, 128–29; following divorce, 91–92; parenting styles and, 136–38; Progressive era and, 19. *See also* childrearing; child well-being; single-mother families; work-family balance
Parsons, Talcott, 11
patriarchal authority: during the 1950s, 26; divorce as liberation from, 29; family change and, 13–14, 15; Great Depression and, 20–21. *See also* gender equality; women's movement
Personal Responsibility and Work Opportunity Reconciliation Act (PRWORA, 1996), 145–47, 172
Pew Research Center, 149, 152
the Pill, 28, 48
Popenoe, David, 31, 32
population aging: care of elders and, 160–62; family implications of, 13, 170–71; family policy and, 142, 158–66; family trends and, 176; fertility rate and, 34; global comparisons and, 163–66.164*fig.*, 165*fig.*; marital status distribution and, 159–61, 159*fig.*; risk of divorce and, 87–88; societal response to, 162–66, 167; stepfamily formation and, 105–6; trends in, 163, 164*fig.*, 165*fig.*; work-family balance and, 158–66. *See also* age level
"posh procreation," 74–75
poverty: in compared OEDC countries, 149–50, 150*fig.*; family policy and, 142, 143–50; family size and, 75; fear of divorce and, 63; increases in, 148–49; marriage promotion and, 147–51; married vs. single Boomers and, 160; maternal education and, 135–36, 135*fig.*; welfare benefits as percentage of income and, 146*fig.*; welfare policy and, 142, 143–47, 148–50, 166. *See also* federal benefits; financial resources; low-wage workers; welfare policy
Progressive movement, 19

Promises I Can Keep: Why Poor Women Put Motherhood before Marriage (Edin & Kefalas), 75
PRWORA (Personal Responsibility and Work Opportunity Reconciliation Act, 1996), 145–47
psychological well-being, 113–14; divorce process and, 91–92, 93; family policies and, 156; marriage advantage and, 111, 113–14, 116; same-sex parents and, 132–33; veterans and, 23; widowhood and, 97–98
public discourse: attitudes toward divorce and, 83–84; attitudes toward marriage, 62–63, 100; definition of family and, 4–5; elder caregiving and, 158; perspectives on family change in, 141–42, 170–73; same-sex marriage and, 4–5, 65–66, 142; welfare programs and, 149
"the pure relationship," 49–50

racial and ethnic groups: benefits of marriage and, 110, 113, 127; birth rate trends and, 67, 68; child poverty and, 149; children's family structures and, 120–21, 123–24, 124*fig.*, 127; cohabiting births and, 72–73; cohabiting relationships and, 94; diverging destinies concept and, 60; divorce patterns and, 81; economic inequality and, 33, 149; marriage patterns and, 39, 60, 61, 102*fig.*; nonmarital births and, 33, 69–71, 72–73, 123–24, 124*fig.*, 143; remarriage and, 100, 102*fig.*, 105; retreat from marriage, 39, 60, 61, 63, 70, 175; stepfamilies and, 105. *See also* African Americans; Asians; Hispanics
racial gap: family stability and, 143–45
Regnerus, Mark, 133
relationship quality: cohabitation and, 57–58, 116; divorce and, 89; dual-earner couples and, 153; health and, 116–17; marriage advantage and, 113; training programs and, 19, 63, 147–51
relationship stability: cohabitation and, 54–55, 94–96; financial stability and, 54–55, 85, 88–89; marriage and, 19, 30, 78; programs supporting, 19, 63, 147–50; same-sex couples and, 66, 95–96; women's employment and, 30, 32, 85–86, 87. *See also* family instability
remarriage: decline in, 79, 100; divorce and, 34, 79, 88, 97, 107, 160; mother-child closeness and, 105; repartnering and,

Temporary Assistance to Needy Families
(TANF), 145–47, 149
tender-years doctrine, 15
TheKnot.com, 59
Today.com, 152
traditional family (1950s), 11–12; concern
about decline of, 12, 170; demographic
trends and, 12–13, 169–70; divorce and,
86–87; educational attainment and, 77;
family patterns and, 24–25; as modern
fiction, 11, 24, 169–70; post-war context
of, 23–25. *See also* companionate family
ideal

*Unequal Childhoods: Class, Race, and Family
Life* (Lareau), 136
UNICEF, 150
union, as demographic term, 52–53
union dissolution: cohabitation and, 8,
58–59, 94–96, 107; consequences of, 95;
distress and, 91–92, 97–99; divorce and,
79–94, 106; family formation and, 78–79;
Great Depression and, 21; remarriage
and, 100–101; same-sex couples and,
95–96, 107; widowhood and, 96–100. *See
also* divorce; family instability
U.S. Census Bureau: 1930 census and, 20;
definition of family, 2–4, 7; distribution of
households by type, 3*fig.;* widowhood
and, 96
U.S.Supreme Court: *Roe v. Wade* and, 28;
same-sex marriage and, 2, 65–66, 95, 142
unwed mothers. *See* nonmarital childbearing
Urban Institute, 146–47

Waite, Linda, 110–11
weddings, 59–60
Weiss, Robert S., 91
welfare policy, 143–50, 172; benefits as
percentage of income and, 146*fig.;* drop in
participation and, 145–47; in early twentieth century, 19–20; marriage promotion
and, 147–48; Moynihan Report and, 143–
44; 1996 reforms and, 32, 145–47, 172;
persistence of poverty and, 148–50. *See
also* family policies; federal benefits
well-being in families. *See* adult well-being;

benefits of marriage; child well-being;
marriage advantage; psychological
well-being
Western, Bruce, 34
Whitehead, Barbara Dafoe, 89–90
widowhood, 38, 79, 96–100, 97*fig.,* 159, 194
Wilson, William Julius, 39, 63
women: marriage rate for, 1890–2011, 60*fig.;*
widowhood and, 38, 79, 96–100, 97*fig.,*
194. *See also* domestic responsibilities;
gender differences; gender equality;
labor-force participation by women;
nonmarital childbearing; single-mother
families; women's roles
women's independence hypothesis, 63–64
women's movement, 27–28, 86
women's roles, 13, 19; mid-twentieth century
shifts in, 22–23, 26–28; separate spheres
doctrine and, 15, 16, 18. *See also* domestic
responsibilities; gender equality; labor-
force participation by women; patriarchal
authority
work-family balance: class divide in, 151–52;
employed wives and, 152, 153–55, 154*fig.–*
155*fig.;* policy and, 142, 151–58; as social
concern, 156–58. *See also* family policies
working class: family-friendly policies and,
156; parenting styles and, 137–38; post-
Civil War and, 16–17; women's roles and,
15–16. *See also* diverging destinies; educational attainment; financial resources
working mothers. *See* dual-income families;
labor-force participation by women;
single-mother families; work-family
balance
Work Revolution and Family Patterns
(Goode), 173
Works Progress Administration (WPA), 21
World War II era, 22–23, 47, 80, 84–85

young adults: birth trends among, 67, 73;
economic situation of, 40–44, 41*fig.,*
42*fig.;* living with parents, 25, 40–45,
41*fig.;* marriage trends among, 39, 62, 73;
trends in intimate relations and, 47–50.
See also Millenial generation (born
1981–2000)